WASTED

WASTED

Inside the Robert Chambers–Jennifer Levin Murder

LINDA WOLFE

OPEN ROAD
INTEGRATED MEDIA
NEW YORK

Cover design by Michel Vrana

978-1-5040-3037-3

This edition published in 2015 by Open Road Integrated Media, Inc.
345 Hudson Street
New York, NY 10014
www.openroadmedia.com

CONTENTS

Prologue: The End of Summer   vii

PART I: JENNIFER AND ROBERT
Chapter One: New Lives   3
Chapter Two: Coming of Age   41
Chapter Three: Valentines   70
Chapter Four: The Summer of '86   101

PART II: WOMAN DOWN
Chapter Five: The Body in the Park   123
Chapter Six: The Interrogation Chapter Seven: Rough Sex   187

PART III: THE PEOPLE V. ROBERT CHAMBERS
Chapter Eight: Hopes and Prayers   208
Chapter Nine: The Long Wait   233
Chapter Ten: The Trial   262

Epilogue   303
Afterword   310
About the Author   313

PROLOGUE:
THE END OF SUMMER

On an August evening in 1986, eighteen-year-old Jennifer Levin, decked out in a white camisole, a pink and white miniskirt, and little glass earrings that shone like diamonds, entered her favorite New York bar and began looking for nineteen-year-old Robert Chambers, a friend she hoped would be there. But the chic Upper East Side pub was crowded and she didn't see him at first. She saw instead the usual masses of wealthy and sophisticated prep school students and graduates who had made the bar their home away from home all summer. Some thronged the old-fashioned jukebox, some sat two-to-a-chair at little gingham-covered tables, some were calling out their drink orders through a three-deep crush at the long wooden bar, some were pushing out through the narrow entranceway to smoke marijuana on the sidewalk. The noise was intense, and the air was filled with the festive abandon of the end of summer.

Jennifer joined in the spirit of the place. She frolicked with her friends, eventually found Robert, flirted with him, and late that night left the bar in his company.

Two hours later, as a warm and brilliant August sun began to rise, she was found in Central Park by an early morning bicyclist. She had been strangled. Her face and body were covered with bruises, one of her eyes was swollen, and her earrings and money, except for a torn dollar bill, had vanished. So had her underpants. She lay on the ground spread-eagled, her bra and camisole pushed up around her neck, and her miniskirt bunched up about her waist.

Someone had raped her, the police thought when they arrived at the scene. They speculated that the attacker had been an unconcerned, callous individual. He had left her breasts and genitals on view. A stranger, no doubt, they concluded.

Yet eighteen hours later, Robert Chambers confessed to having caused her death. It had been an accident, he said. He and Jennifer had decided to have sex in the park but she'd suggested kinky acts, and then gotten extremely aggressive. She'd hurt him, and when she wouldn't stop and he couldn't take any more pain, he'd unthinkingly reached up, put his arm around her neck, and flipped her off him. In the process, she had somehow died.

He spoke casually. "She was a nice girl," he said. "Easy to talk to. She was just too pushy." And he used—with an odd twist—the language of gothic romances. "She was having her way with me," he explained. "Without my consent." But what was most remarkable about his confession was not his words but his tone. He sounded sorry for himself, convinced that although he was alive and Jennifer dead, it was he who had somehow been the victim of the girl who now lay lifeless in the morgue.

In the next few days the killing in the park began to mesmerize New York. Here was flaming youth—and better yet, flaming rich youth. The girl and the boy involved in the tragedy had had all the advantages of being young and all the privileges that money can buy, and yet in the late hours of a single summer night they had lost everything. She was dead. He was in jail. And what had caused the tragedy? Sex, according to the headlines. In the prodigiousness of adolescent passion, newspaper accounts based on Robert's confession implied, the boy and girl had simply lost control. The story struck a chord with the public, reinforced popular beliefs. That having a good time is dangerous. That young people can't handle liquor and sex. And that the rich and the young are no better off than you and me—because look what happened to that pair.

By the time Jennifer Levin had been dead a week, people throughout the city were discussing the case at their breakfast tables, on their coffee breaks, on supermarket lines. And at parties and dinners the subject of what had actually happened between Jennifer and Robert was a principal topic of conversation.

The media fed the public's obsession. What was quickly dubbed "the preppie murder" became front-page and top-of-the-hour news, and battalions of reporters marched forth to dig up any information, however peripheral, that would shed light on the principals and their circle of fun-loving pampered city teenagers. The group's drinking, its drug use, its promiscuity, its extravagance—all were explored as if a new tribe, an anthropological phenomenon, had just been discovered.

In the next two years the preppie killing became one of the most widely covered murder stories in New York's history. Yet still people wondered about it, for the story was haunting. It was particularly haunting to parents, who kept asking themselves if Robert and Jennifer could, but for the grace of God, have been their children.

PART I

JENNIFER AND ROBERT

NEW LIVES

In the late 1950s, a pale, skinny young Irish woman named Phyllis Shanley arrived in the United States, her mind ablaze with extravagant daydreams. She had been poor in Ireland, had grown up, the eldest of six, on a back-country farm in which the principal fuel for cooking and even for fighting the omnipresent dampness had been the peat her father and brothers chopped laboriously from bogs behind the house. She had escaped the farm, gone to Dublin to study nursing, learned in the city's dreary Victorian hospitals how to deliver babies for women who couldn't afford doctors and how to care for poor sufferers from tuberculosis and other communicable diseases. But her experience and training had not brought her prosperity. Prosperity did not come easily in Ireland.

America was another story. In this new country she might flourish. Become anything she wanted to become. America was the land of opportunity, a place where what mattered was not what people had been in the past but what they made of themselves once they were here. And if they made of themselves something worthy, their children and grandchildren might never know hard times and might even, God willing, become rich and powerful. Even the children and grandchildren of Irish immigrants. By the time she arrived in the United States, people were saying the country might even have its first Irish-Catholic president soon. John Fitzgerald Kennedy, the junior senator from Massachusetts and a man but three generations removed from Ireland's hardships, was going to run for the office. Learning the ropes in her new country, Phyllis dreamed classic immigrants' dreams, imagining a golden life for herself and her as yet unborn heirs. And in her dreams she took literally the mythic American promise that on these shores a person could be the equal of any man or woman in the land.

She was not averse to hard work, and she quickly began plying her profession here, taking a job at a large New York hospital and doing private-duty nursing as well while waiting for fortune to smile on her. In three years it did. At a lively dance sponsored by an Irish organization, she met a handsome young man who several times during the evening asked her to be his partner and eventually asked her to be his life's partner as well.

The young man's name was Bob Chambers. Members of his Irish-English family had been in America for generations. One of his ancestors had even come before the Revolution. Bob's parents owned a house in Westchester, a cabin on Lake Placid. They'd raised Bob genteelly and comfortably, sent him to private schools and then to Mitchell College in Connecticut and The American University in Washington, D.C. Four years after Phyllis met him—it was 1965—she married him. A year later she gave birth to her first and only child.

The child, a boy, was beautiful, with sapphire eyes and a delicate pearly-white complexion. Phyllis gave him the first name Robert, after his father, and the middle name Emmet, after the great Irish patriot who had been hanged for plotting against the British.

He was a docile infant, his temperament mild and malleable. And he was responsive, an early babbler and smiler. By the time he was a year and a half and had handily learned to talk and walk, taking his tumbles manfully, Phyllis was head over heels in love with him.

She was not demonstrative. She didn't hug and kiss him the way other mothers hugged and kissed their little boys. But she read to him and played educational games with him, and by the time he was three, she had taught him many things, among them to shake hands when he was introduced.

They were living at the time in a vast apartment complex in Woodside, Queens. They didn't have much money. Bob had a good but not especially well-paying job in the credit department of Dun & Bradstreet. Phyllis was still doing part-time nursing. Most of her patients lived on Manhattan's Upper East Side, in sprawling apartments where the walls were hung with exquisite landscapes and family portraits and the rooms decorated with crystal, silver, and woods so highly polished they shone like gems. Woodside seemed depressing in comparison, and Phyllis dreamed of some day living on the East Side herself. Apartments were cheaper on the bourgeois West Side or in the raffish downtown neighborhoods of Manhattan. But the East Side was patrician and grand, its boulevards lined with palatial apartment buildings, its side streets with opulent town houses and discreet residential hotels. Bob's grandmother lived in one such hotel. It had a posh dining room, and sometimes the old lady invited Phyllis and little Robert to dine there in splendor with her.

After several years in Woodside, Phyllis and Bob left the area for a better apartment in Jackson Heights. It wasn't the East Side of Manhattan, but Phyllis was pleased with the move. Husbanding her earnings, she decorated the new apartment tastefully and tended it zealously, often spending hours polishing her handsome dark furniture until it glowed.

She was working at the time not just for the wealthy but for the extremely wealthy. And one day she got a nursing assignment that thoroughly stimulated her dreamy nature. She was hired by her new country's most famous family to look after the nation's most famous little boy, John-John Kennedy, while he recovered from a respiratory illness.

The day after she started working for the Kennedys, Bob Chambers noticed that his wife was wearing a new expensive looking pair of sunglasses, and that she was wearing them not over her eyes but perched on top of her head, just the way Jackie Kennedy did.

The job didn't last—John-John got well—but its effects did. When Robert was four, Phyllis enrolled him in a prestigious Manhattan nursery, the nursery at the St. David's School on East 89th Street, just off Fifth Avenue. St. David's was a Catholic school, although it also took children of other faiths, and the Catholic families that placed their offspring at the school and in particular at the nursery were exceedingly prominent. The Hearsts, the Skourases, the Burkes had all sent children to the St. David's nursery. A few years before Robert entered it, the sons of John F. Kennedy's sisters, Mrs. Peter Lawford and Mrs. Stephen Smith, had attended. So had John-John Kennedy.

On Long Island that year, two-year-old Jennifer Levin was growing up in a small ranch house in the commuter town of Merrick. Out back was a large tree-studded yard. In front of the TV, an undulating waterbed.

She was the second daughter of Steven Levin and Ellen Domenitz, whose families were Jewish and who had themselves each been raised in green and homogeneous suburban towns, Steve in Massachusetts, Ellen on Long Island.

They'd met in Boston while Ellen was going to a junior college and Steve was attending an acting school. Acting was in Steve's blood. His grandfather, who'd emigrated to the United States from Russia in the early part of the century, had made his living in the shoe business, just as Steve's father did after him, but the old man had always wanted to be an actor and toward the end of his life he had even become one, performing with a Yiddish theater group. Steve had his gifts for comedy, could do hilarious imitations, and had consequently set his heart on a theatrical career. But he gave up that ambition after he and Ellen married and went into real estate. By the time Jennifer was born, he and a partner had begun to have some success with a small real estate firm in Manhattan.

Of the two little girls, five-year-old Danielle was the beauty, the neighbors used to say. But Jennifer would be okay. She had personality. Was a live wire.

She spent much of her time trying to join the games of Danielle and Danielle's friends. They slammed doors on her, or ran giggling away on longer, swifter legs. She would howl, but doggedly keep after them, rattling doorknobs or clumsily tagging behind as the group raced ahead of her. And sometimes, miraculously catching up, she'd chant and sing and parade around the older children, and act so antic that they'd laugh and soften and let her play with them.

St. David's, where four-year-old Robert was daily escorted by one of his parents, was a beautiful school with Georgian-style architecture that suggested permanence and stability. It was also utterly different from the institutions Phyllis had attended as a youngster: Irish convent schools. Her teachers, black-garbed nuns, had focused on self-discipline and obedience as much as on academic subjects. The teachers at St. David's, Catholic lay people for the most part, were gentle, lenient, and devoted to inculcating knowledge in their young charges.

Phyllis was pleased that she'd decided to send Robert there, even though it was far from home and expensive. But her life was not altogether happy. Around the time Robert started at St. David's, Bob, who was a drinker—he had started using alcohol when he was a teenager—began drinking more heavily. Sometimes he wasn't home when he was supposed to be home and sometimes he wasn't at the places he'd said he'd be at.

His mother hit him with a strap when he was bad, little Robert told a teacher at St. David's. The teacher thought that no doubt the mother was well-meaning, if a bit old-fashioned and strict.

Cynthia White, Robert's steady babysitter, also found Phyllis a strict mother. But a superb one as well. She had a lot of rules, but they were sensible. Robert had to do his homework before he did any playing, he couldn't watch a lot of TV, and he had to go out of doors every day, no matter how inclement the weather.

Cynthia admired Mrs. Chambers. And she was enchanted by little Robert, who was charming and polite and so obedient she didn't have to tell him twice to put away his toys or go to his room and get ready for bed. But Cynthia was concerned about him. He didn't see that much of his mother—she had started working full-time taking care of the aging Millicent Hearst, wife of the newspaper baron—and he had no friends. Was he lonely? Cynthia worried. And had Mrs. Chambers done the right thing in sending him to St. David's? It set him off from the neighborhood boys, made him a bit of an isolate.

Still, Robert didn't complain. He wasn't one of those whiny, difficult kids. He kept most things to himself. Even pain.

One day he was climbing on the back of a wing chair. "Don't do that," Cynthia warned him. "It's dangerous." He didn't listen, just went on climbing. A second later he tumbled to the floor.

"Are you all right?" Cynthia asked.

"Yes." But then he retreated into his room.

Cynthia waited for him to emerge. But when after twenty minutes he still hadn't appeared, she went inside to check on him. She found him curled up on his bed, straining to hold back sobs. Which took some doing, because the injury turned out to be no small affair. He'd broken his collarbone.

Sequins. Ribbons. Her mother's high heels. In Merrick, four-year-old Jennifer was displaying a passion for dress-up and, once in costume, would strut and sing and spin around like a whirling human top.

Sometimes she was a bit too lively. The mothers of playmates found her hyperactive and difficult to control. One mother mentioned this to Jennifer's father, and he suggested that when Jennifer visited she be given diet soda instead of Pepsi or Coke, because sugar overstimulated her.

But Jennifer's frivolity served her well. It brought her attention, friends. One afternoon when she and her sister were visiting two boys, the elder of whom considered Jennifer a baby and ignored her, she took the younger brother aside, dressed him and herself up in makeup and funny costumes, and began cavorting around the room. The older boy, eager to reject her, nevertheless cracked up, laughed till he thought his sides would split. "You can be our court jester," he said, and explained how kings kept attendants just to make them laugh.

In the summer of 1972, just before Robert turned six, Cynthia traveled to Ireland with him and his mother on a visit to Phyllis's parents. The three Americans flew to Shannon, then took a trip deep into the Irish countryside, to the town of Bournacoula in County Leitrim, where the Shanleys lived and Phyllis had grown up. Leitrim is one of Ireland's poorest counties, a long narrow spade of land that has a remote, forgotten feel to it. The Shanleys' farm also, to Cynthia at least, seemed forgotten, a thing of the past. The farmhouse was a rambling four-bedroom affair. There was a paved road in front of it, but behind were pens for chickens and ducks, and beyond that, fields in which cows and horses grazed. Further still in the distance were desolate peat bogs. Phyllis's father drove by wagon to the bogs and brought back the peat, and Phyllis's mother cooked with it on a big blackened stove. She stewed and simmered on the stove's surface, and baked loaves of delicious bread inside its ancient oven. She baked daily, telling Cynthia, "The bread's not the same if you eat it when it's old. Even a day old."

The babysitter was awed by the amount of labor the aging Shanleys had to expend on tasks that took no time at all back home, where the flick of a knob brought fuel and bread could keep as fresh as new in the freezer. "Life is so hard here," she said.

"It's nothing, nothing at all," Mrs. Shanley replied. "Why, just a few months ago we had to go upstairs to the bathroom to get water for doing the dishes. That or draw the water from the kitchen pump."

It's no wonder, Cynthia thought after the trip to Bournacoula, that Mrs. Chambers wants Robert at St. David's, even though it means his having to travel so long every day, and his having no one his own age to play with after school. She wants him to make up for what she lacked. She has the American Dream.

By 1973 the Levins' marriage was foundering. To some extent the trouble lay in their temperaments. Both were excitable and tempestuous. But they also had different priorities. Ellen Levin liked pursuing artistic and bohemian pleasures—she was "a leftover flower child from the sixties," one of her friends recalled. Steve was sterner and more pragmatic, and increasingly he was focusing on his real estate business.

Eventually, the pair separated. Steve moved into Manhattan, and Ellen remained behind in Merrick with the two little girls. Jennifer was five.

•   •   •

Seven-year-old Robert was starting his religious instruction at St. David's, studying under an energetic and thoughtful priest named Father Thomas Leonard. Leonard's classes were crowded with shy, attentive, well-scrubbed faces. Robert was just one of the crowd. But the boy's mother was another story. She always spoke up at parents' meetings and made her presence felt.

She was, by then, daily leaving County Leitrim behind. She still spoke with a brogue and clung to the stern religious beliefs of her childhood, but she was rapidly becoming ever more Americanized—and in all outward manifestations an American of high social class. Shopping carefully and cleverly, often in thrift shops to which women like those she worked for donated their wardrobes when they were but a season old, she dressed with sophisticated East Side flair. When she entertained at home, she set her table with fine linens and china, just as the women she worked for did, differing from them only in that she purchased her wares in out-of-the-way secondhand shops.

In 1974, when Robert was eight, Phyllis enrolled him in the Knickerbocker Greys, an after-school military drill group that taught discipline and patriotism to well-to-do boys and had come to be nicknamed the

Social Register's Private Little Army. She knew that the Greys weren't what they had been. Once they were so elite that even some of New York's richest boys could not join. Once they were a training ground for the city's princes. Frederick Warburg and Cornelius Vanderbilt had been Greys. So had Nelson Rockefeller, John Lindsay, and Thomas Hoving. But things had changed. The most socially eminent families in the city had turned away from the group, and their defection, combined with the antimilitaristic sentiment that had swept the country during the Vietnam war, had made the Greys easier to join. Nevertheless the corps still drew its members primarily from Manhattan's most exclusive private schools. Phyllis was aware of this, and she was eager to see Robert enter the ranks and make the right sort of friends.

Robert was nervous the first time he passed through the massive wrought-iron gates and majestic wooden doors of the fortresslike armory on Park Avenue in which the Greys met. For years he had seen older boys at his school wearing the Greys uniform to class, and he had dreamed of wearing one, too. But he had heard he would have to take part in a competition on the first day, and he was fearful he wouldn't pass muster. He needn't have worried. His first day went off without a hitch, he was accepted into the corps, and his parents bought him the coveted uniform. He began dreaming right after that, he wrote in a school essay, of becoming a sergeant. Sergeants got to carry swords.

Separation had hung heavy on Ellen Levin. She'd been stuck in the suburbs with their emphasis on nuclear family solidarity, and all the drudgery of child care had fallen on her shoulders alone. When Jennifer was around six, she decided to move to California. She'd heard that people lived differently out West. There were whole complexes inhabited by single people, or by divorced people living with their children. There were communes and colonies and carefree styles of life. She went to Los Angeles with her two little girls.

In L.A. she rented an apartment on a sprawling estate that was rumored to have belonged at one time to Rudolph Valentino. The estate was filled with separated parents, many of them writers, singers, and actors. They understood one another's hardships and assisted each other with child care and domestic chores. Their companionship alleviated Ellen's loneliness and maternal burdens. Soon she went to work, getting herself a job in an advertising agency.

The Greys met for drill twice a week, and throughout the year for dress reviews and outings to ballgames and army bases. Robert, at eight and a half, attended Greys functions regularly, and soon became an exemplary cadet. He learned to pivot and parade, march and maneuver. He learned to handle the sword he had dreamed of wearing. And, joining the group's Saturday rifle club, he even learned to fire a rifle.

At the end of his second year in the organization, his parents decided—perhaps because they were spending so much time ferrying Robert to Greys events—to move to Manhattan. Phyllis found an apartment in a redbrick high-rise right on Park Avenue itself—just blocks from the armory. It was small, with low ceilings and few architectural details, and it was located in the least fashionable section of the fashionable boulevard—the mid-nineties, only a few streets south of Spanish Harlem. But Phyllis told friends her new address with a quiet but unmistakable pride.

She was still working as a nurse, but she was taking short-term assignments. Mrs. Hearst, for whom she'd worked exclusively for several years, had died. Phyllis's hours were long and stressful. But the move to the city gave her more time to invest in her outside interests. She had always enjoyed organizational and charitable work, had been active when she lived in Queens in the County Leitrim Society, a group which raised money for immigrants from her home county. Now she began raising money for St. David's, and she joined the Altar Society of the Church of St. Thomas More, which was near her new apartment.

Monsignor James Wilders, the priest of St. Thomas's, came to know
Phyllis well. He felt they had a great deal in common. He, too, had in-
vested himself in the care of the sick and dying. Before coming to St.
Thomas's, he'd been the director of hospital chaplains for the Archdiocese
of New York, a job that had put him in charge of Catholic priests at hundreds of local hospitals and nursing homes, and for years he'd immersed
himself in helping patients and their families bear the prospect of death.
The worst thing was the youngsters dying of leukemia. He always said
to their mothers and fathers, You know, this isn't easy, it's a trauma, but
the little one is going straight home to heaven without ever having done
anyone any harm. The worst cross, you know, is for a child to grow up
and bring disgrace and dishonor on the family.

At first in the city ten-year-old Robert was timid. Leaving the apartment,
he stayed close to his mother's side, often clutching her hand or a corner
of her skirt. But in time he got used to his new environment and began
going out on his own to meet boys he knew from St. David's. When he
was with them, he was sometimes shy, speaking softly and waiting till
other boys addressed him first. But he wanted to be liked, and he made an
effort to go where the other kids went, do what the other kids did.

After a while, Phyllis noticed with pleasure that he had made a sizable
circle of friends in the neighborhood. He was popular, she told friends.

Billy Markey, a new student at St. David's, also saw that Robert was
popular, and hoping to be popular too, he considered inviting Robert and
his friends to his tenth birthday party. He wanted to have them, but he
wasn't sure they'd come. They were different from him. He was a scholarship student and lived on the West Side. They were rich and lived on the
East. He had just come to New York from a small provincial town. They
had lived in the city for years. More, they smoked marijuana already. He'd
seen them doing it in school bathrooms. It frightened him. But still he
took the plunge and asked them. And to his surprise and pleasure, they
came.

The party made Billy feel wonderful. He and his guests listened to records, played with his birthday gifts, gobbled cake and ice cream until they felt ready to burst. There was a lot of laughing and joking, and for the first time in months Billy didn't miss his old school and his old friends. But afterward, when the party was over and he was straightening up his room, he noticed that his piggy bank had been emptied of its contents—twenty dollars' worth of coins he had scrupulously saved from his allowance. He wasn't sure who had taken the money, but he thought it was Robby Chambers or one of his close friends. He'd seen the group eyeing the bank.

One afternoon that year, Andy Lockheart, a ten-year-old who went to a different East Side private school from the one Robert and Billy attended, telephoned a friend of his. He'd gotten lucky, he said excitedly: he'd persuaded a man on his way into a liquor store to take his money and bring him out a bottle.

Andy and his friend had been drinking since they were eight, nicking shots from their parents' liquor cabinets. But recently they'd started feeling that a shot here and a shot there was no fun at all. They'd wanted a whole bottle of hard liquor, but had been afraid to swipe one from their parents, so they'd taken to hanging around outside liquor stores wearing their neat little brass-buttoned blue blazers and politely asking customers to help them out. Everyone had turned them down, but today Andy had at last been successful. "I knew it would happen sooner or later," he exulted to his friend.

"It figures," Andy's friend said, "this being New York." Then he asked Andy what store he'd gotten lucky at. Andy told him it was a shop he'd heard about from some St. David's boys, one of whom was a kid named Robby Chambers.

Billy Markey kept his distance from the boys he thought had robbed his piggy bank. But he couldn't avoid them altogether. He was in some classes with them. He did sports with them. He was even in a school pageant with them. Robert Chambers has the best part, Billy sulked. He's a Civil War general, all decked out in a uniform.

Billy himself was just a foot soldier. He was supposed to horse around and ruin the orderly march of a column of soldiers, and the general was supposed to give him a push to make him get in line and behave. When the cue came, Billy did the horsing around, and Robert did the pushing. But it wasn't like a playacting push. It was a real hard shove. Robert's trying to hurt me, Billy worried for a second. Then he thought, No, it's more like he's been drinking or smoking grass and he doesn't know how hard he's pushing.

In California, Jennifer was attending public school. She was as extroverted and irrepressible as she had been as a toddler, a little girl who loved attention and had no qualms about reaching out for it. One day she paraded down Hollywood Boulevard in a big hat and her mother's high heels. Another day, visiting a restaurant owned by a friend of her mother's, she played waitress, clearing tables and, not yet comprehending the principles of tipping, amusingly telling guests she hoped they'd return soon while at the same time handing them quarters.

She saw her father from time to time. She and Danielle went east to visit him during their Christmas and summer vacations, and he flew out to the coast three or four times a year.

He was doing well. His real estate business was flourishing. He was living in the East Sixties between Madison and Park avenues. And he had a girlfriend.

She was Arlene Voorhust, a young Catholic woman who had been widowed and had no children. Jennifer thought her beautiful. Not that her mother wasn't beautiful, too. In fact, Arlene and Ellen Levin looked something alike. But Arlene was darker, slimmer, more glamorous. Jennifer admired her. But like many little girls who imagine when their fathers divorce their mothers that they have won the Oedipal battle only to discover they have a new rival for their father's love, she also resented her.

When she was eight, Steve and Arlene married. The wedding took place at New York's City Hall. Whether it was because Ellen Levin didn't want her daughters to attend the ceremony, or because Steve and Arlene didn't want them to, or because they themselves preferred to stay away, Jennifer and Danielle were not present at the wedding.

Robert grew tall and broad in the next year or two—taller and broader than most of his agemates at St. David's or in the Greys. His face took on a new, almost mannish handsomeness, and his body, firmed up by marching in the armory, became strong.

He brought his parents great joy. He became an altar boy at St. Thomas's and was confirmed there under the sponsorship of Father Theodore McCarrick, an up-and-coming priest who had been an adviser to Mrs. Hearst and with whom Phyllis had stayed in contact after the old woman died. He won a public speaking contest at St. David's, earned several medals for marksmanship at the Greys, and was made a member of the group's elite Honor Guard. The Guard, dressed in sparkling white trousers and braid-bedecked tunics, carried the troop's colors at parades and public ceremonies. One day Ronald and Nancy Reagan were escorted by the Guard to a Woman's Republican Committee luncheon at the Waldorf-Astoria. The presidential hopeful shook Robert's hand.

Phyllis talked about her son obsessively. He was becoming in her eyes everything she had once dreamed a child of hers could become.

She herself was also becoming the kind of person she had once only imagined she might be. She had been invited to join the Greys' fabled board of directors, a group that was, historically, composed of society women, even acquaintances of governors and presidents. But for years she had turned up regularly on drill days to take attendance and on review days to make sure the cadets' shoes were shined and their purple sashes tied just so. And always she'd worked hard at using the wealthy contacts she made through work to get donations for the organization. She was an extraordinary fund-raiser, and the Greys had recognized this and wanted her on the board.

In the spring of 1979, a few months before Robert turned thirteen, the Greys went further, elected her their president. It was a dubious time to have won the title, for the group was suffering recruiting problems. But it was also an exciting time, as the organization would soon be a hundred years old. Elevated, Phyllis began working immediately on getting publicity for the group and on arranging the centennial.

In the fall, she opened her first presidential season with a luncheon at the "21" Club. It was a festive day. The cadet officers, Robert among them, wore medals and carried plumed headgear. Distinguished guests—Phyllis's old friend Father McCarrick, who had recently been named a bishop, was one of them—made toasts, and board members and supporters of the organization gave inspiring or droll speeches. "The point is not to train these boys for social leadership," a former president said, "but leadership for life."

"What this really is," a successful alumnus said, "is a tunnel leading into the old boy network."

Ellen Levin had friends in the film community, and sometimes she took Jennifer and Danielle with her to parties at which they met Hollywood's aristocrats. Producers and movie stars. The party Jennifer liked best was the one where she met Chevy Chase. He was so handsome. So funny.

One night some friends of Ellen's who were sleeping over told Jennifer they'd take her to Disneyland the next day. In the morning she ran into their room and excitedly tried to rouse them. But they wouldn't get up, wouldn't move from the bed. They were stoned, she later complained to a friend.

For Bob Chambers, who was working now in the credit department of MCA, the period of his wife's ascendancy in the Greys was a melancholy one. Although he had several times attempted to give up alcohol, and had even attended the acclaimed Hazelden Foundation clinic in Minnesota for a while, he had fallen off the wagon and begun spending his evenings making the rounds of neighborhood bars. One of his favorite bars was Sheehan's, on Third Avenue.

Mike Sheehan, the proprietor's son, was a detective with the New York City Police Department. He often dropped by the bar when he was on his way home from work, and one night—it was around the time Phyllis started heading up the Greys—he popped in and saw Bob Chambers there. He liked Bob. Liked the way he was a well-behaved drinker who didn't get sloppy or pissed off but just quietly downed his scotch and watched the games on TV, or did crossword puzzles with a friend. Bob wore big muttonchop whiskers and looked so smart and did so many puzzles that Sheehan had dubbed him "the intelligentsia." I'm gonna see how the intelligentsia is, Sheehan decided this night and, strolling over to Bob, said, "Hey, how's it going?"

"Well, you know," Bob said. "Okay." Then he said something about his wife. Something about how he was having problems with her.

"Yeah, well, I guess the best thing is, you never get married," Sheehan said.

Bob nodded, laughed.

He's a really sweet guy, Sheehan thought. Most of the regulars are. And they follow my career as if they're my fan club.

Sheehan had made the regulars real proud this year. He'd gone after a black kid over on Columbus Avenue and 108th who'd looked like he was up to no good, and when he'd pulled up alongside him, he'd seen the kid had a long-barreled .38 in his hand. Sheehan had pulled out his own gun, shoved it at the kid's face and screamed, "You pull the trigger, I'm gonna blow your fucking head off! You wanna be a tough guy, go ahead and shoot me, but I'm gonna take you out, too, I'm gonna take your face right off." He'd never been so tough in his life. Things like that just started pouring out of his mouth. And the kid had backed off, begun running.

Sheehan had run after him and later, his heart pounding, tackled him, cuffed him, and brought him in. Then, lucky him, it turned out the kid was a guy the whole police force had been trying to catch for weeks, a guy who'd shot the city's first female police officer.

Tonight Sheehan told Bob Chambers and the rest of the crew a few more of his adventures, and some of the guys told his parents, the way they always did, that they wished they had a son like him.

Bob Chambers didn't say that. He never says anything like that, Sheehan thought. Maybe he doesn't have a son.

"Go ahead and play," Bob Chambers said to eight-year-old Chip Jones one afternoon that fall. Bob had agreed to babysit for the boy because Phyllis, who'd promised his parents that she'd do the job, was too busy. Bob had taken Chip to the local video arcade, where he'd changed several dollars into quarters, and now he offered the silver to the boy.

Chip got going. The machine lit up and he made his moves and shot down a bunch of space ships. Then he looked around for Mr. Chambers, so he could show him his score. He wasn't there. "He went outside for a minute," the video arcade's change-maker said.

Chip went on playing, but after a while he ran out of money. He stood around wishing Mr. Chambers would come back. After about an hour, when Mr. Chambers still hadn't returned, he got a little scared. But then, there was Mr. Chambers. Big and kindly. "Let's go down to the South Street Seaport now," he suggested.

Chip thought it was a great idea.

They took the subway downtown, and Mr. Chambers bought him lunch in a restaurant. Then Mr. Chambers said he knew a bar in the area that had a model of the *Titanic* in it, and if Chip would just be patient and wait a bit, he'd go out, find just where it was, and take him to see the model ocean liner.

Chip sat in the resturant and played with the remains of his lunch. Mr. Chambers didn't come back. Chip waited and waited. And then after a while, even though he was ashamed of himself, he started getting scared again. If anything happens to Mr. Chambers, he worried, I won't be able to get home. I don't know the way. But then at last there was Mr. Chambers. He looked a little flushed and he was perspiring heavily, but he was cheerful and as kindly as ever. "I'm awfully sorry," he said. "I've been into all the bars, but I couldn't find the *Titanic* anywhere."

If Phyllis was dismayed by Bob's drinking, she didn't let it interfere with her life. She continued going to her nursing jobs and continued to throw herself into her Greys presidential duties, organizing outings for the cadets to the Columbia-Dartmouth football game, and to West Point, where they met a brigadier general and ate their lunch in the military academy's mess hall.

She was well liked by the boys now officially under her command, but she could be very stern when they disappointed her, paraded poorly, or behaved boisterously. With Robert, she was sternest of all. When he failed to carry out an order, she would chew him out royally, criticize and humiliate him even in front of other people. One afternoon in the armory the mother of another Greys cadet witnessed one of these dressing-downs. Phyllis was scolding Robert about a purchase he'd failed to make. Her voice was icy, her words cutting. Robert, towering over her, listened silently.

Isn't he going to defend himself? the observer wondered. My son certainly would.

But Robert merely eyed his mother blankly and kept on saying nothing.

Pressure. Demands. His mother's expectations were grinding him down, thirteen-year-old Robert told a friend that year.

He had lots of friends by then, many of them girls. Girls liked his looks, his military bearing, and the mischievous, playful way in which he teased them.

One day a girl teased him back. She made fun of him verbally and then turned physical, prankishly kicking at his rear end. Robert responded to the humiliation with sudden explosive anger. He whirled around and grabbed the girl's arm, twisting it so hard she felt it was about to break.

That fall—it was 1979—Jennifer, a gangly eleven-year-old with crooked teeth and limp hair that she tucked impatiently behind prominent ears, moved back East. Ellen had soured on California and decided to rent a small house in Manorhaven, a somewhat shabby enclave in the posh Long Island suburb of Port Washington. She enrolled Jennifer in the sixth grade of Manorhaven's public elementary school.

Jennifer barely remembered Long Island, and she wasn't happy about being a new girl at a new school. But she tried to find friends, flinging herself into the chore by making the first gestures. "I'm Jennifer Levin," she would say, scribbling her phone number on a sheet of looseleaf paper. In a short while her efforts bore fruit and she was invited for sleep-overs and backyard swimming pool parties.

At the Greys, Robert's proud record was showing signs of deterioration. By that autumn, he was a steady if secret drinker, accustomed to meeting his thirteen-year-old friends at an East Side bar where the proprietor allowed them to order drinks, or turning up at parties and dances with a flask of cheap whiskey in his pocket. Perhaps as a result of drinking, he had frequent bouts of vertigo at the armory. And one afternoon, while carrying the Greys' cross at a patriotic service at the Presbyterian Brick Church, he passed out.

Parents who witnessed the event whispered among themselves that alcohol or marijuana might have caused Robert's fainting spell, and hinted as much to Phyllis.

She said no, there's nothing wrong with Robert except a touch of flu. And if she was angry at him, she readily forgave him when at Christmas he performed exceptionally well at the 99th Annual Review. She even wrote him a formal letter of congratulation. "You exemplify and demonstrate the fine values which make fine and good men," the note said. "There is no greater compliment to apply to any man other than to say that he is a good man."

One day that semester, Leilia Van Baker, a leggy butterscotch-blond twelve-year-old who went to a private school across the street from Robert's home, visited him at his apartment. In the living room she saw a mammoth gloriously framed three-quarter-length portrait of him. The painting depicted Robert in a blazer, a snowy white dress shirt, and a striped tie. His brown hair was filled with highlights, his smile was radiant, his tapered fingers rested lightly on a chair back, and his tailored torso leaned gracefully forward. He looks, Leilia thought, exalted, like a young duke.

She stared at the painting. Robert began to blush. His mother had commissioned it.

Could he work with Robert on his prep school applications, Phyllis asked a friend that spring. Robert had his heart set on boarding school, she told the friend, particularly Choate, where a number of boys he knew were hoping to go. But the boarding schools had elaborate application procedures, and she felt the boy needed some manly guidance if he was to get his in on time and in the proper fashion.

Why me, why not Bob? the friend, John Dermont, asked himself. But he knew the answer. Bob was hardly ever at home, and when he was, he was less than alert. Dermont agreed to oversee Robert's applications. Under his guidance Robert filled out questionnaires, obtained recommendations from teachers, and wrote an essay about why he might be an asset to a boarding school community. In the essay he concentrated on his participation in the Greys. "The lessons I have learned," he asserted, "the development of good character, and the responsibilities of assuming command, will benefit me in boarding school and throughout the rest of my life."

The application procedure went so smoothly that Phyllis asked Dermont to help Robert with an eighth-grade history essay as well.

Up at Choate, in Wallingford, Connecticut, the admissions staff was hesitant about Robert at first. The school, nearly a hundred years old, was one of the country's most eminent college preparatory institutions and prided itself on being able to attract to its 500-acre campus the best and the brightest students. Robert had received enthusiastic recommendations from several of his lower school teachers, but his grades weren't particularly good. Nor were his scores on the required Secondary School Aptitude Tests.

Still, the staff reasoned, the boy had been a member of the Greys, which had supplied Choate with a number of its finest alumni, and during his interview he'd come across as exceptionally well-mannered and charming. They decided to accept him.

The news stirred him. Made him proud. He was going on "to other things bigger and better than New York," he wrote in the yearbook of a girl he liked. She had nicknamed him Romeo, and he signed with the nickname. Then he scrawled another goodbye on another page, and this time boastfully appended to his signature, "Romeo, The Great! The Sacred! The Fantastic! Forever Great! Nice Guy!"

• • •

Representative Geraldine Ferraro, whose son John Zaccaro, Jr., had gone to St. David's, gave the commencement address on the day of Robert's graduation. From a podium at the Church of St. Thomas More, she reminded Robert and his classmates of all the advantages they had received and urged them always to remember how fortunate they were and give something back to society.

John Dermont and his wife, Barbara, were at the ceremony. They sat in a pew listening dutifully to the speeches and award presentations. Dermont grew drowsy. Then suddenly he heard that the next award would be for the eighth-grade history essay competition. He sat up straight. "Phyllis didn't tell me when she asked me to help Robert with his history essay," he whispered to Barbara, "that it was for a competition."

"Sssh," Barbara said.

Dermont didn't quiet down. "If she'd told me, I'd never have agreed to help."

"You *only* helped," Barbara said. "You didn't write it."

"That's not the point. I made research suggestions. Contributed ideas. If Robert wins, I'm going to have to tell the school."

A moment later the winner was announced. Dermont was relieved to hear another boy's name. "I guess I shouldn't have worried," he whispered to Barbara. "Because even with help, Robert probably didn't write an organized essay. His porch light is off."

In the fall Jennifer began at John Philip Sousa, a public junior high in Port Washington.

She wasn't happy about the school. Port Washington had two junior highs, Sousa and Weber, and many of the friends she had arduously made in sixth grade were at Weber, because they lived in its district. She complained about being parted from her old companions, and complained too that Sousa was cliquish. "I don't fit in," she wailed to a friend. "I'll never fit in." But her social anxiety made her push herself forward, and soon she was hanging out with girls in the school's most powerful clique.

One Sunday morning that fall, John Dermont's breakfast was interrupted by an urgent telephone call. It was from Phyllis Chambers, who sounded on the verge of hysteria. "Robert's down from Choate," she said. "And Bob's been drinking the whole weekend. He's upset the boy." She rattled on for a few minutes, and Dermont tried to calm her down. But she didn't calm down. And after a while she said, "I want you to come over and put Bob out of the apartment."

Dermont was startled. "That's a pretty drastic thing to do to a man, to put him out of his home."

"I don't care. I want him out."

Dermont hesitated. Bob Chambers was a big man. Not aggressive, but nevertheless big. If Bob was drunk, and he tried to get him to leave, there could be trouble. "What's Bob doing now?" he asked Phyllis. "Is he intoxicated now?"

"No. But you'd better come right away."

Dermont was moved by the distress in her voice and said he'd be right over. But as he was scrambling into his coat, he was as worried that Bob might agree to leave his home as that he might resist. "You can't just throw a guy out of his house," he said to his wife. "You've got to offer him an alternative."

"Of course," Barbara said. "But what?"

"Roosevelt Hospital," Dermont remembered. "Call them and see if they've got a free bed in their detoxification unit. If they do, tell them to hold it." Then he raced out of his apartment.

At the Chamberses', he was let in by Phyllis and Robert, who quickly retreated to a bedroom, leaving him alone with Bob in the dining room. "I've got to use the phone," he said to Bob, and dialed Barbara.

"Did you reach Roosevelt?" he asked when she picked up. "Do they have a bed?"

"Yes. I said you'd be right over."

"Good." Dermont hung up and began trying to explain to Bob why he was here. "Phyllis asked me to come," he said. "She and Robert don't want you here anymore."

Bob stared at him with a face full of sorrow and incomprehension. "*Who* doesn't want me here?" he asked.

"Your family," Dermont said. "They want you to go. For your own good."

Bob put his head in his hands.

"Don't worry," Dermont said. "We're going to go over to Roosevelt Hospital. You can stay there a week, and then you can get into Smithers."

"I don't know," Bob said. And he looked so uncertain that Dermont decided that Phyllis and Robert ought to talk to him now, too. Tell him that even though they wanted him gone, they still cared for him. He called Phyllis out of the bedroom, explained his plan about Roosevelt to her, and stood quietly as she told Bob what a good idea it was and that she only wanted him to leave because it would help him. Then he called Robert out. "Tell your father how much you love him," he said.

The boy didn't speak. Wouldn't speak.

"You do love him, don't you?" Dermont prompted. But still the boy remained silent. Was he angry with his father? Embarrassed? Probably a bit of both, Dermont thought, and remembered that Phyllis had said something earlier about how last night Bob had stumbled and fallen on Robert. "Come on, Robert," Dermont coaxed the boy, still hoping he'd say something supportive to his father. But Robert just shrugged. Then, "All this fuss is taking too long," he muttered. "I've got to be back up at school in a few hours."

At that, Bob Chambers stood up. And a moment later he slammed the front door and was gone.

Fifteen minutes afterward, while Phyllis and Dermont were considering what to do, Robert skittered out of the apartment and began looking for his father. He searched for him in all his favorite bars. He tore through the neighborhood, going up and down the streets. But he didn't find Bob, and a few hours later he returned to Choate.

The glitter of gold on red leaves when the first demure bursts of sun light on them, the silver foil of frost that wraps each sheath of grass. Autumn mornings in Connecticut were breathtaking. But after that weekend in New York, Robert rarely woke up in time to see them anymore. He had begun using cocaine and, enjoying the rush, was staying up late, only to drowse away his mornings. Years later, he would tell his parents that he'd never have used coke except for what he'd gone through that terrible weekend when his father had slammed out of the apartment. He'd wanted to blot out the experience, the memory, he said. But his initial explorations of cocaine may have had nothing to do with that painful weekend, may have been the result of cocaine's new and widespread availability. Once a rare drug, it had become in the early 1980s easy to get, even at boarding school, even at Choate. Some Choate students would soon be financing the smuggling of the drug direct to the campus from Caracas.

Robert's teachers didn't know he was using cocaine, or so they later maintained. But they were worried about his absences from class. They alerted Tom Yankus, the vice principal, who called Robert into his office. "You've been cutting classes," Yankus told him. "You're heading for disaster."

"I'm keeping up with the work," Robert said sincerely. "My grades'll turn out fine."

"I have a favor to ask of you," Phyllis wrote to Yankus early in December 1980. "Your student, my son Robert Chambers, enjoyed many years of active participation in the Knickerbocker Greys. On December 12, the group will hold its 100th Christmas Review. Robert, and a goodly number of other 'old boys,' have shown an enthusiastic interest in putting on their dress uniforms and participating in the review."

For close to two years she had been working on the great event, and now it appeared that her son might not be able to witness her triumph. Choate seemed reluctant to give him time off in the middle of the term. She would have Bob with her, of course. Several weeks after she and Dermont had tried to get him to go to Roosevelt Hospital, Bob had returned home. But she wanted Robert present, too. So she described the event to the vice principal. And she invited him, too, using language that might remind him of his own patriotic past. "I believe that you saw naval service," she wrote, "and our ceremonies may be evocative of that period of your life."

Yankus did not accept the personal invitation, but he did grant permission for Robert to attend. Phyllis sent a limousine up to the school to bring her boy home. She always seemed to have money for treats like that for him.

On the night of the ceremony she was in her glory. She dressed in a pink Nipon frock and made her way prettily to the armory, which had been decorated for the Christmas season in a wealth of tinsel and poinsettias. Scores of important guests—among them Major General Robert Arter, commander of the U.S. Army Military District of Washington, D.C., and the Old Guard, the troops that paraded before visiting heads of state—had congregated in the cavernous halls. Phyllis greeted them, proudly eyed her ranks of meticulously attired junior soldiers, and gave an interview to a *Town & Country* reporter. "Discipline is still the main theme," she said. "The teaching that is given in the Greys trains a boy how to walk properly, tall and straight. How to have respect for people both older and younger than himself, and how to accept responsibility."

Robert, standing nearby, wanted to be in the magazine story, too. "The best part," he spoke up, "is becoming an officer. Then you get to boss other people around. That's a whole lot better than taking orders."

Phyllis was not amused. "It's a very tough world out there," she said, cutting him off. "A boy who receives this training is less likely to fall by the wayside later on."

The review was highly successful. The Old Guard's fife and drum corps provided rousing music, and the boys paraded majestically. But afterward, when the guests made their way upstairs for dinner in the armory's baronial dining hall, Phyllis's triumph lost some of its gloss. Bob decided not to stay for the meal. Just as people were sitting down to eat, he disappeared for the evening.

At Christmas, when Robert came down for his school vacation, his father was once again not living at home. "He's traveling on business," Robert told a friend.

The holiday whirled forward. Robert went to numerous parties, and in the process caught up with numerous old acquaintances. One was a girl on whom he'd had a serious crush the year before. She was younger than he, still in grade school, and perhaps that made him feel secure, for he started seeing a great deal of her and confiding to her that he had problems. But although whenever he was with her he told her she was everything he'd ever wanted in a girl, he didn't—like other fourteen-year-old boys she knew—get physical with her.

She didn't mind. It shows he respects me, she thought.

Sometime that spring, Tom Yankus decided that Robert didn't belong at Choate. He wasn't taking school seriously. His room was a clubhouse. He hadn't made up his missing work. Writing to Phyllis, Yankus informed her that the venerable institution didn't want her son back for the next semester.

Phyllis was dismayed. She looked into other boarding schools. But eventually she decided to let Robert live at home and go to a private high school in the city next year. It was what he wanted.

That summer, bumping along twisting Spanish roads, Riply Buckner, an American prep school student, sat in a tour bus and stared enviously at Robert Chambers. Robert was two years younger than Riply, yet he was surrounded by girls. Some of them were even older girls. Riply wished he knew the younger kid's secret.

He started talking to him after that, got to know him a little. The kid had been kicked out of Choate, which was sponsoring the trip, but they'd let him come to Spain anyway because he'd already paid his deposit.

Riply liked him. It's not his fault all the girls have the hots for him, he decided. He just has this cool air about him, like he's slightly superior to everyone else, and girls go for that. I do, too. It makes you think when you're with the guy that it's something of a privilege.

One night he went drinking with Robert at a noisy little *tapas* bar, where they downed beer by the liter. Then he and Robert sat talking on the roof of their hotel. From the roof they could see a moonlit panorama of red-tiled houses and vaulting church spires. Below was the deserted courtyard of the hotel. Robert was in an expansive mood. Words poured out of him. Riply tried to keep up, hoping he sounded witty and wise. But after a while he got the feeling that Robert wasn't listening to him, was just asking him to be his audience. Still, he was pleased to be up on the roof with him.

While they were sitting there, Robert had an idea. There were big chunks of marble lying on the rooftop. "Let's throw one into the court-yard," he said. "Watch it explode."

Riply got uneasy. But there was no one in the courtyard. Everyone was asleep. "Okay," he said, "sure." And he helped Robert heft a wedge of marble, poise it on the roof's edge, and heave it down. It hit the stones below with a terrific noise and sounded, just as Robert had suggested it might, like an explosion.

"Let's get another one," Robert said.

Riply was frightened of throwing down another block of marble. Someone might hear. Come after them. But he was even more afraid of seeming less than daring. So he helped Robert heft another wedge and cast it over the roof edge. Then he helped him heft another. And another.

He and Robert hurled stones into the desolate night for a half hour. No one heard them. No one came. Then at last, manic energy spent, they left the roof and retreated to an exhausted slumber.

Trips abroad. Private schools for Robert. The occasional limousine. How did Phyllis manage? her friends wondered. They assumed that Bob's family helped out. But they didn't think they helped out to any great degree. If they had, Phyllis wouldn't have had to work as hard as she did. She was always working. She put in twelve-hour shifts. Night shifts mostly.

In the fall of 1981, after his return from Europe, Robert began his sophomore year at Browning, an all-male prep school on Manhattan's East Side that was less renowned than Choate but nevertheless prestigious. The reasons that Choate had asked him to leave were apparently not on his school records, for Browning's assistant headmaster, Dr. Gilbert Smith, had no reservations about the new student, except for not being certain he believed the boy's explanation of his departure from Choate—he'd said he simply wanted to be back in the city. Still, he seemed like a fine young man, his demeanor uncommonly pleasant. Smith decided to give him the benefit of the doubt.

Jennifer re-enrolled at Sousa. But she seemed to some of her teachers to be distinctly unhappy that term. Her schoolwork was poor. And while she wasn't officially classified as a slow reader, she read less swiftly than many of her classmates and showed little interest in what she did read. More, she was on the outs with her clique.

One teacher, worried about her, took it upon herself to introduce Jennifer to her own daughter, who went to the town's other junior high, Weber.

"I wish I could go to Weber," Jennifer told her new friend. "The girls at Sousa suck."

"What's the matter with them?"

"They've been spreading stories about me."

"What kind of stories?"

Jennifer wouldn't say.

"My mother's a doctor," Robert told a friend that year. "My father's the president of a record company," he said to other friends. He was hanging out with a well-heeled group of city prep school students; and power, position, and money were important to them. He had friends who had been promised Porsches for their eighteenth birthdays, friends who lived in twelve-room apartments and weekended in the cold weather at their vacation homes in Florida's Palm Beach, in the warm weather at their homes in Long Island's luxury towns of Southampton and East Hampton. They were a sophisticated, a glittering set. They partied a lot, traveled by limousine to fashionable discos, and wore gold Rolexes with their jeans and T-shirts.

Drugs made their nights go round, their parties soar, their lively cliques click and keep clicking throughout the hours. They had no trouble getting drugs. One girl's housekeeper sold cocaine. So did the tutor from whom some of them took private lessons. All that was necessary was money, and that most of the set, except for Robert, had in abundance.

At a party that winter, a girl saw Robert rifling through the guests' coat pockets. At another, the hostess came upon him opening drawers in her parents' bedroom. Neither of the two girls challenged Robert. But they gossiped about the incidents.

"I'm not inviting Robert to *my* party," a third girl told her best friend one night.

"You can't do that," her friend said. "He's one of us. We go way back. Just tell people to be careful where they put their stuff."

Early in 1982, Jennifer transferred to Weber for her last semester of junior high. Ellen Levin had taken a different, somewhat larger house on a street that was in the Weber district. It was a white stucco two-story house with an attic on top. The shingles on the roof were chipped and cracked. The lawn was small.

The Chamberses moved in 1982, too. Or at least Phyllis and Robert did, for at the time of the move, Bob Chambers was away. He'd at last decided to enter a rehabilitation clinic, this one out of town.

The Chamberses' new apartment bore one of the most prestigious addresses in the city. It was on East 90th Street off Fifth Avenue, a few doors away from the Cooper-Hewitt Museum. They'd been able to afford the move because the modest building on Park Avenue in which they'd raised Robert had gone co-op, and they'd bought their apartment at the advantageous insiders' price, then sold it at a profit.

The building Phyllis chose this time was elegant, its lobby tiled with black and white marble and ornamented with Italianate murals and glistening bronze sconces and chandeliers. The apartment itself was equally imposing. Once the library of the mansion, it had paneled walls and a fireplace. Phyllis took the apartment's front bedroom and gave Robert its back one, a quiet private area that looked down upon the playground of an elite girls' school.

Decorating, Phyllis concentrated not just on her apartment but on the public areas of the building as well. She wanted, she told her new neighbors, to make the lobby even prettier and to have the patch of earth in front of the house cleaned out and planted into a proper flower bed. The neighbors were slow to become involved, but Phyllis moved ahead, installing a luxuriant ficus tree in the lobby and hiring someone to plant impatiens in the sidewalk plot.

Having a good address and a beautiful place to live may have held unusual importance for her that winter, for, her presidency of the Greys over, she was devoting her fund-raising skills to a new cause. It was the Gold & Silver Ball, a major East Side charity event that raised money for emotionally disturbed and disadvantaged young people. On the strength of her Greys experience, she had been made a member of the ball's executive committee and was serving on it side by side with dazzlingly rich men and women. Gloria Vanderbilt was on the committee. So was Donald Trump.

Dr. Smith had his hands full. All autumn, Browning had been plagued by a rash of vandalism and robberies. Graffiti had appeared on pristine walls. Lockers had been broken into and students' wallets emptied. The losses and disturbances were minor, but they were the kind of thing that could drive a headmaster crazy, and Smith worried about them. He determined to locate the culprit or culprits forthwith and mete out swift punishment.

He didn't think Robert Chambers was involved. Robert didn't strike him as a troublemaker, though he hung around with some who were. No, Robert was weak, a follower. Not the fellow he was looking for. One of his good friends was. He called Robert's friend into his office and, certain he had found the wrongdoer, expelled him.

He also alerted Phyllis Chambers to Robert's unfortunate choice of companions. She responded well. Unlike other mothers to whom the headmaster had sometimes had to break unpleasant news about their children, she didn't just pooh-pooh what he was saying but promised she'd keep an eye on her son. She must have her share of problems with him, Smith thought.

He was one of the few people to whom Phyllis communicated this impression. At around the same time the headmaster spoke to her about Robert, Phyllis was using her influence with the organizers of the Gold & Silver Ball to escalate her son's social connections. She was urging them to put him on the charity's junior committee, which helped plan the Ball, and where he could meet and share responsibilities with a von Bülow, a Uzielli, a Rockefeller. She said nothing to suggest that Robert would be less than an exemplary committee member, and her request was granted.

One wintry weekend when the remains of a long-forgotten snowstorm lay gray and greasy at the edges of the city's streets, Robert went skiing at Gore Mountain in Vermont, The trip had been organized by Browning, but students from other private high schools had been invited to participate. Leilia Van Baker, the girl who had some years earlier marveled at the large romantic portrait of Robert that hung in his living room, was fourteen now and in the ninth grade at Miss Hewitt's. She came on the expedition, along with a friend of hers from the fashionable academy. They and the rest of the group traveled by bus and stayed in a pretty hotel.

The trip was a voyage to freedom. The very air, smog-free and tinglingly cold, made the students look back on life in New York as a kind of prison, a place that had been suffocating them. They soared down the mountain, which glistened with powdery snow, and felt themselves to be almost magical creatures, capable of flight. The ecstasy of skiing continued on into the night, when they gathered around a fire to listen to music and talk. Robert and several of his friends had brought along bags of pot and huge bong pipes with which to smoke it. They'd also brought cases of beer and bottles of whiskey.

Leilia had a wonderful time at the impromptu party. So did her schoolmate. But after a while Leilia's schoolmate disappeared. So did one of the boys. Leilia waited for her friend to reappear, but when after a long while she didn't, Leilia went looking for her. Tiptoeing along a bedroom corridor, she opened doors. No sign of her friend. Then, in the dim light of one room, she saw a familiar figure. It was her friend, lying alone on a rumpled bed.

Leilia hurried toward her. Her friend didn't move. She was dead still, her neck covered with hickeys and her face covered with vomit. "Help!" Leilia screamed. Afraid that her friend might have choked on her vomit, she turned her over.

In a moment other girls and boys poured into the room. "Call an ambulance!" someone shouted. Someone else did, and Leilia's friend, comatose, was taken to a hospital.

The next day the group boarded a bus for New York. Leilia was gloomy. Her friend was all right. She hadn't choked. But she'd lost her virginity, still felt sick from passing out, and was being kept at the hospital. As the bus started rolling, Leilia kept brooding about what had happened. Kept thinking that she, too, could have gotten so wasted that she might have had her first sexual experience in a stupor. Had it with a partner so stoned that when it was over he'd wander away, leave her practically at death's door. She was furious with the boy who had seduced and abandoned her schoolmate. But she was angry at Robert, too. He and his friends had supplied the drugs and the booze.

Still, in the middle of the bus ride, Robert came and sat with her, and he was nice and comforting. Sexy, too. He made a pass at her. She didn't respond to it, but she talked to him a good part of the way. And in the end she decided that what had happened to her friend hadn't really been Robert's fault but the fault of the group at large.

She forgave Robert and went on being his friend.

Jennifer went on a ski trip that winter, too. Her friends—as soon as she'd transferred to Weber, she'd made many—tried the trails at Plattekill in upstate New York. It was one of her first attempts at skiing, and she ended up spending a good part of the time tumbling into snowbanks.

Her friends weren't sure how much of her performance was lack of skill, how much of it a show designed to amuse them. She was always fooling around, always trying to make them laugh. One day she doused a slice of pizza pie with Parmesan, took a bite, then grabbed another girl and, holding her tight, breathed a mighty breath of strong cheese on her. The girl struggled to escape, and the rest of the crew broke into peals of laughter. Another time, a group of girls at her heels, she burst into a neighborhood fruit store and shouted at the surprised owner, "Your peaches suck!" The girls behind her fled, afraid of the owner's wrath, but when Jennifer, panting, caught up with them, they hugged and kissed her and shrieked with amusement.

Her crowd consisted chiefly of girls from her junior high and a handful of older boys, high school students already. She didn't think the boys found her attractive. She worried about her skin, which was freckled and sometimes blemished, about her height, which was greater than that of her girlfriends, and about her weight and her figure, stooping her shoulders to minimize her inches and dressing in loose baggy shirts to conceal her burgeoning breasts. But in fact boys in the crowd did find her appealing, and on occasion she went on dates with two of the best-looking.

Dates weren't, however, what her group was really into. Not then. Not yet. Mostly, everyone just got together and hung out. During lunch period they met and ate their sandwiches in a secluded place they called "the dungeon," a stairwell alongside a local church. After school they gossiped and told jokes in the playing field bleachers. And once in a while they cut classes, parked themselves in someone's basement den, and smoked marijuana.

The day Jennifer tried it, she enjoyed it at first, laughed and kidded around. But afterward she acted confused, began running up and down a staircase, and cried that she was looking for something she'd misplaced. She couldn't find it, or even explain just what it was.

"My pocketbook's gone," a primary-grade treacher at Browning told Dr. Smith one afternoon. "It was in my desk, and somehow it's vanished."

The teacher was agitated, and Smith tried to comfort her. "Don't worry. We'll find it," he said. "I'll help you."

But although they searched high and low, the pocketbook didn't turn up.

A week later, Dr. Smith picked up his office telephone to hear Phyllis Chambers's voice. "I was going through Robert's things," she said, "and I found some credit cards. With the name of a teacher at the school."

Smith called Robert into his office. "Did *you* steal that teacher's pocketbook?" he demanded.

"No," Robert said. He sounded polite and composed. "A friend of mine did. But I know where it is. I helped him hide it."

"Where is it?"

"I'll show you."

Unabashed, Robert led the way to the fourth floor. There he pointed to an air-conditioning duct. Smith reached to the top of the duct and found the pocketbook.

What was going on in Robert's mind? The headmaster, regarding him with curiosity, couldn't tell. This boy's got the quality of being behind plate glass, he thought. And he looks blank, looks as if he feels no anger at being implicated in the theft, no surprise, no emotion of any kind.

He didn't hesitate. He expelled him.

Robert took the news casually. "Aw, preppies, the hell with them," he told a friend. "Fuck the whole scene."

It was different for Phyllis. Prep school was what she had always wanted for Robert. Prep school, and then the Ivy League. Now who knew what prep school would take him in. Certainly not the old established, highly competitive ones like Choate and Browning. Not anymore. What was to be done? That Robert had stolen in order to buy drugs must have been apparent to her, for she decided to send him to a drug rehabilitation clinic. No doubt she was hoping that once he was clean she would find a way to pick up the shards of her shattered dreams.

She didn't want her friends to know about Robert's drug use. She kept it quiet. But she packed him off to the Chemical Dependency Unit in Baton Rouge, Louisiana.

By February 1982, Robert was back from Louisiana. Early that month, Ronald Stewart, the founder and headmaster of York Preparatory, a coed school on the Upper East Side, received a telephone call from David Hume, the headmaster of St. David's. "We had this really nice kid here," Stewart heard Hume say. "He's been at Browning. But he's been unhappy there. Would you take him?"

Stewart, a garrulous and cheerful schoolmaster given to thoughts and pronouncements of Dickensian airiness, wasn't surprised that his friend and colleague was asking him to take in a boy who was doing poorly at another school. York, which Stewart had founded only thirteen years earlier, did it all the time. If we only took the surefire successes, was the way Stewart looked at it, what good would we be doing mankind?

"David," he said to Hume, "you got it."

Of course, Stewart also interviewed Robert, met his mother, learned about the explusion from Browning, and looked over the boy's transcripts from both Browning and Choate. They were unimpressive. But the IQ was adequate. It was 120. And Robert's mother had a satisfactory enough explanation of why her son had run into difficulties at Browning. "He had trouble adjusting," she said. "Because it was an all-boys school."

Stewart accepted Robert.

After he did, he was glad he'd done so. He liked the way the boy regularly arrived at school dressed in a white shirt and blazer, the way he never seemed to need prodding to rise to his feet when adults entered the classroom, and the way he quickly joined the soccer team, becoming a star player.

Still, the new sophomore wasn't entirely satisfactory. "Robert is a capable student," Stewart wrote to Phyllis toward the end of the school term. "But he must learn to make a consistent effort."

Jennifer finished her last term of junior high with a drama of betrayal and rejection. A classmate of hers had been flirting with one of her boyfriends, and on the last day of classes Jennifer got furious with her. "You're a fat, slutty bitch," she yelled, even though their teacher was present. Then she confronted the boy. "Did you fool around?" she asked him. "With her?"

"No," he said.

But after that he started avoiding Jennifer, and she became convinced that he had lied to her. Rejection. It haunted her. She couldn't put her hurt feelings out of her mind and wrote bitterly about the incident to a friend.

Summer arrived, hot and muggy. Phyllis got Robert a job with the Wall Street law firm Davis Polk & Wardwell. She telephoned one of the firm's partners, a lawyer she knew because his son had been in the Knickerbocker Greys during her presidency. "Robert's looking for a summer job," she said. "Can you help him find one?"

The lawyer called the office manager, put in a good word, and soon Robert was running copying machines and delivering messages.

Jennifer went to summer camp in the Adirondacks. When camp was over, she moved once again—this time out of her mother's house in Port Washington and into the home of her father and stepmother in Manhattan. Steve and Arlene were living now in SoHo, one of the city's hot new real estate areas, a region where long-neglected cast-iron mercantile buildings were rapidly being converted into dramatic apartments, trendy boutiques, and avantgarde art galleries. Steve was managing numerous SoHo properties. And he had purchased and renovated an enormous loft for himself and Arlene, decorating it with exciting art and expensive furniture.

Jennifer's move to SoHo was abrupt, and it surprised some of her junior high friends, who had always thought her fond of her mother. But years later she would tell other friends that her mother hadn't looked after her properly, hadn't given her the security and guidance she'd needed.

In Manhattan, Steve and Arlene created an area for Jennifer in the loft—a balcony room that looked down on the vast space below. They let her choose the colors and hang posters, and they got her her own telephone and answering machine. They also went with her to investigate city high schools. Visiting several, they settled on Baldwin. It was a West Side private school that was known for providing special help to students with learning disabilities. Jennifer had had difficulties keeping up with Port Washington classmates. The new school, the Levins hoped, would give her the kind of academic boost she needed.

COMING OF AGE

Fourteen and in high school. The surge of hormones that turns gangly adolescents into comely young women had done its covert work, and Jennifer had blossomed, grown graceful and more poised. She no longer stooped and slumped, no longer tried to hide her height or her ample breasts. Indeed, she showed off her new, almost womanly, figure, wearing skin-tight jeans and shirts. She also changed her coiffure, shaving and spiking her hair into an up-to-the-minute punk cut. In part she altered her hairdo for fear of looking too suburban. She had heard, she told her old Port Washington friends, that kids in the city made fun of kids from the suburbs, calling them "B and T's"—the Bridge and Tunnel crowd—and she dreaded being viewed as an outsider by her new classmates.

Still, despite her fears, she had a coterie of friends by the time she had been at Baldwin only a few weeks. Carl Morgera, who hoped to be an actor or a playwright, was one of the first. He introduced Jennifer to his friends, and after classes went with her and the gang to nearby Central Park, where they let off steam by playing Frisbee or engaging in mock fights. The park was filled with autumnal light. The leaves were red and copper. Carl would heft Jennifer onto his shoulders and give her racing, tearing piggyback rides, her voice shattering the park's tranquillity with shrieks of feigned terror. He was very fond of her, but she didn't become his girlfriend. Not long into her first semester at Baldwin, she met another boy upon whom she conferred that privilege.

He was Brock Pernice, a slender boy with an animated, mischievous face. A grandson of the famous Broadway producer Alexander Cohen, Brock went to York Prep. On the day he met Jennifer he was visiting friends in the Baldwin gym. She was sitting on a wooden gym horse, her black-jeaned legs dangling over the sides. Her lips were painted a vivid pink, and on her head was a big jaunty hat. Transfixed by her dramatic good looks, Brock invited her to go with him to a Billy Idol concert.

She accepted. He took her to the concert and then to the lively Peppermint Lounge. There he danced with her and kissed her, and after that he began dating her regularly.

Robert, who had turned sixteen that fall, was often surrounded by girls. They flocked to him, attracted by his extraordinarily handsome face and tall, long-limbed body. At parties or in Central Park—where his friends, too, generally gathered after school—girls came up to him, encircled him, and pressed their attentions on him. He did little, just passively accepted their giggles and embraces, and reaped envious stares from less favored boys.

He was in the park constantly. After the trip to the Louisiana clinic, he'd gone right back to drinking and drugs. And his favorite place to get stoned was the park.

He had his preferred spots, a grove of trees behind The Metropolitan Museum of Art, where as a little boy he'd congregated with his St. David's friends, and a grassy slope at the side of the Museum, where the ancient glass-encased Temple of Dendur stood eerie guard over the drug-dazed, sparking their fantasies with visions of mystery and science fiction.

When he himself was drug-dazed, he sometimes hallucinated, talking aloud to a tree or a lamppost. A handful of girls were so struck by the sight that they dubbed him "The Boy Who Talks to Lampposts." But nevertheless they found him cute.

Not so his father. Bob, who had returned sober from the clinic to which *he'd* gone, had been taking a fresh look at his life. He saw with sudden clarity the trouble his son was in.

Phyllis refuses to, Bob told his AA group. She refuses, even though the parents of some of Robert's friends have told us he's no longer welcome at their homes. She just keeps denying his problems and saying he'll straighten out soon.

Phyllis was no doubt counting on college to do the straightening out. Certainly she was turning a blind eye to Robert's failings and pretending to herself and the outside world that he was still the promising child of her daydreams. When York sent her a junior-year questionnaire asking her to which colleges she would like to see her son apply, she wrote down, "Dartmouth, Brown, Duke, and Columbia"—all of them colleges with very high admission standards. She also mentioned on the form that she had "pull" at three of those schools. For Columbia, she noted, she had a friend who was a big contributor. For Duke, she could count on the good word of General Robert Arter, commander of the Military District of Washington, D.C. And for Brown, why, "the Kennedy Family."

That same autumn—it was 1982—Jennifer, Carl, and some of their Baldwin friends started going in groups to Studio 54. Fourteen-year-olds from all over the city were there. Studio, as its regulars called it, had once been the most fashionable disco in town, a place where celebrities and jet-setters rocked and rolled on a strobe-lit dance floor dominated by a neon man-in-the-moon snorting cocaine through a giant spoon. But Studio had fallen on hard times. Its original owners had been jailed for tax fraud and its doors had been shut for a year. In 1981, it had reopened under new management, but its former habitués had moved on to other pleasure palaces. Realizing that a new clientele was necessary to fill the cavernous premises, the new management had begun distributing free or discounted passes at the city's high schools, hoping that the club's former association with the Beautiful People would attract young, and therefore authentically beautiful, people.

By the time Jennifer's group began going to Studio, so many young people were begging for admission that doormen fierce as Cerberus guarding the gates of Hades blocked the mob behind wooden barriers. The doormen picked and chose among the young people, or at least gave the impression that they were picking and choosing, letting in only a few at a time while the rest of the crowd groaned or growled. Those who got in felt honored, assumed they'd been chosen because they looked better than the others, looked like the club's real insiders.

The insiders—generally they were the children of families whose names had publicity value—never had to wait on line. They got into the disco as soon as they arrived. They also got invitations to the club's private parties. And they got free drinks—the management permitted teenage drinking provided teenagers had IDs that falsified their age. The insiders constituted Studio's A-list, and the rest of the crowd, no matter their discounted or free passes, a gigantic, clamoring B-list.

Jennifer was, in her first forays to Studio, a B-listed girl. She didn't complain. It was exciting just to get in.

You felt like a grown-up there, she and her agemates said. But of course that meant you had to dress like one. Wear fancy clothes. And good shoes. Preferably heels. Definitely not sneakers. The bouncers could tell a lot about people from their feet. If your shoes were wrong, you'd *never* get in.

You also needed makeup. Plenty of it. And that could be a problem if your parents thought you'd gone out just to sleep over at a friend's house. But it wasn't insurmountable. You could always just bring your makeup with you and put it on once you arrived. Or even leave your makeup at home and use the expensive brands that were available free in the bathrooms. Studio had these great bathrooms, with big mirrors and pretty cloth-covered vanity tables. The really cool people stashed their coats under the vanities so they didn't have to pay for checking them.

Outside, the music was so loud that you didn't so much hear it as feel it throbbing through your body. And there were sights! Boys wearing jewelry and blond wigs. Older men—a lot of them looked like lawyers—smoking grass or snorting coke. Sometimes they'd offer you some. And then try to pick you up. But if you stuck with the people you came in with, you were okay. You could dance.

Jennifer and her friends knew, of course, about the private parties. How could they not? Calvin Klein's daughter, Marci, had her sixteenth birthday party at Studio and invited scores of Manhattan prep school girls. The invitations were adorable. Little Plexiglas boxes holding sixteen bright red candles, delivered by a messenger in a limo. And at the party there were candles six feet high and dancing girls in fishnet tights and tuxedo jackets, and a raft of celebrities—among them Mick Jagger, Timothy Hutton, and Treat Williams. Jennifer and her friends knew girls who'd gone. And they knew, at fourteen, that at Studio 54, there was glamour and *real* glamour.

Steve Levin didn't like Jennifer staying out late. But he was aware that nothing started in New York until after eleven at night. He gave her rules. No going out on school nights, period. And when she went out on weekend nights, she was to take taxis, no public transportation. He also insisted that if she said she was going to sleep over at some friend's house and then changed her plans, went to someone else's place, she call and let him know where she was.

She always called. And on the few occasions when he had something to tell her and telephoned her at the place she'd said she was going to be, she was always there. She was an honest kid.

As the December date for the Gold & Silver Ball approached, Phyllis was far from happy. For one thing, Robert hadn't gone to even a single planning session of the Junior Committee. He hadn't wanted to be with a bunch of charity-minded kids assigning each other chores. He'd stayed away from the meetings and hung out with his own circle—York boys or street kids he'd met in the park who were heavily into drugs. For another thing, Bob didn't have a proper job. MCA had let him go, and he hadn't been able to find another suitable position. Strapped for money, he'd started working as a deliveryman for a local liquor shop.

The ball was held that winter of 1982 in the ballroom of the brand-new Grand Hyatt Hotel. Phyllis's fellow executive committee member, Donald Trump, owned the hotel and had made it available for the charitable event. Phyllis dressed beautifully and tried to have a good time. But Robert didn't come. And although Bob did, he'd been out ringing doorbells and collecting tips practically up to the moment they left for the great affair.

By Christmas, Phyllis's neighbors were gossiping about the irony of her circumstances. But she kept up a bold front. She purchased a shop-decorated Christmas tree for her apartment from an expensive neighborhood florist. She also got the florist to provide holiday flowers for the lobby. They were not run-of-the-mill small potted poinsettias but two enormous poinsettia trees.

How can she afford them? the neighbors asked one another. Her salary as a nurse, even a nurse to the wealthy, can't be very high. But they decided not to look a gift horse in the mouth—particularly as the lobby needed perking up. The intricate bronze chandelier and sconces that had once been its high point had disappeared. They'd been stolen, a few people in the building feared, by Robert and his friends.

On New Year's Eve, Bob Chambers worked for the liquor store, and Phyllis saw friends. When she returned to her apartment that night, she was greeted by a horrendous sight. The apartment had been burglarized and many things she cherished had been stolen. Jewelry, cameras, and a typewriter were gone. Even some of her clothes.

The neighbors, learning about the burglary, suspected Robert of having committed it. But Phyllis, who wore hand-me-downs for several weeks afterward, told them she believed she'd been robbed by the superintendent or else by some cat burglar who had scaled the back walls. She lobbied to get the super fired and she bought a mercury vapor light for the back of the building. "It's as powerful as a streetlamp," she told the neighbors. "It'll keep any future burglars away."

"It's finished. It's really over," Phyllis said to Barbara Dermont over tea sandwiches at the elegant Carlyle Hotel a few months after her apartment was burglarized. She was speaking about her marriage. Bob Chambers was moving out. A moment later tears welled up in her eyes.

Barbara was astonished. She'd never seen Phyllis cry before, had always imagined her as a tower of strength and a fortress of guarded emotion. She felt embarrassed and tried to comfort Phyllis, but Phyllis was inconsolable. "I didn't want much. All I ever wanted was for Bob to take me for a walk on a Sunday afternoon and hold my hand," she cried. "Or just take me out for a cup of coffee."

He can't, Barbara thought, because you always take control over everything when you're with him. But she didn't say this to Phyllis. Phyllis doesn't *see* herself as controlling, Barbara mused. She doesn't see herself clearly at all. She lives in a kind of fantasy world. Suddenly Barbara felt tears in her own eyes.

Toward the end of that winter's ski season, Brock Pernice made his way to Robert's house on East 90th Street. Brock wasn't at York any longer. He'd transferred to another school. But he'd known Robert at York, and when they'd run into each other recently, Robert had mentioned that he had some terrific skis to sell. Brock had been interested.

At Robert's, Brock went down to the basement with him. There he saw numerous pairs of skis.

"They're old family skis," Robert said, although in fact he and some friends had stolen them from a ski chalet in upstate New York.

"How much do you want for these?" Brock asked, selecting a pair.

"Two hundred dollars."

"I've only got a hundred."

"That'll be okay," Robert said.

Brock took the skis.

Several days later, he saw Robert again. It was at his school cafeteria. He was sitting there when suddenly he looked up and noticed Robert standing over him. He wasn't alone. He had two black guys with him. Strangers. "We came for the money you owe," Robert said.

Owe? Brock felt confused. "I thought you said a hundred dollars would be okay."

"No." Robert shook his head. "It's two hundred."

Brock realized he must have made a mistake about the price and said he'd pay up. "But not now," he explained. "I don't have the money on me."

"You got a bank account, don't you?" one of the strangers suddenly interjected.

Brock nodded unhappily.

"So let's go to the bank."

Brock hesitated. But the stranger who had spoken was broader and more muscular than he. So was the other one. So was Robert for that matter. Getting up from the table, Brock left school and headed for his bank.

Robert and the other two young men went with him. And the whole time he was drawing out his money, they stood ominously at his shoulders.

In the summer of that year—it was 1983—Jennifer went for the second time to the Adirondacks camp. Canoeing, sailing, and struggling up winding wilderness trails, she was, like adolescent campers everywhere, hungry all the time. One weekend Steve and Arlene visited her and, taking her grocery shopping, allowed her to buy thirty-five dollars' worth of snacks. The largesse, the attention made her so joyous that she described the shopping expedition in a letter to one of her old Port Washington girlfriends. She also mentioned in the same letter that she was going out with a boy at camp. "His name is Jeremiah," she wrote. "He is fifteen. Blond hair, blue eyes! Gorgeous!"

"If only I could be like her," a young Colombian woman named Julia Zapata said about Phyllis Chambers to several of her friends that August. Julia's English was poor, her clothes were shabby, and she was perpetually anxious, but she had landed a job as cook for an extremely rich but elderly and ailing couple, Samuel and Irene Coyne, who lived on Park Avenue. Phyllis Chambers was managing the household, supervising Julia and a staff of several nurses, but her principal job was to serve as companion to old Mrs. Coyne, who had had a debilitating stoke. Phyllis attended her with devotion, talking to her, bathing her, and even painting her lips and cheeks and wiggling her into a girdle and dressy clothes so she could go out to lunch to the Carlyle.

Mrs. Coyne's son and daughter-in-law didn't altogether approve of Phyllis. They felt she was extravagant and domineering, rather as if she were the lady of the house, not an employee. But Julia adored her. Sure, Phyllis acted like a lady, not a servant, was the way Julia looked at it. But what was wrong with that. Nothing said that because you scrubbed floors or washed pots or emptied bedpans, you couldn't be a lady. Julia wanted to be one, too. So did all her friends who worked as servants to the rich.

Julia was thrilled when Phyllis began to tutor her in the essentials of ladydom—gave her advice about clothing and hairstyles and lectured her about improving her personality. "You must learn to celebrate yourself," Phyllis told Julia. "You must say to yourself, 'This is Julia, and I'm beautiful.'" Phyllis had learned to say things like this about her own self in a self-help group called The Pursuit of Excellence. She attended numerous self-help groups—among them Freedom Institute and Scientology.

Julia was also thrilled when Phyllis invited her to accompany her and Mrs. Coyne to the Carlyle.

Phyllis had been working for the Coynes for a long time when Julia met her at their home in the summer of 1983. But in the fall Phyllis was fired. Years later a member of the Coyne family would tell a public official that she'd gotten into trouble because, try as the family did to point out to her that her elderly charge no longer could appreciate gourmet dining, she had refused to listen to them and persisted in going to costly restaurants with her.

Losing her position with the Coynes was a blow to Phyllis. But she soon received a nursing assignment that made up for the disappointment. She was hired to care for New York's beloved prelate Terence Cardinal Cooke, who was suffering from leukemia. She looked after the cardinal until his death in mid-October with a devotion and attentiveness that did not go unnoticed among his friends in the Church's hierarchy.

"I miss you terribly. I'll die if I don't see you," Jennifer said over the phone to Marjorie Harvey, one of her old Port Washington friends, late in October 1983. "Promise me, swear to me you'll come and visit me in the city."

At Halloween, Marjorie accepted Jennifer's invitation. So did several other Port Washington girls whom Jennifer had been imploring to come. The group took the half-hour train ride into the city, went downtown to Jennifer's loft in SoHo, and donned their costumes. One girl dressed as a rabbit, another as a bum, several as black cats. Then they went to Washington Square Park, bought a couple of bottles of Riunite red, and sat drinking on a stoop near the park.

They had a wonderful time until the black tights and twisting tails of the girls impersonating cats caught the eye of a group of rowdy young men. "Here pussy, here pussy," the men sniggered. Alarmed, the Port Washington girls scattered and began to run away. But Jennifer turned on their tormentors with an obscene comeback.

"Don't *do* that," Marjorie said, grabbing Jennifer's arm. "One of these days you're going to get yourself killed saying things like that."

Jennifer shrugged. "This is New York. You have to know how to handle yourself here."

Marjorie bristled. Jennifer's telling me I'm unsophisticated, she fretted. Her irritation lingered, and later she decided that all evening Jennifer had kept implying that her old friends were too provincial and tame for her.

They may have been. By the night of the Halloween visit Jennifer was not just going to the occasional disco but to lively and at times turbulent parties. At one, she and two city girlfriends consumed a bottle of vodka. Afterward they got sick and hurried into the bathroom. There Jennifer made them all laugh by lying down in the bathtub with her feet and arms sticking out.

She drank a lot. One night she came home from Studio so drunk her father grounded her.

Despite her flirtations with self-help groups, Phyllis counted most on God to see her through her troubles with Robert. She was very pious— "perhaps even overly pious," a priest who counseled her would one day tell an interviewer. Her beliefs were stern and narrow. One night toward the end of 1983, John Dermont, who was also a Catholic, became aware of this. He and Phyllis were at dinner together, and he had just waxed philosophical and said, "I believe in God. But sometimes I wonder. I mean, where was God during the Holocaust?"

Phyllis said, "What do you mean?"

"Well, you know," Dermont replied. "All those people died."

"Those were Jews," Phyllis said.

Dermont didn't see the relevance of her answer. "I'm not talking about what religion people had," he said, "but about God's concern for humanity."

Phyllis had no problems with the topic. "Oh yes, John,", she said. "But those people had turned their backs upon Christ."

Jennifer, nearly sixteen, fell in love with the rock star Billy Idol in the spring of 1984. Billy had blue eyes. A pouty mouth. A tattoo. She adored his music, the way he scowled, the way he swaggered. BILLY, she wrote in big block letters in her friend Joan Huey's journal, and drew hearts with his name and hers entwined.

She and Joan talked about boys all the time, and daily they went on what they called "guy-searching" walks, strolling eagerly among the crowds of young people on 8th Street in Greenwich Village. They also planned a trip to Florida, a trip which, Jennifer scribbled in Joan's journal, would net them "Tan guys! Epcot Center! Disco! Everything! Sex, sex, sex!"

"I know we would have the best time with blonds," Joan scribbled back. Blonds with "bluish-green eyes."

But Billy Idol was their ruling passion, and at last they managed to find out where he lived. For weeks afterward, the two teenagers spent hours in front of his Village apartment. And soon they began writing each other letters in which they fantasized romance with the surly singer. "Can you believe we got Billy's real name-n-address?" Jennifer wrote. "I happen to love him. . . . Billy Idol rules!"

"I happen to love him also," Joan wrote back. "A lot." Then she spiced up her correspondence. "You and I will get Billy Idol and we will have massive sex with him, okay?" she suggested. Then, later, "All right. We're gonna go back there and Billy will be by himself and we're gonna have a threesome right away."

One day Jennifer told Marjorie Harvey, her old Port Washington friend, that while shopping in Tower Records she'd actually met Billy, and what's more, he'd kissed her. "That's not all," she said. "The best part was that after he kissed me, the manager told him he shouldn't have done it, not with all these diseases going around, and Billy just sneered and gave the manager this look like, Hell, it was worth it!"

It may have been true. But it may just as well have been a fantasy. Marjorie believed it. But she didn't know that Jennifer was busily inventing a new life for herself that spring, a star-studded, stud-starred life in which she was no commonplace schoolgirl but a creature irresistible to handsome tanned guys and even to celebrities.

She was also writing poetry. Her poems, awkward rhymed verses, were generally about love, especially love gone sour or awry. One, written about the boy she had found "gorgeous" at camp, went:

> *I loved to look into his eyes,*
> *To hear his voice,*
> *Or even just to see him smile.*

Another, written to a boy she felt had mistreated her, mourned:

> *That playing games*
> *Is for little boys.*
> *Girls were never meant*
> *To be treated as toys.*

When she wasn't composing verses, she scrawled giddy letters and notes to her girlfriends. "I love you so much!! We are the closest two buddies can ever get," she wrote to one. "I know we'll remain friends forever!!" "I love ya," she wrote to another, "for good times and bad. I'll be on your side forever more 'cause that's what friends are for."

She was increasingly preoccupied by love—or, rather, being loved. As her sixteenth birthday approached, her longings crystallized around the notion of losing her virginity. It was a burden carrying around her virginity, fighting off boys who wanted to relieve her of it, hearing girls she knew who'd given up theirs when they were fourteen and fifteen start to exchange secrets about their experiences, then clam up when she said she hadn't had sex yet. But more important to her than social acceptance was the idea that she would at last, once she had sex, truly experience love.

The guy she had in mind, she told a school friend, wasn't Brock. "Brock's always fighting with me," she said. "He doesn't really love me. And for the first time to be good, the partners really have to be in love."

Soon afterward she and the boy she had chosen had sex. It was her sixteenth birthday present to herself—a present even more exciting than the one Arlene gave her, which was a trip to the Bahamas. She was exultant about giving up her virginity. "I'm *so* happy," she bubbled over the phone to one of her old Port Washington buddies. "I've done it, and it was great. I'm so glad I planned it, didn't just get drunk at a party and end up in bed with some guy, like happens to a lot of girls."

But for all her planning, her first sexual experience brought her misery as well as happiness. Only a few days after the event, she arrived at a party and saw the boy with whom she'd made love greeting another girl with a hug. She sobbed with jealousy and stormed and screamed at him.

She never fully forgave him. Not long afterward she went back to seeing Brock again. And to seeing other boys, too.

"Robert does not do his work nor does he deal realistically with his situation. There is a possibility, therefore, that he will not graduate with his class," York headmaster Stewart informed Phyllis Chambers toward the end of that school semester—Robert's senior term. It was but one of many discouraging notes he had sent to Phyllis. He hated having to write it, because Mrs. Chambers was such a concerned parent. Always volunteering to serve on school committees, always helping out on parent-teacher days. But although he liked her, there was a limit to what he could do for her. Ultimately Robert would have to pass his courses to be entitled to a diploma. And no one could assume he'd pass. As he always said to his kids, never assume! Assume makes an ass out of you and me.

Of course, part of the problem was the way parents these days didn't control their kids. They let them hang out all night doing God knows what, and the kids came to class more asleep than awake. As he always told the parents: If you lose control of your kids, you're running a hotel, not a home.

Still, it was his job to try to get Robert through high school, and he made up his mind to get really tough with him. He'd keep him after school, give him detention. Maybe then he'd recognize the seriousness of his situation.

Day after day that spring of 1984 Robert stayed late after school while much of the rest of the senior class, cans of beer or paper cups of mixed drinks in their hands, made their way to the park and lazed in the sun, smoking pot, playing Frisbee, and listening to music. Only weeks before, he'd been one of them. And now he was a prisoner. Despising Stewart's efforts at disciplining him, he, too, wrote a poem:

> *This detention is not working.*
> *I no longer care.*
> *I'm going insane, slow but sure.*
> *My condition is terminal.*
> *There is no cure except . . . let me out!*

But Stewart wouldn't let him out. And his parents, he complained to his friends, wouldn't get off his back. It was shape up or nothing. They'd even told him that unless he got into some good college, they wouldn't give him financial support. The problem with parents, he charged, was that they were always pushing, pushing, pushing you.

One day, inspired, he wrote another poem, this one entitled "Our Parents." In it he painted a romanticized portrait of a generic mother and father, a portrait in which self-pity and mockery were hidden behind lines of card-shop sentimentality:

> *Strength and security, laughter and fun,*
> *He's a prince to his daughter, a pal to his son.*
> *A storyteller to girls and boys,*
> *She's seldom dismayed by the family noise.*
> *He's an "everyday Santa" who brings home surprises,*
> *The man to consult when a problem arises.*

> *The truest of friends in times of need,*
> *She's eager to help her child succeed.*
> *He's a living instructor who struggles to teach,*
> *All the goals his child someday can reach.*
> *They know deep in their hearts that day after day,*
> *It was all worth the bother*
> *Just to hear their children say,*
> *"I love you, Mother and Father!"*

Then, at last, graduation time arrived. Robert, dressed in a cap and gown, went to the ceremony, which was held in the auditorium of The Metropolitan Museum of Art. He strode up to the podium to receive his diploma case and shook Stewart's hand as he reached for it.

But the diploma case was empty. He hadn't, despite the detention, completed all his course work and wouldn't be getting the actual diploma unless he made up the work at summer school.

That night Robert celebrated with his classmates at a graduation party. It was held in a loft, where a reggae band entertained the graduates. Robert got drunk. But that didn't bother his admirers, the flocks of tittering, dewy-eyed girls who hugged, kissed, and cuddled him as if he were a pasha with a harem.

Phyllis knew that girls sucked up to her son. "It's girls that are at the root of his problems," she had several times told a friend. And, determined to see to it that Robert didn't spend his summer dallying with girls, she went out and found him a job. It was with a woman she knew who owned a yacht and gave parties on it. "Robert's strong," Phyllis told the yacht owner. "And energetic."

The boat, spanking white and 120 feet long, was anchored at a marina in the East River. Robert reported to work and spent several days readying the yacht for the first parties of the summer. He scrubbed the decks, polished the woodwork in the cabins, loaded the pantries till they were full of expensive wines and exotic delicacies.

The setting and luxury inspired him. "Maybe," he said to a friend one evening, "I'll make a ton of money one of these days and buy Malcolm Forbes's yacht. Give parties on *that!*"

But his daydreams came to an abrupt end. After he'd been employed on the yacht only briefly, the owner noticed that bottles of champagne and cases of liquor were disappearing. She began to suspect Robert of being involved in the thefts. She didn't want to confront him with her suspicions. She knew his mother. But on a weekend when a full round of parties had been scheduled and Robert failed to arrive for work, she fired him.

He didn't have a job after that. But he did go to York's summer school, did sit in hot classrooms and struggle to make up his missing work.

A girl who met him at summer school thought he was great fun to be with. And because of that, and because all the girls she knew oohed and aahed when she said she had a class with him, she went bar-hopping with him several times and one night told him boldly that she wanted to make love with him.

"You're too young for that sort of thing," he chided her.

The girl—she was only sixteen and he was nearly eighteen—accepted his rejection and, like other girls before her, figured it showed how much he respected her. But afterward she began to think that he wasn't, when you got right down to it, as interested in sex as other boys were. He talked about it just the way they did. But he held back. Maybe that's why so many girls like him, she decided. He's safe.

Marilei Lew Lee, twenty-four years old and as petite as a doll, had been a nutritionist back home in her native Brazil; but when she came to America in 1984, the only work she'd been able to find was as a domestic. That spring she took a job as a live-in maid for Dorothy Hammerstein, widow of the famous lyricist. Mrs. Hammerstein, who was in her eighties, had been an interior decorator when she was younger, and her Park Avenue apartment was stuffed with a pirate's ransom of treasures. She had museum-quality portraits from England, lacquered screens from China, hand-painted secretaries from Venice, and myriad exotic knickknacks that required constant and meticulous dusting and cleaning. Marilei threw herself into the work, Mrs. Hammerstein praised her for her application, and after she had worked there for four months, Marilei almost ceased wishing that she knew English well enough to go back into the field of nutrition. She was happy, at least for now, with what she was doing. And she liked the rest of the staff, liked Mitchell, the valet and cook, and especially Phyllis Chambers, the new nurse. Phyllis wrote a letter to the Department of Immigration for her, saying that she too had once been a stranger in America, but had worked hard and made a success of herself and was sure that Marilei would, too.

Not everyone connected to the household liked Phyllis. Mrs. Hammerstein's other nurses didn't. Nor did Mrs. Hammerstein's doctor. But Phyllis didn't care. She told Mrs. Hammerstein that she ought to fire the other nurses and switch to Dr. Kevin Cahill, a prominent physician who had treated the late Cardinal Cooke and even Pope John Paul II, and whose office had frequently found Phyllis jobs. Mrs. Hammerstein did it.

The old lady always does whatever Phyllis asks her to do, Marilei thought. Me, too. Because Phyllis takes such charge of things that after a while everyone around her thinks they can't even take a breath without her at their side.

Forty-room houses and two-passenger cars. A wealth of broad beaches, chic little restaurants, and gorgeous suntanned guys. Long Island's Southampton enchanted Jennifer, who was staying at Joan Huey's country home and working in a store that sold Moroccan jewelry and fabrics.

She and Joan spent a lot of time together, but she made new friends, too. One was Leilia Van Baker a wealthy, WASPy girl with blond hair, a lean body, and long, gazellelike limbs. She'd been an A-listed girl at the discos ever since she was a little kid, she told Jennifer, and frequently entertained her with stories about her adventures on that A-list. She knew a girl who'd snorted coke with a famous movie star at one disco party, she said. She knew another who'd lost her virginity to a world-renowned rock singer twenty years her senior. "Do you realize," she trilled, "that there are girls our age who live in the Midwest and read in *Seventeen* about the kinds of people me and my friends actually know? Do you realize there are girls who would give their eye teeth to be part of our scene, to go to the parties we turn up our noses at?"

Jennifer knew.

One day Leilia told Jennifer that she'd been feeling a bit jaded with the scene before they'd met, but that now, seeing things through her new friend's eyes, it had become wondrous and new again. Jennifer had a rare gift, Leilia marveled, the ability to make life seem fresh.

They palled around often, and when the summer began drawing to a close, Leilia swore to Jennifer that she'd remain friends with her in the city. "We'll go to Studio together," she said. "And to the other discos. I'll introduce you around."

Leilia knew everybody. She knew the men who managed the discos. She knew the doormen who guarded the gates. She knew Amy Lumet and Cosima von Bülow and all the teenage girls who got written about in society columns. And she knew, and was good friends with, the teenage boys who were the most talked-about escorts, guys like Nick Beavers, whose family owned a lively disco, and John Flanagan, who was forever throwing the most wonderful parties, and Robert Chambers, who was the best-looking in the bunch and terrifically popular.

"You'll meet them all," Leilia promised.

"Would you mind ironing some shirts I bought for Robert?" Phyllis asked Marilei one day toward the end of that summer. Marilei said she wouldn't mind. She'd become good friends with Phyllis, and she'd met and become fond of her handsome, polite son. She liked doing favors for Phyllis and the boy, whose name she could never quite pronounce. "Hrobert," she always called him.

She took the shirts from Phyllis. They were soft cotton broadcloth from Brooks Brothers. Phyllis, she noted, buys Hrobert only the best. Laying them lovingly on her board, she made sure to press them both on the inside and on the outside, so that they would be perfectly smooth.

The next week Phyllis gave Marilei some more of Robert's shirts to iron. She did those, too, and soon it was taken for granted that she would always do Robert's laundry.

At the start of the fall, she did a great batch of laundry for him. Robert was leaving for college. He'd gotten into Boston University's School of Basic Studies.

Leilia was true to her word. By the late fall of 1984, Jennifer started turning up at private parties at Studio 54. She always seemed to be having a good time, a young man who hosted some of the parties noticed. Well, why not, he confided to an interviewer. His parties were wondrous, if he did say so himself. Everything went. Drinking, drugging, girls fellating their boyfriends right out in the open, up in the balconies. And the clothes! There was this one woman, she was worth a fortune, she used to go home in her limo every hour and change her clothes and come back in a different outfit.

He was always throwing parties. Well, he had to, he always said. He had no money. His father had cut off his trust fund. But he got paid by the discos. They paid him for bringing in the right kinds of people.

Jennifer wasn't the right kind of people, though she was, you know, *okay.* *His* people were, like, Courtney Duchin and Carter Burden, Jr., and Al Uzielli and John Flanagan. They attracted the others.

What times those parties were! The boys would get so drunk they wouldn't know what they were doing. And the girls would fight over them. At least they'd fight over the ones who were status symbols. The girls were terribly immature. They always screwed things up. Like the time he invited Prince Albert of Monaco to a party, and Prince Albert took a fancy to one of the girls, and then she wouldn't sleep with him. If he were a girl and a prince asked him to bed, well, he certainly wouldn't have stood on ceremony. But these girls, you couldn't rely on them.

Parents? Personally, he'd never noticed any parental supervision of the kids who came to his parties. The parents were blasé. They were parents who were out all night themselves. Or else they were the kind who were afraid that if they told their kids they couldn't go, the kids would have no social lives. You had to be one sonofabitch of a parent to tell your kid he or she couldn't go to these parties and risk that your kid would grow up *unpopular*.

Jennifer? He wasn't impressed with her. She looked like a lot of other girls. Just another Madonna clone.

· · ·

Why did he have to read *Hamlet*, Robert sulked at his family's Thanksgiving dinner. *Hamlet* was boring. And he'd read it already at St. David's or York or someplace. That was what was wrong with Boston University's School of Basic Studies. The curriculum was dull, repetitious.

He'd started the semester full of enthusiasm, happy to be up in Boston and pleased by the program, which had seemed designed for people like him.

"Many young people glide through high school at half-speed," the college's brochure had blazoned in big heart-warming type, "never realizing the promise of their own potential, seldom feeling the pride of having done their best. There is a college that exists for no purpose other than to help such students become the best that they can be." He'd enrolled for his classes—a smorgasbord of psychology, rhetoric, humanities, science, and social science—and tried to keep up with them. But he couldn't. He was partying a lot, drinking, doing coke. Sometimes he'd spread the white powder out on his hand in the shape of his initials and snort away his identity. By the time mid-term exams came around, he'd fallen so far behind in his assignments that he'd been warned that unless he quickly made up his work, he wouldn't be allowed to continue at the school.

He didn't tell the assembled relatives of the warning. He just said he didn't like B.U. and didn't want to go back.

Several days after the dinner, Phyllis called John Dermont and asked him, "Do you think Robert could get into Oxford?"

Dermont was astounded. He'd always viewed Oxford as the intellectual capital of the world and Robert as totally muddle-headed. "I don't really think," he said, speaking measuredly as if breaking bad news, "that Robert has what they look for."

Phyllis was undaunted. "What about for a summer session?" she asked.

Dermont thought, Of all the mothers I know, Phyllis is the one with the most undying optimism about her offspring. He shook his head. Then he said, "I think the only way kids get into Oxford for the summer is through a program sponsored by their schools. Maybe his school has such a program."

Dermont didn't know that Robert was about to be a man without a school. Nor did he know until long after the phone call about the Thanksgiving trashing of *Hamlet*. When he did hear about it, he said to his wife, "Can you imagine? Phyllis wanted to pack Robert off to Oxford. Oxford, where he'd never have to be troubled with English literature again!"

In December, Phyllis told Marilei that through no fault of his own Robert had been asked to leave Boston University. "He got into trouble," she said. "They found drugs in his room. Marijuana. He didn't put it there. Some girl did. She was jealous of him because he wouldn't pay attention to her, so she played that trick on him."

Poor Hrobert, Marilei thought. It's not his fault girls find him so attractive.

Phyllis didn't tell Marilei that Robert had stolen a roommate's credit card and used it to buy dinners for himself.

"Did you see that girl in the Maidenform ad that ran in the New York Times Magazine?" Bob Chambers said to John Dermont one day at around the time Phyllis told Marilei about the marijuana. Bob was doing all right. He had a place of his own—an apartment on the West Side—he was still on the wagon, and he had landed a job in the credit department of HBO.

"Sure I saw her," Dermont said. "She was a real pistol."

"I know her. She's a girlfriend of mine."

Was it true? Dermont wasn't sure. But he said, "Not bad!"

"I showed the picture to Robert," Bob went on.

"You showed it to *Robert?*" Dermont looked askance.

"Yeah. I was visiting. And I had the magazine with me. I told him, 'Here, take a look at your father's girlfriend.'"

"How come?"

"Just wanted him to know."

What had Bob wanted Robert to know? Dermont wondered afterward. That he was a macho guy? Or that he was no longer under Phyllis's control.

During Christmas week, Julia Zapata came to Mrs. Hammerstein's to do some work. Through Phyllis's recommendation, the former cook had been hired as a seamstress. She chalked and pinned Mrs. Hammerstein's skirts, then toured the apartment with Phyllis. In the kitchen she met Marilei who, with her shabby clothes and halting English, reminded her of herself just a few years ago, when she had first come to America. Marilei had tears in her eyes and, drawn to her, Julia asked worriedly, "Why are you crying? What's wrong?"

But Marilei wasn't sorrowing. "I'm crying happiness," she said.

"What do you mean happiness?" Julia said.

"Phyllis gave me a fur coat for Christmas," the girl explained. "All my life I wanted a fur coat and Phyllis went to a thrift shop and got me the nicest one and now I'm crying for three days."

Just like Phyllis, Julia thought. Always so thoughtful. So generous. She'd just negotiated for Julia a far higher price for her sewing than she herself had intended to request of Mrs. Hammerstein. Leaving the kitchen, Julia went into Phyllis's room—it was filled with fresh flowers—sat down, and began telling her what a good soul she was. But Phyllis was glum.

"I'm having trouble with Robert," she said, and explained that he'd gotten into a scrape having to do with money and credit cards. "Ever since Robert was a little boy," she went on angrily, "I've done so much for him. But nothing makes any difference to him."

Poor Phyllis, Julia grieved. She's always worked so hard, so many hours, for that boy. She's the kind of mother like my own, who washed me and bathed me and took the lice from my hair, the kind who, if she had only one jewel, would give it to her child. How could Robert not see this? How could he not say to himself, My mother works so hard to give me the things I want that I am going to be good because of her sacrifices.

Should she speak her mind to Phyllis? At last Julia decided she would. "Maybe you give him too much," she said. "I grew up with nothing, and it made me a decent person. It taught me to want to learn, to work, to become somebody. But children that have everything, they don't learn this."

Perhaps it was because of Julia's words, or perhaps it was on the advice of one of her self-help groups, or perhaps she was just finally fed up with Robert, but toward the end of 1984 Phyllis banished Robert from their apartment on East 90th Street and sent him to live in the basement. There was an empty apartment down there, a two-room flat that sometimes served as superintendent's quarters but was presently empty. It was a dreary place, the bedroom windowless and the living room damp and dark, but it was habitable. Robert would have to live down there, Phyllis told him, until he found himself a job and started paying his own way.

One day a neighbor noticed the door to the basement apartment ajar and peeked inside. He saw the open-out couch that served as a bed, and the posters that decorated the dismal walls—a Modigliani, a turn-of-the-century Gibson Girl print, and a pin-up of two women making love, one of them with her legs spread wide apart and her vagina fully exposed. In the semidarkness, he also saw Robert sitting on a chair. He was staring into space.

At a Christmas party in the SoHo shop of the sportswear chain French Connections, Connie Davies, who was in charge of merchandising and buying, chatted with Jennifer. She was happy that Jennifer, who had worked in the shop briefly earlier in the year, had come. She had enjoyed training the young girl, who seemed to have a flair for selling and an innate sense of style. She dressed like a little newspaper boy, with cropped denim pants, oversized sweaters, and a peaked cap turned backward on her head, or she'd twist a scarf just so around her neck, or she'd turn up with the funniest jewelry, like her long black earring that said, like Madonna's belt buckle, "Boy-Toy." Connie had started teaching her the ropes of the fashion business, and Jennifer had been such a willing pupil that Connie had begun to feel as fond of her as she did of her own nieces.

Today Jennifer asked Connie to give her a piece of the white lace with which the shop's Christmas tree was decorated.

"What for?" Connie asked.

"To wear," Jennifer said. "White lace is the look of the eighties."

Connie was struck by the words, but she wasn't sure why. Maybe it was because the teenager was so clued in, or maybe just because the phrase "the look of the eighties" sounded so amusing and portentous coming from her young lips.

.   .   .

Phyllis couldn't stay firm with Robert. Early in January she let him stop living in the basement. He'd caught the flu down there, she told Marilei. She put him in his bedroom once again and, because he'd gotten nowhere with finding himself a job, she began reading want ads, preparing resumes, and telephoning her contacts for him. "Do you know of any jobs that Robert might qualify for?" she asked a woman she'd known on the executive committee of the Gold & Silver Ball. "He's taking a year off from college. To find himself." She didn't mention that he'd been asked to leave Boston University.

Robert had made it clear to her he didn't want a dull job, or a poorly paying one. He wanted something in television or the fashion industry. Maybe he could be a model, he suggested. Phyllis agreed, asked a friend who was in the business to recommend him to photographers and agencies, and sent him to an expensive dentist to have his teeth prettified. And all the while that she worked at helping him get a job, she continued to try, just as she had when he was a little boy, to expand his social connections. The actress Mary Martin was a friend of Mrs. Hammerstein's. One day Phyllis suggested to the actress that Robert and her grandson ought to meet and go out together. They'd like each other, she insisted, and pressed to arrange a date.

But all her efforts came to naught. Robert and Mary Martin's grandson didn't hit it off, and none of her contacts came up with a proper job. After a while she decided the best thing would be to enroll him at Hunter College in the upcoming semester.

Far-out hairstyles were in, that early winter of 1985. Leilia Van Baker shaved off a chunk of her butterscotch locks, then bleached the rest sheer white, and Jennifer streaked her brown hair with flashes of blond. On weekends the two of them went out on the town with a third girl, Kitty Schoen, who was a year older than they were. They went not just to Studio but to West Side bars like MacGowan's and the West End Cafe, and the new downtown club, Area, where the elaborate decor was changed every few weeks and the bathroom stalls were often used for quick sex or quicker drug fixes. At Area, Kitty and Jennifer had the most startling experience of their young lives. Someone offered them heroin. It was a shock. They were used to people offering them coke and pot and Ecstasy. Those drugs were middle-class. But heroin!

Kitty and Jennifer didn't smoke cigarettes, but occasionally they sampled some of the middle-class drugs that were offered to them. Still, for the most part they preferred to get high on liquor. And on attention. They got plenty of that. Wherever they went, they made sure to dress eye-catchingly.

Jennifer was the most eye-catching of the three of them. She wore tiny miniskirts or ripped jeans—bought them long before Kitty and Leilia did. And she dangled a big cross around her neck, just the way Madonna did. The cross didn't go over too well with her Jewish family, but she wore it anyway.

But no matter how many compliments girls and boys alike paid Jennifer for her trendy outfits, she didn't feel altogether attractive. Often she'd stand in front of a mirror and bemoan her face, her figure. "God, I'm getting so fat," she'd say. She was five feet seven and weighed about 140 pounds. Staring at her stomach, she'd promise herself she'd go on a diet to get rid of the little bulge beneath her belly button. Thin was what those East Side boys she'd been meeting lately really liked. Thin was what all their girlfriends were.

Kitty felt Jennifer's obsession with being thin had something to do with her being jealous of Leilia. Or of her stepmother. She told Jennifer to forget about being thin. "Plump is in your genes," she said. "You're Jewish. Me, too. We'll never look like lanky Christian girls. Anyway, even if you were thin as a rail, those preppie guys would never *really* accept you. They fool around with girls like us, but they don't fall in love with us." Still, Jennifer started to diet, shunning meat and gobbling carrots, celery sticks, and lettuce leaves until she felt like a rabbit. You had to be skinny if you were going to really make it on the scene.

"Yo, Jennifer!" a girl named Sally Hopper, who hadn't seen Jennifer since camp two summers before, called out to her excitedly when she ran into her in MacGowan's shortly after the start of 1985. Jumping up to greet her old camp friend, Jennifer accidentally knocked over the drink of a boy she was sitting with, and the liquid went spilling into his lap. Sally's first thought was My God, if I did that, I'd be so embarrassed. But Jennifer wasn't embarrassed. She was cool. "I'm really sorry," she said to the boy. "Do you want me to buy you another drink?" Sally admired her for that, and afterward she took to hanging out with Jennifer.

One night at the West End Cafe, Sally and Jennifer got drunk and pretended to be having a fight, pantomiming being cats about to scratch. They got so into the game, they didn't realize how loud they were being until a bartender objected and one of their friends made them go ouside. But what the hell. It was so much fun they just carried the pretend fight out onto the street.

Sally loved goofing around. So did Jennifer. One weekend Jennifer went on a ski trip with a bunch of friends and goofed around in front of a fireplace, posing for outrageous photographs. Lying on the floor alongside one of the guys, she held the fireplace tongs to his genitals and smiled a silly gleeful smile.

Tables with red and white checked clothes. A fireplace with a roaring fire. An old-fashioned wooden bar and behind it a display of cunning little toys—dolls and cars and brass knickknacks. Dorrian's Red Hand was one of the homiest, coziest bars Jennifer had ever been in.

It was Brock who had first suggested they go there. He and she had gotten back together again, and he'd been taking her out to little French restaurants and even to a couple of shows. He knew she liked to do sophisticated things. And Dorrian's was, no doubt about it, sophisticated. Her girlfriends had been talking about it for weeks. They said you had to dress up to go there. Wear nice shirts, good leather boots, and your *best* ripped jeans, because there were girls there who came in fur coats. Minks. Maybe their mothers', but maybe their own. They were loaded, those girls. They carried hundreds of dollars of cash in their wallets, and some of them even had their own credit cards. Jennifer had been curious to see the place.

Then, the first time she went, she didn't like it all that much. At least not at first. She felt uncomfortable, because she didn't know anybody, whereas everyone else seemed to know everyone else. They'd been friends since grade school, had met each other years ago in fancy East Side schools like Spence and St. David's. Some of the people she met said they'd never even *heard* of Baldwin, and treated her as if she was a nobody, a "wannabe." That's what people there called girls who wanted to get into their set.

But in the end she had a good time. She met a few girls with whom she clicked, recognized a couple of guys she'd seen at other bars, and told Brock she'd like to go to Dorrian's again.

They did go back. They went again and again. They went so often that Brock tired of Dorrian's, and sometimes he'd say, "Let's do something else. Let's try a new bar." But they always wound up at Dorrian's.

VALENTINES

On an April afternoon in 1985, Patricia Fillyaw, a personnel manager for a major communications company, went into the kitchen of her Roosevelt Island apartment and flung herself into an orgy of cooking. Her elder son, twenty-one-year-old David, was coming home today after a year and a half in prison.

Pat was a community-minded woman who had helped establish Roosevelt Island's first day-care center. She was also a devoted mother. She'd helped David with his schoolwork when he was a little boy, she'd encouraged him to paint when he showed an early talent for art, and when he'd entered junior high and begun to have scholastic problems, she'd raided her family's small savings and put him in a private prep school—McBurney, on the West Side. He was one of the few black children there.

Pat's husband, Jerry, who worked for a cash register company, had approved the expenditure. He wasn't David's natural father. Pat had David out of wedlock when she was just a girl. But Jerry, with whom she had another son, had adopted David, looked after him like a real father, and tried, like Pat herself, to do for David whatever would ensure him a good future, whatever would keep him from drowning in the whirlpool that sucked up so many promising young black men.

Still, despite Pat and Jerry's sacrifices, David hadn't done well at Mc-Burney. He'd kept having problems, McBurney had asked him to withdraw, and around that time, Pat had learned that he was using cocaine.

She'd been shocked, and consumed with guilt. What kind of a mother was she that she hadn't realized earlier what was wrong with her son? she'd asked herself. But the parents of other drug-abusing teenagers, whom she met in the support groups she began attending, had made her feel better. What did she know about coke? they said. What did most parents know? How could parents spot the effects when all they saw, if they saw anything at all, was that their kid had a runny nose? Anyway, the important thing was not to brood about the past but to rescue the future, do something to ensure that the kid got rehabilitated.

Pat had tried. She'd consulted a psychiatrist and put David in a good residential treatment center. But David had kept on using drugs. And when he was seventeen, he and some friends had broken into a house and David had been sent to Camp McCormick, a state-run correctional center for youths. Then, when he'd been released from Camp McCormick, he'd committed another burglary and ended up in jail. But now at last he'd served his time. And he was drug-free.

Awaiting his arrival, Pat sautéed a chicken and peeled a mound of vegetables. Then she began sifting flour for her dessert, the special pound cake David had adored when he was little.

The cake was in the oven when she heard him at the door. She ran to him with open arms.

Soon after Pat Fillyaw welcomed David home, Robert applied for work at the Fulton Street Cafe, a restaurant in New York's newest tourist area, the South Street Seaport. Roberta Dillon, a young manager, interviewed him and was impressed with his good looks and courtesy. He'll make a perfect host, she thought, and offered him a summer job.

•   •   •

Parties. Girls getting so stoned they'd strip to their panties and dance with each other. Guys getting so wasted they didn't even pay attention to the girls. George Hannaford, a shy young preppie who lived in a vast apartment on Park Avenue, started giving parties that summer whenever his parents went to their vacation house. Coke was the big thing with the boys. The girls preferred Ecstasy, which cost about forty dollars a hit but lasted six hours and made them feel in love with the world. When they felt that way, they'd screw whoever wanted them, even two or three guys in a row. But there wasn't that much sex. Sex wasn't what it was all about.

George worried about his parties sometimes. There'd be thirty, forty, even fifty kids camped out on the Aubusson carpet and the Billy Baldwin print sofas. Suppose his parents got wind of the bashes? But he kept on giving them. They made him feel popular.

The only bad thing was the mornings. He always got this let-down feeling, because he'd wake up and see that he didn't know half the people who'd slept over. That would make him start worrying again. Suppose something got stolen? What would his parents say?

Robert Chambers came to a lot of the parties. George didn't worry about him. Robert's okay, was the way he looked at it. He's one of us.

A few weeks after she hired Robert, Roberta Dillon noticed that he was not, in fact, an ideal host. He was chronically late to work, and when he finally arrived, he moved so lethargically around the dining room that his efficiency was close to zero. He was deep into drugs, some of the waiters and waitresses told her. And what's more, he was stealing their tips. Dillon wasn't sure she believed the stories about Robert. He was so clean-cut and well-mannered. She kept him on.

"I'm going into business," David Fillyaw told his mother excitedly one evening in August. "Me and two friends. We're going to get discos to sponsor fashion shows."

"Where are you going to get the money?" Pat Fillyaw asked. "It costs a lot of money to start a business."

"Not this one. Not East Side Productions," David said. "All we have to do is get some stores to contribute clothes to us and a disco to agree to show the clothes, and we'll start turning a profit right away."

Pat wasn't keen about the plan. For one thing, she didn't believe it would work. For another, she'd been hoping that in the fall David would go to college. He'd been poring over school catalogues ever since he'd returned home, and watching him do so had filled her with joy. But he was so enthusiastic about his business idea that after a while Pat decided that maybe business was right for David. Besides, East Side Productions seemed viable. The sportswear chain Benetton had shown an interest in the idea, David said, and the Cat Club, a downtown disco, had given him and his friends the go-ahead.

Still, Pat wanted to see the disco. And one night she persuaded David to take her and Jerry to it.

As soon as they entered, Pat's stomach sank. The disco looked more like a warehouse than a nightclub. It had black walls and beer-sticky carpets. The mirror on the back wall was smeared with dirt. There was something about the atmosphere that told her it was wrong for David to be hanging out there.

She told David this. "Go to school," she said. "Get a career." But he got angry. "East Side Productions *is* my career," he said.

Robert ran into David that summer. He'd met him years ago, back when David used to hang out with friends who went to York Prep. Now he found out David had just gotten out of prison for stealing. He knew a thing or two about stealing, too, Robert told David. He'd burglarized his own building twice, he boasted, as well as an apartment on the West Side. Not only that, but all summer long he'd been managing to pay for his coke by copying names and numbers off credit cards he handled at the restaurant he was working in. What he did was, he used the information on the cards to get Western Union to wire him money. He didn't have to show the card, he said. All he had to do was have the cardholder's name and number.

David and Robert hit it off.

. . .

Jennifer was summering in Southampton again, where she was working in a boutique. Some of her friends were staying at their parents' vacation homes, others—the ones whose parents didn't have houses in the Hamptons—were crashing wherever they could. Kitty Schoen even crashed one night at the Meadow Club in Southampton, spending the hours in secret in the women's locker room. But Jennifer had a place of her own. She was sharing a house with Leilia and several other young people.

One of the boys in their group house, a preppie with a penchant for outrageous pets, had brought his boa constrictor with him. Jennifer hated the loathsome creature at first. It looked slimy and thick, and it ate live mice. She watched the owner feed it, and she shrieked with disgust.

"It's a snake," the boa constrictor's master grumbled. "What do you expect it to eat? Pizza?"

Jennifer laughed despite herself. And eventually she came to enjoy the snake's acrobatic gyrations and voracious appetite. She also began to enjoy its owner, who was strikingly good-looking. And soon they became lovers. Their affair was glorious at first. He told his friends Jennifer had a really hot body. She told her friends that he was the first guy who had truly awakened her sexually. Not that she had orgasms. But that wasn't the point. The snake's owner paid more attention to her body than any guy she'd been with previously, she explained, and that in itself made her feel wonderful.

In the middle of the summer she started keeping a diary. And at the height of the summer her friends noticed a change in her. She stopped worrying about her figure, wore bikinis all the time, and seemed infinitely more sure of herself than she'd ever been before.

But her self-assurance didn't last long. When the cool weather set in, her bronzed and virile boyfriend broke up with her. She felt betrayed, and returned disheartened to the city.

Money and coke. Coke and money. By the fall of 1985, Robert was obsessed with both. He was enrolled at Hunter College, but he rarely went to his classes. He'd started freebasing, and when he wasn't high he was thinking about how to afford getting high.

He had lots of ideas. They came to him easily when he put his mind to thinking about the rich people among whom he had moved throughout his life, and soon he began trying out some of his ideas. One day he went home with a girl he knew and, when she wasn't looking, fixed her front door so that it would remain unlocked while he and she went into her bedroom to neck. While she was moaning in his arms, a friend whose help he had enlisted entered the apartment through the unlocked door and removed whatever valuables he could grab in the foyer. Another day, Robert gained entry to the well-guarded Park Avenue building where another of his girlfriends lived by having the doorman buzz the girl's apartment; her maid, recognizing his name, said it was all right for him to come in. Once in the lobby, he took the elevator to the top floor, got out, climbed a service staircase to the penthouse, and burglarized an apartment. This time David Fillyaw came along, and they stole thousands of dollars' worth of silver, jewelry, and electronic equipment. They fenced their catch in midtown and shared the proceeds.

Afterward, Robert felt pleased with himself. And one day he bragged about the exploit to a new girlfriend.

She was impressed. He's suave, she thought. Just like Cary Grant in *To Catch a Thief.*

Back at school and starting her senior year, Jennifer became more experimental. She used drugs on occasion—coke, Ecstasy, and LSD. And she had sex with a number of lovers. None of them gave her the kind of ecstatic experiences she'd had with her summer boyfriend. Nor did they assuage the pain she still felt about that breakup, the hurt that clung to her heart like moss to a stone. But when she slept with guys, she told her friends, they'd always tell her afterward how wonderful and beautiful she was, and for a little while, for the time they were staring into her eyes and saying the words, she'd believe it was true and at least momentarily feel good about herself.

She was having a hard time that fall. Her schoolwork oppressed her. Her scores on college admissions tests were very low. And she was fighting a lot with her father and stepmother. The quarrels were over the usual adolescent issues—late hours, unmade beds, unwashed laundry—but they made Jennifer furious, and she'd storm out of the apartment and go to friends' homes to sleep.

Her father and stepmother were impossible, she'd complain to these friends, sometimes falling into such a rage that she'd pound clenched fists against furniture and walls. Her father was erratic, she'd fume, loving and indulgent sometimes, strict and punitive at others. Her stepmother was a witch who had enchanted him and stolen away his love. They went off on fascinating trips together without inviting her along. Worse, if she objected to being left behind, they assumed she didn't want to be alone in the loft and asked friends of theirs to stay with her, as if what she needed was a babysitter. Then, when they didn't leave her alone, when they were all three together in the loft, they made her feel like an intruder. They'd yell at her if she left even a few dishes in the sink, say she had no respect for their space. And if she so much as went near their collection of musical instruments, picked up one of their little flutes or African shakers, they'd shout at her to stop. "I get into trouble if I so much as move anything!" she'd sob.

But if she was down on her father and stepmother, she was also down on her mother. Her mother was her best friend, she'd say. But she was irresponsible, more a pal than a parent. Still, she loved seeing her, and one night she and a girlfriend, who were going out for the evening to a club that was in Ellen's neighborhood, made arrangements to stop by and visit her on their way home.

It was late when they got there. Nearly two in the morning. "She's up," Jennifer said. "The lights are still on and there's music playing." She knocked on the door.

No one answered, and Jennifer went on knocking. Still no one answered.

Jennifer didn't give up. She knocked for half an hour. But at last she said harshly, "Maybe my mother passed out from booze."

After that the girls left and went to Jennifer's loft, where they stayed awake talking till dawn. Then, just as they got ready to go to sleep, the telephone rang. Jennifer picked it up. "It's my mother," she signaled her friend.

Her mother began to talk and Jennifer listened. But a moment later she said, "Fuck you, Mom," and hung up the phone.

"What did your mom say that made you so angry?" Jennifer's friend asked.

"She said, 'I'm so sorry I didn't hear you, but I was wasted,'" Jennifer replied.

Her girlfriend felt sad for her. Poor Jennifer, she thought. She has no adult figure she can count on. No wonder that when she comes to *my* house, she never relates to my parents, but just talks to them rudely or ignores them altogether.

"Can we go into your building with you?" Robert said to the younger brother of one of his friends. It was not long after he'd robbed the Park Avenue penthouse. He and David, each carrying an empty canvas satchel, were standing in front of the kid's apartment house on East 72nd Street. The kid was nervous. He'd heard stories about Robert's exploits. But Robert assured him that he and David weren't going to steal from anybody in his building. They were going to leap from the roof to a building across the way.

That made it all right. The kid agreed to help them out. He led them into his lobby and past the uniformed doorman.

They all took the elevator together, but the kid got out on his floor. Once he was gone, Robert and David stayed on and continued to the top of the building. But they didn't try to leap over to the building across the way. Robert was afraid of heights. They just stayed in the kid's building, making their way onto the terrace that ran behind the penthouse apartments, and, breaking the glass panes in a terrace door, slipped into one of the apartments.

They'd gotten lucky, they saw. The apartment was filled with treasures. They stuffed their bags with silver cups and ashtrays, gold jewelry, a magnum of Moët & Chandon, and a huge soft fur coat. Then, flushed with accomplishment, they hotfooted it outside and tried to hit a second apartment.

They went into it the same way, from the terrace door. But just as they were sizing up the place, they heard a noise. Someone was home! That was the bad part, and it almost ruined everything. They had to run, had to try to reach the kitchen, where there was a window leading back put onto the terrace, before whoever was home spotted them. They managed. They found the kitchen, raised the window, started to scramble away. But just then, just as they were halfway out, a man entered the kitchen. They were so terrified when they saw him that they almost dropped their bags with all the loot from the first place.

Still, they didn't. They held on and squeezed through the window. Then they jumped onto the terrace and began running, getting as far away from the man as they could.

He didn't come after them, and a few moments later, their hearts pounding, they were ringing the doorbell of the kid who had let them into the building. Would he escort them out, they asked.

The kid didn't ask any questions. He said sure and rode down in the elevator with them.

When they reached the front door, the doorman stopped them. "Do you know these boys?" he asked the kid suspiciously, pointing at David and Robert.

"Yes," the kid said coolly.

The doorman opened the door for them and let them out.

One night at around that time, Jennifer was at Dorrian's. She saw a good-looking guy at the bar.

"Who's that?" she asked a girlfriend.

"Robert Chambers."

"He's gorgeous."

"Yeah," Jennifer's friend said. "And he's had this real hard life and all." Then she lowered her voice and whispered to Jennifer that she felt sorry for Robert because people were always telling stories about him, saying he stole from his friends, and even that he'd broken into some apartment someplace.

A rascal—he sounded fascinating. Jennifer tucked the information away in a corner of her mind.

On the evening of October 9, 1985, David Fillyaw told his mother not to expect him home that night. He'd be sleeping up at Columbia in his friend Peter's dorm suite, he said. Then he left the apartment, met Peter, and went with him to the Cat Club. They listened to music, had some drinks and some coke, and around 3 A.M. taxied to Peter's dorm. There they had a few beers, and David did a little more coke. And then Peter said he was sleepy and went to bed.

David wasn't tired at all. He decided to buy some more beer. He put on his jacket and, reasoning that because it was still dark out he might need some protection, grabbed a cooking knife from the suite's kitchen and shoved it into his pocket.

He was heading for the elevator when he passed the television room of the dorm. He heard the set, glanced in, and saw a pretty blond girl in a bathrobe sitting there all alone. "Whatcha doing up so late?" he said to her.

"Watching TV," she answered shyly.

He told her his name, and she said hers was Sarah and that she was studying engineering. "What about you?" she asked.

He said he didn't actually go to Columbia, but he had this good friend who did and that he often stayed in his suite. Then he asked her if she wanted to do some coke.

She sounded interested, he thought, so he suggested they go to her room, and they did. But once they were there, it turned out she didn't want any coke, and anyway, that wasn't what he wanted now either. He wanted to kiss her. He told her so, and she let him put his arms around her, and he gave her a kiss, and she kissed him back. Then he began fondling her body. It felt terrific, but he'd gotten himself so stoned he couldn't do anything. Couldn't have sex. Maybe if he held her for a while longer, though, he'd be able to, he hoped. So he started feeling her all over, and she didn't seem to mind, and he was just starting to think that maybe he was going to be okay, maybe he'd be able to do it, when all of a sudden she said, "No. I don't want to have sex."

He couldn't believe it. "I thought you did," he said.

"No. Just get out."

"Get out?"

"Yeah."

It made him mad. "What'd you bring me here for?" he demanded. And then he gave her a piece of his mind. Called her an asshole and a few other things.

She went wild. Slapped his face. He wanted to slap her back, but he didn't, just told her again what he thought of her. But that didn't settle her down. She lifted her arm and struck him again. Then everything went haywire. She wouldn't stop hitting, so he pushed her down onto the bed, and before he knew it he'd grabbed her bra and tied up her hands with it, and then he pulled the knife out of his jacket and thrust it into her, and then he thrust it in again and he heard her cry out, but he couldn't stop and he did it again. He sliced her in the liver and he perforated her lung, but it was like someone else was doing it to her, like he wasn't even there. He stabbed her at least six times, and then, as if he were hearing the soundtrack of a movie or something, he heard the shrieking and knew he had to get out of there.

He left her, crawling on the bed and screaming, and ran down a staircase to Peter's suite. Peter was asleep, so he didn't wake him. He just peeled off his bloody shirt, threw the shirt and the knife in a corner, and lay down on a mattress on the floor. He lay there, and he got drowsy, and after a while he just went to sleep.

Pat Fillyaw heard from David at about five that afternoon. The police had searched the dorm for Sarah's attacker and had found David, his hands still bloody, asleep in Peter's room. They'd taken him to a station house, and he'd confessed. But when he called Pat, he didn't tell her what had happened. He just said, "Mommy, please don't hate me. I've done something terrible." And then he told her he needed a lawyer.

She called her father. "David's in some sort of trouble," she said.

"Yeah, I know. It's on the news."

"The news?" Pat's heart tumbled to her shoes even before her father told her about the stabbing. When he finished, she couldn't believe it. It couldn't be David who'd done that. But it was. She didn't believe it, but at the same time she knew it was true. She started sobbing, and what was strange about her tears, she would remember long afterward, was that they weren't just for David, but for this girl, this Sarah. Why, she kept thinking as the tears poured down her cheeks, did women always have to suffer at the hands of men?

"Mommy, can't you get me bail?" A week later, in the visitors' room at Rikers Island, the infamous and overcrowded prison in the middle of New York's East River, David was mournful.

"They're not letting you have bail. You know that," Pat said to him sharply. She was worried that Sarah, who was still alive, might die of her wounds. "Anyway, what for?" she sighed. "So you can take my clothes and my money and clean me out of everything we've got in the apartment?"

"So I can come home. I'm homesick." David sounded as if he really meant it.

Pat softened. "You know," she said lightly, "that if they gave you bail, you'd be on the first boat to China."

David burst out laughing.

Pat laughed, too. And the visit made them both feel better.

Jennifer didn't go out on the town all the time. There were evenings she had dinner at home with Steve and Arlene, nights when she babysat for the children of friends of theirs, weekend afternoons when she went to family gatherings. At one of these gatherings, both her mother and Arlene were present. It was a reception in honor of her sister Danielle. Danielle had just returned from Hawaii, where she'd gotten married. She'd married one of her high school teachers.

Jennifer thought he was cute. And she was proud of her big sister for becoming a bride.

Her own romantic prospects were not very promising. By that late autumn of 1985, it seemed to her friends that she had become a specialist in rejection. She kept getting crushes on unsuitable guys, only to reap disappointments and repudiation. Still, she never stopped falling in love. And she never fell in love without falling, afterward, into despair.

The pattern was apparent even with Brock. She kept resuming her connection to him, then a fight would happen, and he'd tell her he wanted to break up. She'd say fine, she never wanted to see him again anyway. They'd part. And then, although the relationship was so tempestuous that her closest girlfriends couldn't understand why she wanted it at all, she would once again start seeing Brock.

In November he was back in the picture. She went with him to a reggae concert at Radio City Music Hall, and then to a sweet sixteen party at the home of Margaret Trahill, a new friend.

She looked grown up that night, her body sleek in a snug Betsey Johnson number that laced up the back. Margaret's mother thought the garment inappropriate. All the other girls were wearing decorous little cocktail dresses. "Jennifer looks vulgar," she said. "Sluttish."

Margaret defended Jennifer. "Nobody," she said to her mother, "knows as much about style as Jennifer."

Sarah, with all those wounds in her, didn't die. For that, Pat Fillyaw would ever afterward be grateful. The girl was hospitalized for weeks after David stabbed her, but by mid-November it was clear that she would soon be well enough to return to Columbia and resume her engineering studies.

It was David about whom Pat was worried now. A few weeks after his arrest he had begun talking about killing himself, and he'd sounded so determined to do so that he'd been transferred from prison on Rikers Island to the forensic unit at Bellevue Hospital. There, Pat visited him every day, sitting with him in a crowded lounge and trying to make small talk. But no matter how hard she worked at cheering him up, he remained distant and blue.

She believed in her mother's heart that he was suffering from remorse. He'd told the police the night they arrested him that he hadn't meant to hurt Sarah, that he'd been so stoned he'd been out of his mind. "It was like it wasn't me there," he'd said. "It was not something I would have done in a sober or conscious state." Now he was sober. Conscious. The horror of what he had done must surely, Pat was convinced, be flooding him hourly with guilt and shame.

He may have felt those emotions. But the charges facing him were in themselves severe enough to warrant depression. He had been indicted for attempted murder, and there was talk that he might be indicted, too, for the East 72nd Street burglaries. The police had been speaking with the boy who'd let him and Robert into the building, and by now had gotten both their names.

On a gray November afternoon David took a belt from a hospital bathrobe and concealed it in his pocket. An attendant noticed the belt and took it away from him. But at six in the evening he got hold of another belt. He tied one end of it around his neck and attached the other to a window lock.

He was found with his feet still on the ground. But nevertheless the hospital placed him on a suicide watch, and attendants monitored him round the clock.

Jennifer could tell her mother anything, Joan Huey noticed at around that time. They were as close as friends. Best friends. That was because Ellen was so warm, so giving. She'd moved to Manhattan, gotten an apartment not far from Steve and Arlene's loft, and she'd take Jen and Joan out to dinner in restaurants, fun places where there were crayons and paper tablecloths you could draw on. Jen's father was fun, too. But he was strict. Gave Jennifer curfews. Grounded her when she came in late. "Don't you wish you lived with your mom?" Joan asked Jennifer.

Jennifer's answer surprised Joan. She said that if she lived with her mom, she might not have the curfew problem, but she liked having a curfew. Wanted discipline. Then she said, "Anyway, at my father's, I've got my own room. At mom's, I'd have to share her bedroom."

"My partner and I would like to come over and have a few words with you," Detective Theresa Enterlin said to Robert over the phone early in December. Robert said his mother was out, but that it was all right with him if the detectives stopped by.

Enterlin and her partner went over to East 90th Street and took the elevator to the Chamberses' floor. It deposited them right in the foyer of the apartment. Nice touch, Enterlin thought. She had been on the force for thirty years, seen all sorts of people and places, but still was amazed at the plushness of the Upper East Side. This place looked especially nice. Meticulously neat and tasteful. There were antiques, a couch with really puffy cushions, a cut-crystal chandelier. Classy, Enterlin told herself. Nothing from Seamans here.

When Robert showed her and her partner to a seat, she began asking him questions. "A paper with your name on it was found outside the terrace of a burglarized apartment on Park Avenue," she said. "Any idea how it got there?"

Robert had been missing a registration receipt from Hunter College. But he hadn't realized he'd lost it the day he and David did their first burglary together. "Can't imagine," he said.

Enterlin moved ahead. "What were you doing at 245 East Seventy-second Street the day two apartments there got burglarized?"

East 72nd Street? Robert knew better than to deny that he'd been there. His friend's kid brother, the one who'd let him and David into the building, had told him he'd talked to the police. "I was there," he said. "I was with my friend David Fillyaw. But I didn't steal anything. David did all the stealing."

Enterlin noted this down. Then she said, "How come you were along with him?"

"He forced me to come. He threatened he'd hurt my mother or my girlfriend if I didn't help him get into the building, and I was scared to say no."

Enterlin laughed. "Why should *you* be scared? You're a big, tall fellow, and David's small. Half your size."

"Yeah," Robert said, "But you never know what *they* can do."

Enterlin knew he meant blacks. He had a black friend, but that didn't seem to keep him from making racist remarks.

"*They* have gangs," Robert went on. "I'm still afraid of David. Even though he's in jail now."

Enterlin didn't buy his account. But she had five grandchildren and hated to see kids in trouble. She let him talk on, and after a while he said that in any event nothing particularly valuable had been stolen. "Just a few pieces of silver and a ratty-looking fur coat." He made a disdainful face. "The collar was ripped and the fur was shedding. It came out in bunches without even being touched."

There wasn't enough evidence to arrest the boy, Enterlin decided. But when she got back to her precinct, she recommended that the case be kept active.

Right after Christmas, sixteen-and-a-half-year-old Dave Silverstein met Jennifer in the West End Cafe. He was a little drunk that night. At the beginning of December, New York had raised the drinking age from nineteen to twenty-one, and Dave had thought he'd never be able to get a drink again. In fact, the day the law went into effect, he and his friends had gone nuts. They'd kept calling each other up and saying, "Can you believe it?" and, "What's gonna happen to us now!" The whole thing was so tragic it reminded Dave of that time his father always talked about, the day President Kennedy got shot. By Christmas, though, Dave and his friends had discovered they could get drinks at the West End Cafe if they had ID saying they were twenty-one; that's why he was drunk. He was making up for lost time.

The way he met Jennifer was, she smiled at him from across the bar and he smiled back. And then later, even though she looked older than him, she came up to him and said, "There's something about you. I don't know what it is, but it's something really special." Then she said, "Could you call me?" and gave him her number.

He was flying for days, it was so flattering. Especially considering she was seventeen and a half! So he called her. And she was very friendly. Casual, like they'd known each other a long time. She wanted to come to his house that very evening, but since he had a rehearsal for a school play, they made plans to go out on Friday. She wanted to go to this place America, but he didn't have the money. But he had free passes for the Hard Rock Cafe, and he suggested they go there instead, and she said fine.

He picked her up in front of a girlfriend's building on Park Avenue, and they took the subway downtown to her place in SoHo. She was the first girl he'd ever been out with that didn't mind the subway. The rest of them were so Jappy they'd only go places by cab. But not Jennifer. She was so nice.

Her neighborhood startled him. He'd never been down to SoHo before. There were all these iron buildings, and they were covered with graffiti. He felt he was in that movie *After Hours*. And then it got more and more bizarre, just like in the movie. Her apartment was a loft. It was so big it looked like the gymnasium of his high school. And then she took a shower, and afterward got dressed right in front of him. She wasn't *all* naked when she came over to where he was waiting for her, but she wasn't all dressed, either. And she just acted casual and took about an hour getting into her clothes. She said she couldn't find the right blouse to put on.

Nothing happened. Not then. They just hung out in her room, which was plastered with pictures of male models and Billy Idol, and talked about people they knew in common. He was surprised to learn that there was one, a friend of his cousin's who looked like a real thug, whom she'd gone out with. She didn't seem the type. Still, he didn't let it throw him, and after a while they stopped talking and walked all the way uptown to the Hard Rock.

One funny thing happened there. They'd been told they'd have to wait a half hour for their table, so they'd put their names on the list and gone outside to pass the time. They were sitting on a stoop not far from the club when they were approached by three girls from Long Island or New Jersey—you could tell they were B and T by the way they talked—and one of the girls said, "Which way's the Hard Rock Cafe?" He started to point to the place, but Jennifer interrupted him. "It's right down that way," she said. But she was pointing in the wrong direction. He said, "Jennifer, are you sure?" and she said, "Yes, I'm positive." So these Bridge and Tunnel girls went the way she'd said to go. Well, sure enough, five minutes later they were back, and when they turned up, Jennifer sent them off in another wrong direction. It made him think Jennifer had an attitude. That she liked to make fun of people. But maybe she just liked to make fun of people from Long Island or New Jersey. Though that would be odd, because she'd told him she came from Long Island. Well, maybe she was trying to live it down. Anyway, it didn't matter. She didn't make fun of *him*.

The Hard Rock was great when they finally got inside, and afterward they went back to Jennifer's place. Her parents weren't coming home, she told him, and she asked him to sleep over. That was fine with him, though he had to call his parents and lie to them, tell them he was at a friend's house. But later he didn't feel so fine. They started fooling around and it didn't work out. He just couldn't bring himself to fool around all the way. She wanted him to. She didn't play games like other girls. There was no bullshit about her. But he wasn't used to girls being so direct. He was still a junior, and he hadn't even begun to figure it all out yet, and here all of a sudden he was with a girl who just asked for what she wanted, and it just threw him for a loop.

He didn't feel proud of himself for the way it turned out. But she was nice about it and told him to call her again sometime.

He did. He took her out to the show *Plenty*, which they both hated, and afterward they went back to his house and fooled around there. But it was no different the second time, and they ended up just talking and looking at photographs. She asked to see a picture of him as a little kid, and that kind of touched him.

After that they made a date for another night. But his cat died, and he couldn't get to a phone, and he kept thinking about his cousin's friend and the things Jennifer had said she'd done with him, and with other guys, too, and he figured he wasn't old enough for the hassle of teenage romance, so he just went out with his friends.

She called him the next day. She told him she was upset at his standing her up. But when he told her what he felt about himself, about how he was ashamed of himself for being afraid to have a girlfriend just yet, she couldn't have been nicer. She didn't carry on about being rejected. She didn't say, "Please, please." She acted real understanding, and she just said, "Well, okay. But let's stay in touch. Call me every once in a while." He never did, though.

Later that month Jennifer told a friend that a guy she'd thought was really cute had rejected her. "Boys are so strange," she said, her voice sad. "When you haven't had sex yet, all they want is to get you to do it. But if you've had it, they're scared of you."

Early in February of 1986, Robert and a friend stole traveler's checks from a Brazilian visitor to the United States. They went out on the town with this bonanza, cashing the checks in bars and restaurants along crowded Columbus Avenue.

They got away with the theft, just as Robert had gotten away with his burglaries, and he began to feel clever. "I'm wasting my time at Hunter," he told Joel Coles, one of his Hunter classmates. "I want to get back up to Boston."

"Why? What'll you do up there?" his classmate asked.

"Go to Harvard."

"Harvard? How're you gonna get in there?"

"It's easy," he said. "All I gotta do is take some classes in their extension program, like John Flanagan's doing. Once I'm in the extension program, they'll move me along, and next thing I'll be going to Harvard."

Coles wasn't sure you could do that, but Robert was so cool he didn't want to argue about it.

• • •

"You've *gotta* ask Robert Chambers," Jennifer said to Kitty Schoen just before Valentine's Day. Kitty was planning a combination birthday and Valentine's Day party.

At first Kitty was reluctant about asking him. She knew that people said he sometimes stole when he went to parties. Suppose he ripped something off from her parents?

"I can't ask him," she told Jennifer. "I don't even know him."

"Leilia does," Jennifer said. "Let's get her to ask him."

Kitty still wasn't sure she wanted Robert, but Jennifer begged Leilia to invite him, and after a while Kitty decided that having him at the party might be fun. He was so good-looking and popular. She joined Jennifer in imploring Leilia to ask him.

Leilia did, and on the night of the party, she picked him up and personally escorted him to Kitty's. Jennifer was ecstatic. She was there with another boy, but she talked to Robert awhile and told Kitty he was really nice.

It was a great party, to Kitty's way of thinking. Everyone got really ripped on champagne. And there was music and dancing and people looked terrific. Not the boys. The boys didn't give a damn about dressing. But the girls were really *dressed*.

Things got a little out of hand, though. A friend of Robert's took one of those four-foot-high Think Big pencils and started writing on the wall with it. It didn't have any lead, but it made marks just the same. And Kitty's father came in and saw the marks and told the guy to leave. Which he did. And Robert left with him. And then afterward one of the girls discovered she was missing twenty dollars from her coat pocket, and everyone thought Robert had taken the money. Everyone except Kitty and Jennifer. They blamed his friend.

After a while Robert and his friend came back. But nobody said anything about the money. There wasn't any point. The guys came back stoned. They were so bombed out you couldn't really talk to them. They were so out of it that although Jennifer was really excited about Robert's being there, he never even remembered afterward that he'd talked with her at the party. "Jennifer?" he said to Kitty when she mentioned that he'd met her at her house. "I didn't notice her."

• • •

The forensic unit at Bellevue is like no other floor in the giant hospital. Prisoners enter it through an electronic gate that deposits them in a tiny claustrophobic closetlike area. There they wait till a second electronic gate swings open with a ferocious clang. Then they are on the unit, a warren of small wards and private rooms. These wards and rooms are as big as those on other floors, and no more drab in color, but their outside windows are barred, and along the corridor side each has a viewing area made of shatterproof glass to permit surveillance by hospital personnel and corrections officers.

David Fillyaw kept returning there. He preferred the conditions to those at Rikers Island, hospital personnel believed, and they held firm to the view that his frequent talk of suicide was just an effort to frighten corrections department authorities into hospitalizing rather than jailing him. They saw in him the classic outlines of the sociopath, a man whose stated emotions were a sham and who was forever making excuses for himself. When he talked to them about Sarah, he persisted in saying that if it hadn't been for cocaine and what he called "Long Island iced tea"— a concoction of various white liquors he had mixed with a shot of a red liqueur—he never would have hurt her. And when he talked of his penchant for drugs and drink, he blamed his habits not on himself but on the fact that he'd never known his real father and that his stepfather hadn't loved or understood him.

Pat Fillyaw was unaware of the degree to which David held her girlhood transgression and her choice of a stepfather for him responsible for the wreckage he'd made of his life. Nor did she view her son as a sociopath. When she visited David, which she did every day, she saw only a sad, disheartened boy, a child to whom she had given life and who now no longer wanted that gift. His despair seemed authentic enough to her, matching as it did her own now that he was in such trouble.

On March 19, David once again obtained a bathrobe belt and, knotting it around his neck, attempted to hang himself. He was found before he had succeeded in altogether choking away his own breath. This time he had made a real suicide attempt, a corrections officer promptly informed the district attorney's office. It was serious.

When Pat learned what had happened, she was distraught. She blamed the hospital. How the hell had David gotten the belt? she kept wanting to know. And why, when he'd said he was fed up with life, had the staff not protected her boy from himself?

Sleek Vuarnet sunglasses. Velvet-soft sweatshirts. On March 21, as he was wandering along Columbus Avenue, these things caught Robert's eye— perhaps because his old friend John Flanagan had invited him to visit him over Easter at his vacation home in Palm Beach, and looking good was on his mind.

Many days when he window-shopped, he felt envious of his wealthy friends, and a feeling of self-pity overtook him. He would ask himself why it was that he, who was as worthy, as deserving, as those other young men, didn't have all the clothes, the accessories, the accouterments they had. On this particular night he set out to rectify matters. He had the means. He had stolen a credit card from a girlfriend while they were at a party together. The card was her mother's. He would take care of his needs with it, he decided. Entering store after store on the busy avenue, he shopped to his heart's content. He bought the sweatshirts he'd admired. He bought the fancy sunglasses. And he even got himself a shiny state-of-the-art stereo.

The next night he used the card again, treating friends to dinner in an East Side restaurant. Then later, while he was walking alone on 42nd Street, it occurred to him that he needed new sneakers. Reeboks, Nike, Adidas—footgear made the man. He went into a shoe shop, tried on some sneakers, made his selection, and handed his credit card to the salesclerk.

He was standing there waiting for the clerk to finish checking on the card and give him his parcel, when suddenly the clerk put down the phone and began striding toward him with an angry expression on his face. He panicked. And a second later he tore out of the store.

The clerk came after him. But he hid himself amid the crowds on 42nd Street. Once he was sure he was safe, he made his way uptown to Dorrian's and bought himself a couple of drinks.

The next day, Palm Sunday, he flew to Palm Beach. When he arrived, the air was moist, the breezes scented. He took a taxi to John Flanagan's home. But when he reached the house, he couldn't get in. No one was at home, and all the doors and windows were locked and shuttered. He waited around for a while, but no one came. And at last, late at night, he made his way back to the airport.

In the morning, at 7 A.M., he telephoned his mother, hoping that perhaps Flanagan had called and left a message for him saying why he'd been delayed and when he'd be arriving. His mother barely listened to his account of looking for Flanagan. "Come home at once," she told him.

There was something in her voice that warned him he'd better not argue with her. And, not knowing why she sounded so peremptory, he boarded the first New York-bound flight he could get.

As soon as he was home, he understood her insistence. The mother of the girl from whom he'd stolen the credit card had called while he was away and accused him of having taken it.

"There must be some mistake," Phyllis had said.

"I doubt it," the woman had answered. "I'm going to press charges."

Phyllis had been imploring, conciliatory. "Please wait," she'd said. "I'm sure that as soon as Robert gets back he'll be able to explain everything."

He wasn't home for more than a few hours before the irate woman came to his apartment. His father came too. Phyllis had asked him to be present so that they could handle the matter together.

"Why did you steal my credit card?" the woman asked. They were sitting in his living room, amid the antiques and paneling.

"I was forced to," Robert said. He had made up his mind that admitting the theft was the wisest policy. But he didn't intend to be blamed for the entire thing.

"Who forced you? What do you mean forced?" the woman said.

"My friends. They made me take it. It was their idea. And as soon as I did it, I wanted to give it back. To your daughter."

"Then why didn't you?"

"I was too ashamed. If I gave it back, she'd have known I'd taken it."

The woman shook her head. Her daughter had told her that Robert was a druggie and that he lied all the time. He was lying now, she felt sure. And trying to pull the wool over her eyes. "If that's the case," she demanded, "why didn't you just cut the card up? Destroy it?"

Robert had no response to that question. He stared at her.

"You don't have to answer that," his father said.

His father is trying to rescue him, the woman thought. He shouldn't. If he really wants to rescue his son, he should face up to the truth about him and do something about it. "I don't believe you wanted to give the card back," she said. "If you had, you wouldn't have used it."

"I didn't use it," Robert shot out. "Only my friends did."

The woman whose card had been stolen remained unconvinced. But, a mother herself, she felt sorry for Phyllis and Bob. She struck a bargain with them. "If you acknowledge his cocaine addiction and send him to a rehabilitation center," she offered, "I'll let the matter drop."

Phyllis and Bob were grateful, and the next day they shipped Robert off to the Hazelden Foundation in Minnesota, where years before Bob had once briefly shaken his drinking problem.

Around the time Robert went to Hazelden, Jennifer spent a few days at the Ritz in Boston with a new girlfriend, Alexandra LaGatta. She loved the stately old hotel from the moment she entered the ornate lobby, and she was elated by the spacious bedroom she and Alex would be sharing. But best of all, she discovered as the porter was carrying in the luggage, the room had its own little bar. "Look!" she called out to Alexandra. "We've got a bar!"

Alexandra said, "Sssh!" She was afraid that the porter might notice they were under the drinking age and report them to the management. But a moment later she felt foolish. Jennifer was scoffing at her timidity. "We can do what we want," she said. "It's *our* room. *Our* bar."

The two of them were in a great mood that afternoon. They went shopping in a mall, bought themselves new clothes, wore their purchases right out of the store, and, giggling, ordered huge bags of jellybeans at a candy shop and consumed the entire quantity while riding an escalator backwards. At night they went to a party that John Flanagan was throwing, flirted with some boys, and stayed late.

It was raining when they left the party, and the streets were deserted. "Let's take a cab," Alexandra said.

"Back to the hotel? What for?" Jennifer said. "It isn't that far."

Alexandra didn't want to walk. She felt frightened of the dark and empty streets. But she chided herself for not being as daring and courageous as Jennifer was and, not wanting to seem fainthearted, faced into the rain and made her way to the Ritz on foot alongside her friend.

Hazelden treats its youthful addicts in an attractive sprawling building called Pioneer House, which seems more like a ski lodge than an institution. Outside are acres of verdant lawn; inside, a massive fireplace, multileveled carpeted public rooms, and small attractive collegelike dormitories with beds, bureaus, and desks.

A structured schedule, counseling, peer-group support, and the self-help principles of Alcoholics Anonymous are the pinions of Pioneer House's program. Robert settled in and began to follow the program, rising early in the morning, attending lectures and meetings all day, and going to bed just a few hours after dark. But he felt sorry for himself. He complained bitterly about the rules and regulations. And one evening when he discovered that someone had stolen a gift his family had mailed him, he broke down and cried at having to live among thieves.

Jennifer was trying to decide where to go to school. She was interested in a career in fashion, but she didn't want to go to the Fashion Institute of Technology in New York. Not yet. Not now. She might go there later, she told one of her teachers. But for the present she wanted an out-of-town school. High on her list was Boston's Chamberlayne Junior College, a two-year institution that gave courses in fashion design and illustration. One weekend she went up to Boston again, this time with her friend Betsy Shankin, and looked the school over. She and Betsy stayed in John Flanagan's apartment near Harvard, and Jennifer fell in love with Harvard Yard and the collegiate atmosphere that pervaded both Cambridge and Boston. Yes, she'd go to Chamberlayne in the fall, she decided.

Late in April, Robert, having completed Hazelden's program, flew home from Minnesota and went to see a New York lawyer, Henry Putzel III. Phyllis went with him. While Robert had been at Hazelden, Detective Enterlin had called her to say that Robert would have to participate in a line-up on the burglary matter. Phyllis had asked friends to recommend a lawyer.

Putzel was a serious, gentle Yale man, with two teenagers of his own. As soon as Phyllis and Robert walked into his modest Midtown office, he recognized that he'd met Phyllis before. It had been at the home of a wealthy former client of his. Phyllis had been his client's nurse, a dedicated caretaker who had worried over every detail. She's a wonderful woman, Putzel thought. And after he talked to her, he felt the same. Her boy had had some problems, he realized. But she'd attended to them, sent him to rehab, and now he was straightening out.

He agreed without hesitation to take Robert's case.

Robert remained in New York after his appointment with Putzel. Hazelden had recommended that he not consider himself cured of drugs, and that for a time he live in a halfway house where he could avoid old temptations and bad companions. But he didn't want to go to a halfway house, Robert told his mother. Couldn't he live at home? He'd be all right, he promised. He'd get a job, he'd attend Narcotics Anonymous meetings regularly, and he'd manage on his own, without the support of a halfway house, to stay clean.

Phyllis yielded to his entreaties. But soon after he settled into his old room, with its night-long silence while she was away at work, and its view of the private school playground that even when empty must have seemed haunted by the figures of girls he had once known, he started going out to bars and discos. One night he made his way downtown to the Palladium, the East 14th Street rock club that had replaced Studio 54 and Area as his friends' favorite nightspot.

The club was swinging that night, its undulating entrance walls and dizzying translucent staircase crowded with young people. On the dance floor, mammoth and dark, more crowds gyrated to the sounds of explosive music, and overhead banks of video screens rotated, descended, climbed high again. Robert took in the sights and sounds, then made his way into one of the smaller rooms where there was a private party. There he ran into Leilia Van Baker.

"Got any dope?" he asked her.

She was surprised to see him, but even more surprised at the question. She knew he'd just returned from rehab.

"I don't," she told him. Then she said, "Anyway, getting baked is so boring."

He looked at her as if he didn't believe what she was saying.

"No, I mean it," she said. "Sure it's okay once a month. Or once every two months. But that's it. I just don't get baked."

He took her remark for a put-down. "Look, Leilia," he said, "don't give me a guilt trip. I've been dry for seven weeks!"

"I'm not giving you a guilt trip. I don't care what you do. You can do whatever you like."

"Good."

He wandered away toward the crowds and the music, and Leilia forgot about him. But fifteen minutes later he was back. "I got some Ecstasy," he said. Then, "I hear you're going up to Vermont to live."

"Yeah."

He smiled seductively. "I'd like to live with you up there."

Leilia shrugged. She wasn't interested in him.

Still, they were old friends, and at the end of the party she said goodbye to him pleasantly.

"Call you soon," he promised.

But he didn't call, and when a few weeks later she ran into him again at a friend's house party, she snubbed him. She didn't need friends who didn't keep their promises, and besides, he was acting real weird. Wasted.

Jennifer was still keeping up the diary she had started in Southampton. It was a small black spiral date book, and in it in a childish handwriting she scrawled fervent descriptions of sexual encounters she had had or wanted to have. She alluded to using cocaine. And, writing in superlatives, she caroled the charms of various young men, terming this one or that the greatest lover. The diary was graphic and feverish, and she didn't like to leave it lying around in her room at home, where it might be found by her father and stepmother. So instead she carried it with her to school. But she didn't mind sharing its contents with friends, and at times read them choice passages.

She had always shared her secrets with friends, and now as graduation approached, she poured out her love for some of them in a torrent of impassioned yearbook inscriptions. "I love you so focken much it would scare you," she wrote to one old friend. "You mean more to me than anyone else in my life! I dearly cherish all we've shared from *driving* to boys to

DRUGS. From laughter to *complete* tears (Area). . . . You are a huge part of my life and a person too dear to me to ever forget."

To Leilia Van Baker she wrote, "You have a heart the size of any mountain and the intelligence and beauty every girl envies. I can't really explain the feeling of closeness I feel toward you. If we don't speak for a month, a year, a century, the feeling and specialness between you and I will never fade. I'll always be in your footsteps, and you'll always be in my heart."

But despite her ardent, cheery yearbook inscriptions, Jennifer was not happy as the school year drew to a close. She had contracted vaginal herpes, and the virus made her feel loathsome and blue. "Why are our bodies so *disgusting*?" she cried out to a friend over Memorial Day weekend. "Why am I caught up in all this unhappiness?"

She brooded about her condition throughout the holiday, but the following week got good news. Visiting her gynecologist, she learned that the disease was in remission.

Two weeks later she graduated. Her class had voted her "best-looking," and on the eve of graduation she repaid the honor by distributing woven friendship bracelets to many of her fellow graduates. The ceremony was held in an auditorium at Columbia University's Teachers College. Wearing a white cap and gown, she listened solemnly to a handful of speakers exhorting her class to go out into the world and make something of themselves. At last her name was called. She rose triumphantly, did a little dance as she crossed the platform. Then, just before she took possession of her diploma, she raised her arms and thrust high the fingers of both her hands in a victory sign.

That night she celebrated. She went to the class prom, a dress-up dinner at a Village restaurant, then changed into casual clothes and headed in an entourage of eight cars to Jones Beach, out on Long Island. It took the group hours to find the beach, and when they finally did, they were disappointed to be told by a ranger that they couldn't stay. "You'll have to leave," he said coldly. But Jennifer felt she could get around him. "Leave it to me," she told her friends, and, jumping out of the car, explained to the man that this was graduation night. The ranger, moved by her eagerness and persistence, said he'd escort the group to another beach, and Jennifer's friends praised her for saving the night.

It was still dark when they got to the second beach. They lit a fire and cooked some food. Then two cops came by and told them they couldn't have a fire. They put it out and set up a volleyball net instead and, when the dawn came up, played volleyball and splashed in the cold ocean. Some of the group left after that and went home, but Jennifer stayed and sunned and swam until about three in the afternoon.

She looked beautiful that night, her dark eyes brighter than usual amid the flush of color in her cheeks. Tired, but still high on her new status as a graduate, she met up with Betsy and the two of them went to Dorrian's. There after a while they split up. She wandered around talking to friends while Betsy sat down at a table with Robert Chambers.

Jennifer was startled when a few moments later Betsy came over to her and reported what Robert had just said. "I want you to know," he'd said, "that your friend Jennifer is the most. The best-looking girl in the world."

He'd never even spoken to her since that night at Kitty's Valentine's party when they'd first met. She listened to Betsy with amazement.

"He said he really would like to talk to you," Betsy was going on. "But not inside the bar, because his girlfriend's friends are here. He says to meet him outside in twenty minutes."

The best-looking girl in the world? His lavish praise made her heart leap. In twenty minutes, just as he had bidden, she went outside and talked with him; and when she came back in, she was glowing.

THE SUMMER OF '86

She had made love with Robert Chambers! Jennifer couldn't keep the news to herself. She got on the phone and in a flush of excitement related the details to a whole cotillion of girlfriends. It was their first date, she said. They'd gone to the apartment he lived in with his mother. She was out working that night, so it was okay to go there. Robert was great. Gentle and agreeable. And wonder of wonders, he'd kept on complimenting her. Saying how beautiful she was. She couldn't believe how well things were going. It was the second week of July and she'd graduated and she was seeing Robert Chambers!

"You've reached Hot Choice. This week we featchuh a fabulous assortment of lovelies. Press Numbuh One fuh Amy and huh incredible, uh, pussonality. Press Numbuh Two fuh a waitress with ger-reat specials. Press Numbuh Three fuh Magical Maggie's haht oil treatment."

From his bedroom late at night, Robert sometimes dialed a porno hot line and listened to the soft Southern-accented female voices on the other end of the line mouthing possibilities. He liked the disembodied panting voices that were stimulating without being demanding. A couple of times he finished listening to the tape, waited awhile, dialed again, and listened all over again.

He was spending a lot of time in his bedroom. He had everything he needed in there. Hi-fi. TV. A rolltop desk. He had his history there, too. The mirror whose frame he'd decorated with dozens of pairs of sunglasses. The stuffed animals he'd played with as a child, their vacant button-eyes staring familiarly down at him. He preferred lying on his bed and looking at his old playthings, or just listening to music and thinking about his future, to going out and looking for a job, even though his mother was pressing him to do so. And when she complained that he was lazy, he no longer held his tongue the way he used to when he was a little boy. He cursed her to her face.

Marilei, coming to visit, heard him damning Phyllis and decided that part of his anger had to do with the fact that Phyllis was trying to push him into getting a job, and that some of the job possibilities she'd come up with were beneath his dignity. Things like being a porter in the Trump Tower, or an elevator man on Fifth Avenue. Marilei, nutritionist turned maid, knew how unpleasant it could be to work beneath one's dignity, but she also knew there were advantages to work—any sort of work. She tried to communicate this to Robert, tried to help him understand that if he took a job, any job, he could be his own man. "Hrobert, this is your best time of life," she said. "Why you miss your time? Why you don't change, go, move, make money, have your own apartment, have your mother off your back. *You* can do this. *You* can be somebody. Because you are an *American*."

Robert ignored Marilei, just as he ignored Phyllis. But eventually Marilei heard from Phyllis that Robert had taken a job. He'd be doing some painting, she said. In the apartment of a neighbor, Mrs. Murphy.

Marilei stopped by the Chamberses' building the day Robert was supposed to start his job. She found Robert still asleep and Phyllis in Mrs. Murphy's apartment. Phyllis was wearing work clothes and moving the

furniture into the middle of the room so that when Robert woke up he
would find it easy to start the job.

• • •

Jennifer was having a wonderful summer. Keeping her weight off—she
was down to 135 pounds—by taking over-the-counter diet pills. Working as a hostess down at Fluties in the South Street Seaport. Making good
money. Each week she put her paycheck into a drawer. She wouldn't cash
the checks now, she decided. Better to save them and have a nest egg
when she went off to college in September.

The work at Fluties was fun. She didn't mind the crowds, the heavy
trays she had to carry when she helped clear the tables, the way her feet
hurt at night when she took her shoes off. Besides, she liked her fellow
waiters, and sometimes went out with a group of them.

She saw her old friends, too. And when she was with them, she'd cut
up. Drink, and then do dopey things and make them laugh. There was
the time she raced along the streets of SoHo banging a stick on the cast-
iron buildings to see if any rats would scurry out. The time she went to
a pool and smeared pats of butter from the pool's cafe onto her legs to
protect them from sunburn. That time, her friends told her she reeked of
rancid butter and chased her away from them to the far end of the pool,
the whole bunch of them wet and slippery and convulsed with laughter.

The best thing about the summer was guys. There were a bunch of
guys from Fluties who were always after her. And there was a gorgeous
blond preppie from Dorrian's with whom she'd made love a couple of
times. She hadn't used birth control. She rarely did. The pills made her
nauseous, and a diaphragm was so inconvenient. She hadn't used anything with Robert Chambers either. He was the one, out of all the guys
who were interested in her, that she found the most exciting. She'd feared
her thing with him might prove just a one-time fling, but in the middle of
July she'd gone up to Boston to attend an orientation weekend at Chamberlayne; and when she'd gotten back, he'd left messages on her tape. It

was terribly flattering. She couldn't remember when she hadn't known his name, hadn't heard about how he could have his pick of any of the classy Upper East Side girls he wanted. But he'd called her. Listening to the tape, she'd felt so happy that she'd phoned her friend Margaret, who was up in Boston for the month, and played the messages back to her. "Jennifer, why haven't you called me," he said on one. "Jennifer, *please* call me," he said on another. So she called him.

Nora Bray, a friend of Jennifer and Robert's, let them sleep together in her apartment on the West Side shortly after Jennifer received Robert's messages. She gave them the master bedroom, her parents' room, and in the morning went in to talk to them. Robert was sitting on the bed, and Jennifer was on the phone. She was rating him, telling someone that she'd just spent a fantastic night with the most fantastic lover. It's her mother she's talking to, Nora thought, and was amazed at how open Jennifer could be with a parent.

All right already, Robert told his mother, he'd accompany her to New Jersey. Her friend Father McCarrick had been named archbishop of Newark, and there was going to be a gala installation ceremony. McCarrick was like a member of the family. He'd even given Robert an autographed picture of himself and signed it "Uncle Ted." Still, Robert didn't feel that close to Father McCarrick, hadn't seen him for several years. But to get Phyllis off his case, he adopted the mask of compliance he'd worn as a little boy and promised her he'd go to the ceremony with her.

It was like old times. He sat alongside her in the chauffeured limousine she hired for the drive, and again at the Cathedral of the Sacred Heart, where the installation took place; and when the ceremony was over, he stood at her side during the crowded formal reception and shook hands with all her friends. He even exchanged a few polite words with McCarrick.

That night, however, he dropped the mask. Back in the city, he went to Dorrian's, stayed late, and then walked with friends out onto the avenue, where he shouted happy obscenities at the top of his lungs. Two policemen cruising the neighborhood heard the racket and, parking their car, gave Robert and another young man a summons for disorderly conduct. Robert didn't care. Throwing the day's restraints to the winds, he shouted at the cops, "You fucking cowards, you should stick to niggers!"

They ignored him, walking away.

When he saw that they were gone, he ripped up the summons. Then in a swirling storm of defiance he shoved the torn bits of paper under the windshield wipers of their car.

"Robert Chambers is so cute," Jennifer said over the telephone to Leilia Van Baker a couple of weeks later. Leilia was in New York, but Jennifer had quit her job and taken off for California to spend a week visiting friends. The night before she left, she'd slept with Robert again, this time at the home of another girl she knew. "It was so much fun being with him," she told Leilia. Then she said, "He's the best person I ever slept with in my entire life."

Leilia wondered about that statement. She knew Robert was drinking and doing drugs again. Wouldn't that affect his sexual performance? Make him less than the best? But then she decided that coming from Jennifer, the praise didn't add up to much, since, after all, Jennifer had never really had particularly good sex.

In California, Kitty Schoen, who was also vacationing out West, took one look at Jennifer and just knew something wonderful had happened to her. They were on their way to the Hare Krishna festival at Venice Beach, and Jennifer was looking exceptionally pretty, her skin burned to butternut and her brown eyes unusually radiant. So Kitty wasn't surprised as they sped along the highway to hear Jennifer say, "I have to tell you something. You're not going to believe this. Guess who I slept with?"

"Who?" Kitty demanded. "Tell me!"

"Robert Chambers!"

"Oh, wow," Kitty said. *"Tell* me about it. Like tell me *everything.*"

Jennifer did. She explained how Robert had admired her in Dorrian's and asked her to meet him outside, and how they'd gotten together for their first date not long after that, and how he'd left messages for her when she went to Boston, and made love to her twice after that. And she said, "He's absolutely incredible in bed!"

Kitty was a little surprised at that. She knew a girl who'd recently tried to make it with Robert and reported that her efforts had bombed out. He'd been impotent. She told Jennifer what her friend had said, and Jennifer smiled. "Not with me he wasn't," she said proudly. "He was great. I even had an orgasm. My first!"

"Oh, wow," Kitty said again. "That's *totally* great."

When they got to Venice, the festival was in full swing. Orange-robed Hare Krishnas were parading along the ocean-front walk and theater groups and live bands were putting on shows. Kitty and Jennifer joined the milling spectators and stopped talking about Robert.

That night they went discoing and slept over at Kitty's place with a third girl, someone Jennifer didn't feel all that comfortable about. So it wasn't until the next morning, when Kitty was driving Jennifer to the airport to catch her plane back to New York, that Jennifer brought up the subject of Robert again. "I'll probably see him when I get back," she said.

Kitty smiled. "I'll bet."

"It's casual," Jennifer said. "Just casual. But it's so mellow. And he's so nice."

The day Jennifer flew home, two old friends of Robert's from York Prep ran into him in Central Park. He was with a beautiful blond girl they'd never seen before. He introduced them, and they thought she was so pretty they decided to take pictures.

Robert didn't pose. He wasn't looking as good as usual that day. Although it was almost the end of summer, his skin was deathly pale, as if he hadn't been out of doors in the daylight all season long. Moreover, his eyes had a faraway, stunned look.

"Hey, man, you on coke?" one of the boys asked him.

"Naw," Robert said. "Ecstasy. I did some last night."

Later the boys told Robert how stunning his new girlfriend was, and Robert said he'd been seeing her all week.

The two boys were impressed. And jealous. "What do girls see in him?" one of them asked the other as they were leaving the park. "I mean, this guy's done nothing since high school."

"They want him for his looks, I guess," the other boy responded. "Guys get status from going out with good-looking girls. Maybe it works the other way around, too."

Back in New York, Jennifer went shopping for clothes to wear at college. She bought a few things in her neighborhood, then went uptown to 59th Street, where she stepped into a French Connections shop. Her old boss Connie Davies was working there. Connie was getting married in the fall and Jennifer wanted to wish her well.

"Show me what you bought," Connie said to her after they talked about the wedding.

Jennifer put her parcels down on the floor and began pulling out clothes. "Do you like these?" she asked Connie, holding up a pair of black checked pants. "I got them on sale." Her voice was full of pride.

"They're lovely. Real college girl stuff."

As soon as she spoke, Connie had one of those moments of wonder at time and its swift passage, remembering vividly the way Jennifer had looked just like a little newspaper boy when she'd first met her. Now she was a young lady going off to college. It's sad in a way, Connie thought. But what can you do? Everyone grows up. She snapped out of her mood.

"Come over here," she directed, and led Jennifer past racks of new wools and corduroys. "I've got something that'll look great on you."

At a skirt rack Connie paused and extricated a pink, blue, and white plaid with a houndstooth design on it.

"Beautiful," Jennifer said.

"Perfect for school," Connie said.

Jennifer slipped into the skirt, twirled for a moment in front of a silvery mirror, and bought the skirt. Then, arms laden, she said goodbye to Connie.

She hadn't seen Robert since her return from California and didn't expect that she would until the following week, because she had promised her father and stepmother that she would visit them at their summer home in Montauk, just east of the Hamptons, right after the trip to California.

She did, leaving the city on Wednesday, August 20.

The day that Jennifer went to Montauk, Robert telephoned Monsignor James Wilders, the elderly Irish priest under whom he had served as an altar boy back in grade school. All week he had been edgy and explosive, and at last it had occurred to him that he needed someone to talk to, someone who might be able to help him. He hadn't spoken to Wilders, who had long ago left St. Thomas More Church for a downtown parish, in six years. But he had seen him at the archbishop's installation. Dialing the number of his new parish, he asked for him.

He was out, a secretary said.

The next day he got a call back from the priest, but he no longer felt the urgency that had prompted him to dial him the first time. When Wilders suggested they talk face to face, he didn't say there was any hurry about their doing so, and when Wilders recommended that they speak again on Monday to set up an appointment, Robert said that was fine.

In Montauk, Steve Levin was in a great mood. He gave Jennifer a lesson in driving his Toyota pickup truck—she knew how to drive, but the pickup had a stick shift, and she'd been begging him for instruction. He also took her swimming. The weather was cool, but that didn't faze them. He'd always been in love with the sea, ever since he was a little kid climbing the cliffs at his grandfather's house off Nahant and plunging into the frigid Massachusetts water. Jennifer shared his passion for the sea. She wasn't just a good swimmer. She was a body-surfer. Surfing was his hobby, and he'd taught her how to do it.

At the beach he watched her as she tangled with the roiling waves in the company of a group of inveterate surfers. One of them marveled at her facility, saying, "Wow! Where'd you learn to do that?" She told him her father had showed her how. He heard the acknowledgment and experienced a surge of pride. It felt great to have taught Jennifer to do something for which people admired her.

But later the visit ran into a snag. "All my friends are getting together in the Hamptons," Jennifer said. "Can I borrow the Toyota and drive over and join them?"

Steve didn't think she was ready to take the truck on a long drive. She hadn't really gotten the hang of the stick shift yet. He told her no.

She got upset and lay down on the couch and sulked. Steve tried to cheer her up. "It's no big deal," he said. Then, "Look, I'll drive you to your friends. Or maybe you can get them to come and pick you up."

She didn't want that. She went on sulking. But at last she brightened and told him, "Oh, all right. I'll call my friends."

Not long afterward, Alexandra LaGatta and her mother picked up Jennifer in Montauk and drove her to their summer house in Southampton.

She was confused, Jennifer said to Alexandra when they were alone. She wasn't in love with Robert Chambers. She was in love with Brock. He'd been in Europe all summer, but he was back now, and she'd talked with him on the phone. Yet even though when she'd spoken to him she'd remembered their love, it wasn't Brock she kept thinking about when she let her mind wander. It was Robert. Which was weird. Because she didn't even like Robert as a person.

She tried to have a good time that weekend. On Saturday afternoon, dressed in a little black bikini, she swam and sunned both at the beach and at Alexandra's pool. And on Saturday night she and Alexandra went to a party in East Hampton. There Jennifer got into a long talk with a boy who had just returned from a Minnesota drug rehabilitation clinic. Just like Robert Chambers. She promised him that if he went on trying to stay clean, she'd be his buddy. He could call her any time the going got rough and she'd talk him down. She liked the idea of helping. Of being needed.

Later that night, she drove from East Hampton to Southampton to pick up Margaret Trahill and bring her to the party. She used Alexandra's mother's car and, feeling exhilarated, made the twelve traffic-ridden crowded miles in twenty minutes, even though it was raining. Margaret was impressed and Jennifer felt great and when they got back to the party, she didn't want the night ever to end, so after a while she and Margaret left East Hampton and went to Danceteria over in Water Mill. It was her favorite nightspot in the Hamptons. One weekend earlier in the summer, they'd included her name on an invitation to a private party at the club; when she saw her name in print on the little card, she'd wanted to scream with joy.

Danceteria was crowded. Everyone was there. Even Brock. She went up to him and hugged him and acted really glad to see him. But he was short, and Robert was tall. He was a flyweight, and Robert was husky. He had a toothy open grin, and Robert had a mysterious fleeting smile. He was familiar, like a book she'd read many times, and Robert was the unknown. She danced with Brock and tried to look happy, but inside she was jumpy and out of sorts. When some guy on the dance floor tried to give her a pinch in the rear, she hauled off and let him have it, cursing and screaming at him. She hated when guys wised off.

Brock was protective. He calmed her down and got the guy thrown out. She was in love with him, she was in love with him, she kept reminding herself. And when they parted, she made a date to meet him on Sunday night at a club in Sag Harbor.

Around the time that Jennifer was saying good night to Brock, Robert entered his apartment in the city with Josephine Perry, the pretty blonde his friends had taken pictures of in the park. She was a lot younger than he was, only seventeen, but that was one of the things he liked about her. That and the fact that she always seemed to have plenty of money on her. The first night they'd met, he'd managed to steal twenty dollars from her without her noticing. That was eight months ago, before they'd become lovers.

Tonight his mother was out of town, so Jo and he were going to spend the whole night together. He took her into his room, with its platform bed and shelf of stuffed animals, and, after she fell asleep, began a stealthy search through her wallet. It was thick with bills. He slipped fifty dollars out and hid it away.

In the morning Jo discovered the theft. "You stole from me, didn't you?" she demanded.

He was casual. "It's only money," he said.

If he hoped that would calm her down, it didn't. She stomped home in a fury.

Sunday night was reggae night at the Bay Street in Sag Harbor. Jamaican musicians in dreadlocks and wool caps enthralled the neatly coiffed children of the rich with lyrics about revolution and the impending destruction of the world. Transported, Brock and Jennifer listened to the performance in the dilapidated warehouselike club. But after about an hour, Jennifer wanted to leave. She'd been annoyed at Brock because he'd arrived late for their rendezvous, and although they had made up, she was impatient now to return to Southampton.

Brock said okay, and he and a friend drove her back to Alexandra's house. She was mellow on the way over, listening repeatedly to a favorite Police song on the car's tape deck, and when they got to Alexandra's she invited Brock to come in. He wanted to, he explained, but he couldn't. The car was his friend's, and his friend had to get home. He kissed Jennifer good night, and she got out. She looks beautiful, he thought. She was wearing a black miniskirt and black top, and as she started toward the house she turned around and stood smiling at him for a moment, the headlights catching and holding her like a butterfly.

He waved, and then he and his friend drove off.

From Brock's point of view, the reunion with Jennifer that weekend had been a great success. She'd confessed her fling with Robert, but he'd had some confessions to make, too, and they'd forgiven each other their dalliances. She'd implied that now that he was back, Robert was out of the picture, and she'd even told him, wiping away a small lingering hurt, that being with Robert wasn't "like being with you." Brock felt that everything was good between them now, and that it had probably never been better.

But that was not the impression Jennifer conveyed to Alexandra on Monday morning. "Brock was mean to me," she said. "We had a fight." She sounded disconsolate. And then she was talking about Robert again. How sexy he was. How much he'd pleased her. "I'll be leaving for school in a couple of days," she grumbled. "Am I gonna see him?"

"Let's go into the city," Alexandra suggested after a while. "Let's have some fun. Forget about Brock."

That afternoon Jennifer called her father and said she wanted to spend another night with Alexandra. She didn't say they were going into the city, and Steve assumed she meant she wanted to spend some more time in Southampton. He was disappointed. He'd been hoping she'd spend the night at home with him and Arlene. But he didn't want to chide her." Do whatever you want to do," he said.

Still, she heard his dissatisfaction. "What's wrong?" she said.

He told her how he felt, said he'd been expecting to have extra time with her before she went off to school. But she was full of plans and prospects. "Dad, this is probably the last time I'm going to get to see all my friends together," she pleaded.

He understood what she was saying. She was telling him that high school friends have a way of drifting apart, but one's family will always be around. That's the way kids look at things, he thought. So he gave in, said it was okay.

"I love you, Dad," she thanked him.

"I love you, too," he said.

In Manhattan, that Monday evening, a north wind was blowing and the air was crisp. Taxiing to Alexandra's apartment on the Upper East Side, Jennifer talked about the end of summer and her imminent departure for Boston. She was looking forward to college, she said. But every time she tried to imagine life at Chamberlayne, the pit of her stomach went fluttery. Suppose people up there didn't like her? Suppose it was like Sousa Junior High and she was odd girl out? "You've got to come and visit me every weekend," she told Alexandra, who would still be in the city, finishing high school.

The two girls had dinner with Alexandra's father, then made arrangements with friends for the rest of the evening. First they'd go to Juanita s, a Mexican cafe, with Laura and Larissa. Then the four of them would go on to Dorrian's and meet up with Betsy and Edwina and a few other girls.

Dressing, Jennifer talked about Robert and fussed over her appearance, borrowing bits and pieces of finery from Alexandra's wardrobe. Alexandra was smaller than she was, but Jennifer had been eating carefully and using her diet pills all summer, and she looked fine in Alexandra's white camisole and pink and white miniskirt. She put them on, along with a pair of Alexandra's freshly laundered panties. Cute little white bikini panties. She also put on some of Alexandra's makeup, including a rich, dark lipstick.

Then she fooled around with her hair, pinning it back with a black bow. That way, her zircon earrings showed more. But her hair looked better loose, she decided after a while, and she tucked the bow into a pocket of her jean jacket. She put the dark lipstick in there, too. Then she slung the jacket jauntily over her left shoulder, took a farewell glance into the mirror, and set off with Alexandra for Juanita's.

She was excited when she got there. She and Alexandra ordered margaritas, and Laura and Larissa ordered vodka Collinses, and she kept talking about Dorrian's and how she hoped Robert would be there. Just thinking about seeing him thrilled her. But what should she do when she first saw him? Should she go right up to him and kiss him? Or should she hold back awhile and just talk to him? She laid the question before her friends and asked them to give her advice.

Soon they were all giggling and exchanging romantic tips and revelations. And soon, beach-tanned and merry, one girl more lovely than the next, they were the life of the restaurant. Everywhere people were looking at them. Jennifer had another margarita.

Then suddenly a waiter arrived unbeckoned at the table. He was carrying a bottle of champagne and four champagne glasses. "Someone ordered this for you," he announced.

Who? Jennifer begged the waiter to tell her, but he said he didn't know who it was. He'd simply been asked to deliver it. She glanced around at the young preppies in summer sweaters and the older guys in business suits crowding the bar. But no one's eyes met hers in acknowledgment. Still, clearly, she and her friends had an unknown admirer. They'd been singled out. Noticed. It felt so good that she stood up, and, like a starlet receiving an Oscar, gave a little mini bow, and, addressing the entire room, called out passionately, "Thank you."

While Jennifer was thanking the crowd at Juanita's, Robert was standing on a street corner, talking to a friend outside Dorrian's. He and Jo Perry had had a reconciliation over the telephone, and to make her happy he'd promised to meet her at the pub tonight. But he'd arrived early, there'd been hardly anyone inside, and he and his friend had come out into the cool night air to wait till the place filled up.

Lighting a joint, Robert stared at the traffic racing down Second Avenue and gave himself over to melancholia. "I'm depressed," he grumbled. "I've got nothing. No job. No money. And Hazelden didn't help me. I've been falling off the wagon."

"Look, maybe you should go home," his friend suggested. "I mean, if you hang around here, you gotta fall off the wagon."

Robert shrugged. Going home was no solution. "Naw," he said. "I want to hang out."

He finished the joint, stood outside a while longer, then went back into Dorrian's.

Jennifer and her girlfriends arrived at Dorrian's about midnight. They had the half-drunk bottle of champagne from Juanita's with them, and when they walked in they sipped more of it. The bar was jammed and festive, like a giant cocktail party, and two bartenders were busily pouring drinks. One of them was twenty-two-year-old John Zaccaro, Jr., Geraldine Ferraro's son, who was awaiting trial in Vermont on charges of possessing and intending to sell cocaine. Jennifer asked Zaccaro for a glass of water, looked around for Robert, and not seeing him, made her way deeper into the room. The friends she bumped into welcomed her extravagantly, hugging and kissing her, and she embraced them back and told them she loved them. But all the while she kept searching for Robert. Two boys grabbed her and planted noisy kisses on either side of her neck, trying to give her hickeys, but she ignored them. Was Robert here?

At last, entering the glassed-in porch at the back of the pub, she saw him in the distance, sitting at a table with some people she didn't know. He was so handsome. His face, with its cleft chin, so rugged and his blue eyes so dark and enigmatic. At once all her planning drained from her mind. She didn't kiss him, didn't address him, just went over to his table and started talking to the group at large. She didn't know what she was saying. She just said whatever came into her head.

She's prattling, Robert thought. She's going on and on about her trip to California, and the suntan she worked on in the Hamptons. Who cares? He made faces while she spoke, and then after a while just ignored her, getting into a conversation with one of the guys at his table.

•   •   •

Jennifer didn't linger. But although she was hurt by Robert's response, she decided not to give it too much significance. She'd approach him again and see what happened. Ten minutes later she went back to his table, ordered a drink—a baybreeze, with vodka, cranberry juice, and pineapple juice—and this time she sat down.

Robert rose and left the table.

She didn't follow him, just got up, too, and talked to people she knew. But memories of the stories she'd been telling about Robert all summer flooded her mind, filling her with shame. All her friends knew she'd been to bed with him. All her friends knew how much she liked him. Even tonight she'd been saying that she wanted to leave the bar with him later and have sex. What would people think of her if he ignored her? And why *was* he, when they'd been so good together? It occurred to her then that maybe he didn't know how much she liked him, and that maybe, if she told him, he'd soften toward her. Lots of guys, she knew, needed girls to make the first move. She waited until she saw him standing alone near the back of the bar and approached him a third time, determined to make him pay attention to her.

He was terribly handsome, she told him. And terribly sexy. And then she said saucily, "You were the best sex I ever had."

She hoped that would carry some weight. Guys loved to hear they were the best. But to her astonishment, he didn't seem happy to hear her words. Odd—he didn't even smile. He just looked at her coldly and said, "You shouldn't have said that."

Why?

Betsy saw them talking. They were deep in conversation, and the expressions on their faces were serious.

Jo Perry also saw them, and their being together made her angry. She and Robert had agreed to meet at Dorrian's at ten forty-five, but he'd arrived an hour late. And when he'd finally come, he hadn't even said hello, let alone sat down with her. He'd gone to the back of the bar and done some coke, a friend told her. And now he was not only still ignoring her, he was talking with another girl. He wasn't supposed to be doing that; she and he had an agreement about Dorrian's. If either of them wanted to flirt with someone else there, that was okay, provided they informed each other in advance. He hadn't said anything of the sort about tonight. Yet there he was, engrossed in conversation with Jennifer. Irate, Jo went over to Robert and began to shout at him. In her hand was a bag containing packages of condoms. "Use these with someone else," she said, flinging the bag at his face. "Because you're not going to get a chance to use them with me."

It was embarrassing to Robert to have Jo chew him out. People were listening. Some of them were laughing. Jennifer was laughing. Not only that, now she was talking to some other guy. Flirting with him. She pissed him off. It was her fault that Jo was yelling at him in front of everybody. Her fault, because if she hadn't come over to him, Jo wouldn't have seen them and gotten so furious.

When she stopped shouting and walked away, he shrugged and ignored both Jo and Jennifer.

Why was he being so standoffish? Why, when she'd let him know how much he'd pleased her? Jennifer, utterly wretched, ran through the merry-

making crowd and grabbed Alexandra LaGatta and told her how Robert
had brushed her off. She was on the verge of tears, and she wailed, "Oh,
my God, now look at what's happening between us."

It's probably all for the best, Alexandra thought. She'd never cared for
Robert, and she didn't like Dorrian's all that much either. The way she saw
it, the place was filled with a bunch of kids who didn't know what to do
with themselves except drink and drug and chase after one another. The
guys were insecure, so they went after every girl they saw, and that made
the girls insecure, so in retaliation they went after every guy. The place
was like a circle, with everybody trying to make out with everybody else,
and she'd never heard of people who hung out at Dorrian's being faithful
to one another for longer than a week. If that.

"Forget Robert," she told Jennifer.

But Jennifer didn't want to. When Alexandra lost interest in her plight,
she sought out Betsy and implored her to intercede with Robert. "Tell
him I want to talk to him," she said. "Tell him to meet me outside in
twenty minutes."

Betsy delivered the message. But Robert listened to the words indiffer-
ently. "I don't want to deal with it," he said.

. . .

Jennifer tried afterward to put him out of her mind. She circulated
through the bar with Edwina looking for new good-looking guys. But
most of the guys she met were so unappealing that when they asked for
her phone number, she gave them a false one. She played a trick on Edwina, who had casually left her wallet lying around on a table, by removing the credit cards from the wallet. But although she'd meant it as a
joke, a lesson to Edwina not to be careless, Edwina got angry, and that
spoiled the fun. She took part in an ice fight, letting herself be captured
by a group of boys and dragged under a table. But a bartender broke up
the fight. She went out of doors for a while with Alexandra LaGatta. But

Alexandra got into an intimate conversation with a guy. Jennifer, a fifth wheel, went back inside.

Robert was still there. He looked just as handsome and sexy as ever. Maybe it had been a mistake to give up on him, she began thinking. Persistence had always been her strong suit, and maybe if she stuck to it, stayed at Dorrian's long enough, she'd be lucky. Most people paired off when the bar closed, and if there was no other girl waiting for Robert when closing came, he just might feel lonesome and she just might end up in bed with him after all.

At around two thirty, when Alexandra LaGatta came back inside and said she was ready to go home now, she told Alexandra she didn't want to leave yet, because Robert was still there. Alexandra took off, promising to leave the key to her apartment under the doormat, and Jennifer lingered on.

There was a problem with her plan, though. Jo Perry, the girl who had yelled at Robert and said he'd stood her up, was still hanging around, too. Was she waiting for Robert? Or was she really through with him, the way she'd said she was. Unsure, Jennifer went to Jo's table, sat down, and engaged her in conversation. She kept the conversation light. She didn't say why she'd come over. But she did hint at her reason. "I have a problem," she said. "I know this nice girl. And—and I want her boyfriend."

Jo didn't know what nice girl she was referring to and didn't ask. Jennifer let the subject drop. But in the end it didn't matter, because later, at around a quarter of four, she realized that Jo wasn't waiting for Robert. She was going home.

The bar was pretty empty by then. Only a dozen or so people were left. Jennifer stayed put. And then at last her plan began working. Robert came over to her.

She talked with him for a long while after that. She sat at the bar with him and, toying with the ice cubes in her glass, spoke to him seriously and intimately. While they were talking, a fistfight broke out between some of the remaining patrons, but she ignored the commotion and concentrated on Robert. And then, just as she'd hoped, he said he wanted her to leave with him.

She should have been overjoyed, but she wasn't. A feeling of uneasiness came over her, and she couldn't make up her mind to go. She needed advice, she decided. And noticing that her friend William was still there, tried to get it from him. "I've been talking to Robert," she said, cornering William. "And, I don't know, a couple of things he said worried me."

"Naw, Robert's okay." William shrugged. "He's one of us."

"Should I leave with him?"

"Yeah, if that's what you want to do."

She *did* want to leave with him. She'd been thinking about him for weeks. Or was it years? She knew he'd had lots of girls in his life. And she knew the sort of girls they were—the ones who always got to see their names in print on club invitations, the ones who had perfect skin and bodies thin as rails and who wore little black cocktail dresses to parties and the dun-colored uniforms of fancy East Side academies to school. But he'd chosen her. Made her body feel loved and the rest of her feel something for which she'd always yearned. Feel that she belonged.

She went back to Robert.

About four thirty, looking proud and exhilarated, she stood up and, with Robert beside her, began saying her goodbyes.

"We know what you're gonna do," Betsy, who was still there, teased.

She gave Betsy a wink.

"Where are you going?" Betsy asked.

"Don't worry," she said. "I'll call you tomorrow." Then she tossed her hair bravely and slung her jean jacket over her left shoulder. Robert opened the door for her, and she sailed through it.

PART II

WOMAN DOWN

THE BODY IN THE PARK

The air was chilly and the sky still dark when Pat Reilly awoke at 5 A.M. She turned off the alarm, then sank back beneath the bedclothes, thinking she just might stay where she was and skip exercising this morning. But after a few minutes she got out of bed, ate a hurried breakfast, and went downstairs, where she straddled her streamlined racing bike. She worked such long hours at her job—she was a mutual funds trader—that if she didn't exercise now she wouldn't be able to do it all day.

It was still too dim to ride safely in the park, so she pedaled downtown along Fifth Avenue. But a few minutes past six, when the sun began to rise, she turned the bike, headed uptown, and entered the park.

She was moving fast when, right near the boathouse at 72nd Street, a brown car came hurtling toward her, traveling in the wrong direction on the one-way road. Who is this lunatic? she wondered, and tried to peer into the car. But the windows were tinted and she couldn't make out the driver.

She kept a wary eye out for danger after that. You couldn't be too cautious in the park. Not if you were a biker. Because it wasn't just traffic you had to worry about. It was predators who accosted you for your equipment. Pedaling, she kept glancing to either side of the roadway to make certain no one was lurking in wait for her.

She was just passing Cleopatra's Needle, behind The Metropolitan Museum of Art, when something caught her eye in the trees to her left. There was someone there. Someone sprawled on the ground. Just a bag lady asleep, she told herself, and kept on going. Then she did a double take. It wasn't a bag lady. It was something else. She braked the bike, got off, and began walking timorously toward the spot that had captured her attention.

When she was about forty feet away from a tall elm tree, she saw clearly what she'd glimpsed from the road. It was the body of a young woman, naked except for a few clothes bunched up around her neck and waist and a jean jacket tossed across one of her arms. Her limbs were contorted, and she was lying motionless beneath an overhanging branch. Pat stopped walking. She didn't want to get any closer. If the woman was still alive, she wouldn't know how to help her. And if she was dead, she didn't want to see what it was that had happened to her.

She ran to her bicycle, leaped onto it, and rode frantically back to the boathouse. There were telephones there. She'd call the police.

She tried one. It didn't work. She tried a second. It didn't work either. Someone had pulled out the wires. She tried a third. Broken, too.

Frustrated, Pat jumped back on her bike, raced it out of the park, and found a phone on a street corner.

It was around 6:15 A.M. She dialed 911 and reported to an operator what she'd seen. But she couldn't describe the exact location. She'd help direct the police toward it, she promised the operator; she'd wait on the side of the road near the elm tree.

At 6:21 A.M. Sergeant Anthony Michelak and Police Officer James Mc-Creary, whose job it was to provide security for the park's early morning athletes, were parked in a patrol car alongside the reservoir when a voice penetrated the static of their radio. "Woman down," the voice sputtered.

"Woman down at Eighty-first and East Drive." It was police lingo for a woman in need of assistance.

"Let's go!" said Michelak, who was a certified emergency medical services technician. "Let's see what's happening." Seconds later he and McCreary were careening along the bridle path. Then they turned onto the joggers' road and began heading south.

Before they reached 81st Street, they passed Pat Reilly sitting along the roadway. She saw them and gestured toward the trees. McCreary, who was driving, swerved in a U-turn. As he started the turn, he noticed several people clustered at a stone wall behind the Museum. They were standing, except for one young man who was sitting down. McCreary paid no attention to the spectators. He finished his turn and parked the car.

Michelak jumped out. In the distance he could make out a figure lying under a tree. He hurried toward it, determined to provide the required assistance. But when he reached the figure, he hesitated, wondering if the woman *could* be assisted. Her neck was covered with a welter of garish red bruises and she appeared to have been strangled. Maybe she wasn't dead. Maybe some shred of life still lingered within her. Deciding to check, he reached to take her pulse. But although he'd been trained to take it at the carotid artery, he knew better than to touch the woman's bruised neck. Instead, he placed his hand beneath her heart. It was completely still.

Michelak went to the car and told his supervisors that this wasn't an assistance site. It was a crime scene. He asked for detectives and an ambulance. By then more spectators had gathered. He opened the car's trunk, took out a long sheet of brown wrapping paper, and gave the dead woman some semblance of privacy from the rubberneckers across the road.

Susan Bird, a lawyer in her forties, was one of the rubberneckers. She'd been running near the Museum with a friend when she'd heard sirens and noticed the police car pull over onto the grass. She stopped moving in order to take in the activity across the way. A young man was also watching, sitting on a low stone wall and staring intently at the police. "What's going on?" Susan asked him.

"I don't know," he said. "It looks like they found something." Susan thought him odd. His face had strange vertical scratches on it, and he seemed almost indifferent to her presence. "Like what?" she said, forcing herself on his consciousness. "What could it be?"

"I think they found a body," he murmured.

A body? Susan's mind immediately filled in a scenario. A runner had died. Had a stroke. That's what happens when you get to be forty and exercise too vigorously. You fall down in the park and die, and nobody finds you till morning. "Have you gone to check?" she asked the young man worriedly. "I mean, have you done anything?"

"Well, no," he said.

"Why not?"

"Because if I did, the cops would chase me away."

A strange thing to say, Susan thought. Police in the Midwest, where she was raised, didn't chase away concerned citizens. Still, she didn't go across the road to ask what had happened. The policemen over there were busy removing a length of brown paper from something lying on the ground and replacing it with a sheet. She saw a leg. Whatever had happened, it was all under control now. Susan, no longer keen to linger, walked away.

The friend she'd been running with left at the same time. As they headed out of the park, he said to Susan, "Did you see the scratches on that guy on the wall? How deep and regular they were?"

"Yeah," Susan said. "Like he got scratched by a machine. What kind of industrial accident would you have to be in to get those kinds of scratches?"

Where's Jennifer?

Alexandra LaGatta asked herself that when her alarm clock woke her at 6:30 A.M. But she wasn't particularly worried about Jennifer. Jennifer probably figured I'd forget to leave the keys under the mat, she thought.

So she went home. Or maybe to Robert's. Whatever, I don't have time to think about Jennifer now. Because the boy I left Dorrian's with last night is in my bedroom. I'd better get him out before my father finds out. I ought to get myself out, too. Go down to the Motor Vehicles Bureau, like I was planning to do, and get my learner's permit.

Moving quickly, Alexandra dressed, rushed the boy who had spent the night with her out of the apartment, and headed downtown for her permit.

At 7:45 A.M. Detective Mickey McEntee, wearing running clothes, sneakers, and a glittering diamond in his ear, parked his Starion Turbo in the parking lot of the police precinct in Central Park, the Two-Two. McEntee had been with the Central Park Precinct only nine months. Before that he'd been with Bronx Narcotics, where he'd worked undercover, funky dark glasses on his eyes and fake needle tracks on his arms. He made the marks each morning with red ink and a splash of a coagulant that caused skin to shrivel, and he would never forget the way his adrenaline had surged when one of the dealers with whom he was hanging out reached toward his fake scar and started fingering it. He'd reared back, put on his ugliest expression, and shouted, "Get your hands off me, man! That hurts!"

McEntee missed the action he'd had in the Bronx. Compared to those days, the park precinct was Toys "R" Us. Despite the way the public looked at it. They saw the park as some kind of terror zone. But in fact it had fewer major crimes than any precinct in the city. Which was why he didn't like it. Yeah, he'd helped look for a guy who'd murdered a homeless man up near the Lasker Pool, and for another who'd killed a homosexual outside the Ramble, and he'd helped catch a weirdo who'd stabbed a hooker forty-three times and left her body, if you could call what he saw a body, in a garbage bag at the northernmost tip of the park. But mostly nothing happened. The guys he worked with in the detective squad almost never needed to put on their homicide suits, the two- or three-piece outfits they wore when they went out to face the public. Their homicide suits, and their homicide hats as well, got so dusty that whenever the guys did need to wear them they had to go over them first with a clothes brush.

Still, being bored wasn't what McEntee minded most about the park precinct. What he minded most was that on the rare occasions when something did happen, the boss wouldn't let him catch the case. Even though it had been his turn up for months. The boss gave the assignments to his partner, Joe Kennedy, because Kennedy had been around a long time and had experience. He just got to watch and do whatever Kennedy told him to do. How was he supposed to get enough experience to catch a case if they wouldn't give you one because you didn't have the experience? Catch 22. Catch Two-Two. The only bright side of the park precinct was that it put him in the Great Outdoors, which meant he could barbecue steak in the parking lot for dinner and run around the reservoir before starting work.

He'd have his run this morning, McEntee planned. Then after the run he'd shower and shave and get into the jeans he used for work clothes. He locked up the car and ambled into the precinct house. He was just inside the door when Kennedy saw him and shouted, "Homicide!"

"We got a homicide?" he asked incredulously. There hadn't been one since spring.

"None of this 'we' stuff," Kennedy said. "'We' is a French word. *You* got a homicide. I'm gonna let you have this one."

Yeah, sure, McEntee thought. If the boss don't volunteer you.

The thought of the boss brought him up short. The guy wasn't necessarily there every day, but he'd be in today for sure. He always showed up at homicides. And here he was in his running clothes and without a shave. Racing to his locker, he got out his razor and scraped it hastily across his stubble, bloodying his face in three places before he got himself clean. Then he searched in the locker for some homicide clothes. He didn't have a homicide suit like Kennedy and the rest of the guys had. He hadn't gotten around to buying one yet. All he had were his Bronx Narcotics outfits. Dark pants, skinny leather ties, pastel-colored shirts, and a pearl-gray linen jacket. He slipped on black pants, a mauve shirt, and a black leather tie, then pulled the jacket over his shoulders. The outfit would just have to do. Anyway, it wasn't so bad. It just looked more like *Miami Vice* than the Central Park detective squad.

Moments later the boss arrived, and he and Kennedy and their boss jumped into a car and sped to the back of the Museum.

At a few minutes before 8 A.M., John Cotter, New York Newsday's new metropolitan editor, reported to the paper's offices. It was his first day on the job, and when he walked in he had in mind spending the morning taking it easy, getting to know the staff and how the place operated. But even before he reached his desk, a guy at the teletype machine beckoned him over and said, "Looks like a pretty good one at Central Park."

Cotter glanced at the release from the police department that was coming over the teletype and knew the guy who'd called it to his attention was right. Yeah, this was a good story. The dead girl was white. The death of a white girl always sells papers. By eight, he was assigning a reporter and a photographer to the story. "Let's dance with it," he told them.

Standing behind The Metropolitan Museum of Art in the grove of trees where the girl's body had been found, McEntee told himself that no matter how unlikely the prospects of his catching this case were, he was going to make a try for it as soon as the right time came. That wasn't yet. Right now Nightwatch, which handled the start of all crimes reported between midnight and 8 A.M., was still in charge. Their head, Detective Sergeant Wallace Ziens, was briefing a group of the Central Park detectives. "What we got here," Ziens was saying, "is a girl. Young. White. We also got tire tracks." He gestured at an area where the grass was matted down and explained that the biker who had found the body had moments earlier nearly been run down by a brown car traveling against traffic. "It looks as if," Ziens went on, "whoever this girl is, she was killed by whoever was driving the brown car and then dumped here."

To break his tension, McEntee turned to Kennedy and ribbed him. "Naw, some of our own guys were probably sleeping here in a radio car," he said. "Someone killed the girl. Then our guys woke up and saw the body. And they said, Jeez, it's a crime. Let's drive the other way fast."

Kennedy laughed, and McEntee felt more relaxed. When the briefing was over, he talked to some of the Nightwatch detectives who'd been on the scene for an hour already, then went to have a look at the body. Detectives from the Crime Scene Unit were working on it, taking photographs and looking for evidence. Hairs. Fluids. Fingerprints. They always got first crack on a case, recording and collecting whatever traces of the killer they could find on the body, and any traces of his or the victim's presence at the scene of the crime. It was painstaking and time-consuming work, McEntee knew, so they would take a while to finish. He and the other detectives couldn't examine the corpse until they were done. But in the meantime he could make a few observations. Eager to get going, McEntee stood over the body, which was no longer covered, and tried to figure out what had happened to the girl.

She'd been strangled. That much was obvious. But she'd probably been assaulted, too. Her face was dirty, as if it had been pushed into the ground, her left eye was swollen, and around her nipples were gouges that looked like bite marks. Most likely she tried to resist her attacker. That's how she got so marked up. And most likely she was raped. That's how come her clothes were all shoved up, and her breasts and pubic area exposed.

He was touched by the girl's body. She looked so young. And so well groomed. Somehow, cops were always affected when a dead woman looked well groomed. It made them think about their wives or girlfriends. And except for the dirt and marks on her, this girl looked unusually tidy. Her hair was lustrous, and she had a deep tan, one she'd clearly worked hard at getting. It showed the traces of the straps of several different bathing suits. One of the Nightwatch detectives McEntee had talked to had said the girl was probably a hooker, but McEntee didn't think so now that he'd seen her.

Anyway, it probably wasn't the girl's identity that he'd have to worry about if he caught the case. That would get straightened out when the Crime Scene Unit finished its work and let the rest of the guys search her pockets. There was a jean jacket draped over her arm. Probably there'd be ID in there. The killer was another story. Who could he be? Looking at his handiwork, McEntee figured he already knew a bit about him. The guy was a callous sonofabitch. He had to be. Otherwise he'd have covered the girl up when he was done with her. And he was cruel. He had to be in order to strangle her. Take me, McEntee said to himself. I could shoot someone, but if I had to go hand to hand and choke a person to death, I'm not sure I could do it. To choke someone, you had to stand right up close to them and actually squeeze out your victim's life.

The clues he was getting made him feel better, even though he knew they weren't much. But he went on regarding the body, hoping he'd find more. And then something odd struck him. The girl had a pierced ear, but no earring. That in itself wasn't strange. He didn't wear his earring all the time. But when he didn't wear it for a while, the tiny hole in his lobe seemed to tighten up and grow almost imperceptible, whereas when he wore the earring and then removed it, the hole looked slightly stretched for quite a while afterward. The hole in the girl's lobe had that stretched look he'd seen in his own. "Hey!" he shouted suddenly to the Crime Scene Unit detectives. "You guys remove an earring?"

They hadn't.

After that McEntee decided to search for earrings. He didn't know why he decided that. Maybe it was because when he turned away from the Crime Scene guys, he noticed a group of news photographers stampeding onto the roadway and said to himself that the last thing the Police Department wants to have are camera crews photographing guys standing around with their hands in their pockets. Whatever the reason, he said to Joe Kennedy, "Hey, she was wearing earrings. I'm sure of it. Let's look for them." Kennedy agreed, and the two of them began shuffling around the elm tree, peering into the thick layer of twigs and leaves that covered the ground like a rug.

They saw nothing, so they kept on looking, moving their search to other trees in the area. They were checking beneath a crab-apple tree about forty-five feet north of the body when they saw something white on the ground. A dirty handkerchief, McEntee thought, and bent toward it. But it wasn't a handkerchief. It was a pair of soiled panties. He studied the area. A few feet away from the panties, the ground looked peculiar. The twigs and leaves covering it had been scattered, leaving bits of earth visible. Maybe the girl struggled with her killer here, McEntee said to himself, maybe she tussled with him under the crab-apple tree and then ran away, only to be caught and killed under the elm. Or maybe she was even killed here and then dragged to the elm. "C'mere," he called to the guys from Crime Scene. "Take a picture of this! Looks like there was a struggle here."

They refused to come over. "Naw, this was a dump job," one of them called back. "The girl was dumped from the car that made the tracks."

"Her panties are here," McEntee said. Behind him, cameramen were being kept back by park police and reporters were craning their necks. "How'd her panties get over here if she was dumped where the tracks are?"

"Those aren't her panties, that's how."

"Whaddya mean?"

"We looked at them. Too soiled. Those panties have probably been here for days. Anyway, we already got panties. A blue pair. From over near the tire tracks."

Two pair of panties so close to the scene? The park was really something! No matter. The panties he'd found were the right ones, McEntee was sure. What did the Crime Scene Unit know? They were a bunch of old hairbags. A bunch of guys who'd been on the job so long, they'd forgotten how to think. The girl *had* to have been over here, under the crab-apple tree. Not far from the panties were other signs. A lipstick case and a little black hairbow. "This wasn't no dump job," he grumbled to Kennedy, and Kennedy agreed.

A few minutes later they discussed their theory with some Night-watch detectives. A couple of them agreed; they, too, had noticed the lipstick, the bow, and the ground disturbance. One of them had even gotten the Crime Scene Unit to dust the lipstick case and the bow for fingerprints. But when none had been found, Crime Scene had refused to collect the items. Still, the Nightwatch detective continued, there were now two factions in Nightwatch, a bunch of guys who believed the body had been dumped dead from the car and another who were seriously considering the idea that dumping wasn't involved, that the victim had reached the park alive and struggled with someone under the crab-apple tree.

McEntee was glad to hear about the factions. He felt certain the girl had run, or been dragged, from the crab-apple tree, and he felt absolutely certain the white panties, not the blue ones, were hers. Being something of a dude himself, he knew a bit about how people put their outfits together. The skirt that was pulled up around the girl's waist was pink and white and made of a knit fabric. She'd never have worn dark blue panties under it. They'd have shown through. If Crime Scene won't collect the panties, he decided, I'll just have to do it myself. He bent down and, not wanting to touch them, lifted them up with the eraser end of a pencil. Then he shoved them into an envelope and put it into his pocket.

By then, the Crime Scene Unit had finished processing the body. It was time to find out who she was. A couple of Nightwatch detectives lifted up the jean jacket draped across the arm and started looking through the pockets. They found a Pierre Cardin wallet with no money except, oddly, half of a dollar bill. But there were free passes to stylish clubs, a check stub from Fluties, and several pieces of identification. One listed the girl's name and address. She was Jennifer Dawn Levin and she lived in SoHo.

Once the information was recorded, the contents of the wallet were passed around. McEntee stared at a learner's permit and a miniature diploma. Both permit and diploma had birthdates on them, but they weren't the same. The learner's permit said 1968, which would have made the girl eighteen. The diploma said 1964, which would have made her twenty-two. The diploma was a phony, McEntee thought, made so she could buy drinks. Then he noticed the day of her birth, May 21. "Unbelievable! Whata coincidence," he said to Kennedy. "Same as my wife's."

"You sure it's not your wife?"

"Sure I'm sure."

"Oh, yeah? Where was your wife last night?"

Joking about dead people was SOP. McEntee laughed. But he was only listening to Kennedy with half his mind. He was thinking that Nightwatch would be leaving any minute, and Ziens would be turning the case over to the Central Park Precinct. He had to keep his wits about him for that. Had to be ready to reach out for the case the moment Ziens passed it.

Seconds later, it was time. Ziens called his men over, instructed them to return to headquarters, and told a couple of detectives from the Manhattan North Homicide Squad, a special detective unit assigned to help local precinct detectives do their work, to notify the girl's family. Nightwatch was pulling out, he said. Then he looked over at McEntee's boss and shouted, "Whose is this?"

"Mine," McEntee yelled. Kennedy looked surprised, but he didn't say anything. Neither did the boss.

"Spell your name," Ziens said.

McEntee called the letters out loudly. And then he was smiling. His first homicide! The thing had gone down like baseball. Finally it was his turn up.

Carrying a bag stuffed with rubber gloves, aprons, specimen bottles, death certificates, and an automatic camera, Maria Alandy arrived in the park a little before ten o'clock. She had been with the medical examiner's office for just two months, but was already well versed in the science of determining the causes of unexpected death. After leaving the Philippines, where she had attended medical school, she'd taken a residency in pathology at New York's Metropolitan Hospital, and while there she had studied forensic pathology at the ME's office. When her residency was over in June, the office had given her a fellowship to work downtown with them.

Virtually every day since her fellowship had begun, she'd had autopsies to conduct or crime scenes to visit, even though summer wasn't the ME office's busy season. That was around Christmastime, when there was a rash of traffic accidents and suicides. Or in the spring, when the ice melted and floaters turned up in the rivers. There were lots of floaters. The Hudson alone washed up about a hundred or so bodies every year. It was New York's Ganges, the watery resting place of numerous dead, many of them victims of stabbings, shootings, and strangulations that had taken place elsewhere. Central Park was like the rivers in that respect, a place where the dead weren't actually killed so much as deposited afterward.

The dead girl in the park was Dr. Alandy's first body of the day. After introducing herself to the police officers at the scene, she got out her camera and took photographs. Then she examined the body, making notes as she did so. The skin was cool. She saw abrasions on the chin and neck, the cheeks, forehead, nose, and right upper thigh. She saw a contusion above the left eye. She lifted the eyelids and saw pinpoint hemorrhages in their linings. The tiny hemorrhages, she knew, indicated that the neck had been compressed, causing an interruption in the blood flow to the brain. Strangulation, she wrote. Then she went on to the next body. She had lots of them on her assignment sheet today.

• • •

Steve Levin was in his office on Lafayette Street, a spacious suite of rooms with an unobstructed, panoramic view of lower Manhattan, when two detectives entered the reception area and asked an assistant, "Can we speak with the boss?" He came out and invited them into the conference room.

"Better sit down," they told him.

He did. Then slow and deliberate, one of them said, "Do you have a daughter named Jennifer?"

"What's wrong? What's going on?" Steve asked.

"She may be hurt."

Hurt? "Where is she?" Steve demanded.

The second detective drew a breath and said, "Jennifer may not be with us any longer."

The detectives showed Steve Polaroid pictures of Jennifer taken in the park. He was stunned when he saw her face staring out at him from the shiny prints. He'd spoken to her less than twenty-four hours ago, told her he loved her, and that he'd see her tonight. For a moment he couldn't believe that the pictures were really of Jennifer. Then his face crumpled. Beneath his tan, he went deathly pale.

A few minutes later the detectives led him, a man grown suddenly old, out of his office and over to the loft on Mercer Street. If he'd be so kind, they told him, they'd like to look through Jennifer's room on the chance her possessions might provide some leads to her killer.

At about 10 A.M., Alexandra LaGatta, returning home from getting her learner's permit at the Motor Vehicles Bureau, stooped in front of her doormat and checked beneath it. The key she'd left for Jennifer was still there. Hey, wait a minute, where's Jen? she thought. Inside her apartment, she dialed Jennifer's number.

Mr. Levin answered, and at once Alexandra sensed something was wrong. Jennifer's phone number was different from her family's, and her phone was in her bedroom. What was her father doing on the line? But even as she was thinking that it was strange, Mr. Levin started firing questions at her. "What happened to Jennifer?" he said. "When did you see her last?" He sounded distraught.

"Last night," Alexandra said. She wanted to ask Mr. Levin why he was so upset, but before she could do so, a detective got on the phone. "We'd like to come up and ask you a few questions," he announced.

He didn't say why, but she told him all right. Then, *What's going on?* she wondered. *What's happened to Jennifer? Did she get busted for being drunk?*

A few moments later she decided to see if Betsy Shankin had any idea of what was happening. She called her, awakening her out of a deep sleep. When Betsy said she didn't know anything, Alexandra said, "I've got to get hold of Jennifer. Where can I find her? Who was she with last night?"

"She was with Robert," Betsy, still drowsy, murmured.

"Thanks."

She'd call Robert, Alexandra decided next. But she didn't know his number. Was it in Jennifer's diary? Jennifer had left the little black spiral book in her bedroom last night, and now Alexandra got it out, leafed through the pages, found Robert's number, and dialed.

A woman answered. She said she was Robert's mother and that Robert was taking a shower.

"Ask him to please call me back," Alexandra said.

A few minutes later he did. "Is Jen there?" she asked him.

"No."

"Do you know where she is?"

"No."

"Well, I've got to find her. Her father is worried about her. He's really upset. And there are detectives coming up here."

Robert was no help. "I was with her at Dorrian's," he said. "But she left me to go see Brock." Then he said, "She's with Brock."

Alexandra felt relieved. "Thanks," she said and hung up. But right afterward it dawned on her that Brock was still out on Long Island. There was no way Jen could be with him.

She was getting worried all over again when the doorbell rang and the detectives arrived. They'd made it uptown from SoHo in just fifteen minutes or so.

She told them what she knew. She said she'd been with Jennifer at Dorrian's, but that she'd left before her. She said she'd called Robert, who'd reported that Jen might be with Brock. And she gave them Jennifer's diary so that they could get the phone numbers of her friends.

But although she helped the police all she could, they wouldn't tell her anything. Not even why they were asking questions about Jen. "Please tell me," she begged. "Please tell me what's happened to Jen."

"Her father has to be the one to tell you," one of the detectives said. "And by the way, don't call any more of her friends. We'll call them. We want to judge their reactions."

Then they were gone.

Alone, Alexandra grew increasingly worried. Maybe Jen got hit by a car, she thought. Or raped. Whatever, it was something awful. Picking up the phone, she called Betsy again, just to tell her what she was thinking. "Something really horrible has happened to Jen," she said when she got her.

Betsy, who wasn't alarmed, told her she was going to go shopping. But Alexandra went on worrying. And after a while she dialed her father at his office, told him about the detectives, and said that something must have happened to Jennifer but she didn't know what.

"I'll see what I can find out," her father said.

Ten minutes later he called her back. "A girl was killed in the park," he said. He gave her a description of the girl—and then she knew what had happened to Jennifer.

Her father came home right afterward, but she didn't want to talk to him. She wanted to talk to her friends. To the people who had loved Jennifer the way she had, the people whom Jennifer had always made smile and laugh and feel happy. But she couldn't talk to them. The police had warned her not to. She went into her room and just sat there.

She stayed in the room for hours, not speaking to anyone and not doing anything, and the whole time she stayed there she kept thinking that
if only she hadn't left Dorrian's early, if only she'd waited till Jennifer was
ready to leave, the whole thing wouldn't have happened. Jennifer would
have come home with her.

. . .

Marilei, arriving at the Chamberses' to have lunch with Phyllis, said hello
to Robert, and noticed that his face was scratched.

"What happened to Hrobert?" she asked Phyllis.

"The cat scratched him," Phyllis said. "He was playing with it last
night, and it dug its claws into him."

"Poor Hrobert. He could get an infection."

"He'll be all right. I put peroxide on the scratches."

In a few minutes, she and Phyllis strolled over to a coffee shop for
hamburgers. Phyllis was chatty. "Robert's decided to go to Columbia in
the fall," she said.

"To university?" Marilei's thin face broke into a wide smile. "Just you
wait and see. He'll make good yet."

"Umm," Phyllis murmured and nodded cheerfully.

"Detectives," a gruff voice coming over the house phone shattered Phyllis's daydreams right after she and Marilei returned from lunch. "Is Robert
Chambers at home?"

"Which Robert Chambers?" she said.

"Robert Chambers Senior," she thought she heard. Robert Chambers
Senior? He hadn't lived at the apartment for years. Still, she buzzed the
detectives in.

A few seconds later they were stepping off the elevator. And then she
realized it wasn't Robert Senior they were asking about but Robert Junior.
"We'd like to talk with him privately," they said.

She didn't go to get him immediately. She stood stock-still. And then she demanded to know what business they had with Robert.

"We're investigating a missing girl," one of the detectives, Al Genova, said evenly. He didn't say "dead." When you said dead, people got hysterical. "We believe she was an acquaintance of Robert's and that he may have been with her and some other people last night."

Phyllis said she'd fetch her son and showed Genova and his partner into her living room. The two men parked their haunches on a soft couch and waited for the man they'd come to see to appear.

A few minutes later, he did. But he wasn't a man. Not really. He was a teenager. A hulking one. About six feet four and two hundred pounds. He had on sneakers, sweat pants, and a T-shirt. And his face was emblazoned with scratches.

Genova, seventeen years with the Police Department, didn't blink an eye. "We're investigating a girl who is missing," he said, repeating the words he'd used with the youth's mother. "Her name is Jennifer Levin. Do you know her?"

"Yes, I know her," Chambers said.

"We're trying to identify as many people as possible who were with her last night," Genova went on. "So we can find out what her movements were." Then he asked Chambers if he'd mind coming with him to the precinct house to help investigate Jennifer's disappearance.

Chambers said he'd come.

"Do you have the phone numbers of any of her friends?" Genova asked.

"Yes, in my phone book," Chambers said. "I'll go get it."

In his room, Robert got out his black spiral phone book with the numbers of his and Jennifer's friends. He knew now that what had happened between him and Jennifer was real. He hadn't when he'd first awakened. Nothing had hurt him. Not the scratches Jennifer had given him, not his fingers, where she'd bitten him, not his right hand, which was beginning to ache him now. No wonder everything that had happened in the park had seemed like a dream. But he was sure now that it wasn't a dream.

He didn't hurry out to where the police were waiting. Instead he dialed Jo Perry, as if he were thinking that if only he'd been nicer to her none of what was happening now would have come to pass.

"It's been a bad day," he said when he got her on the phone. "And it's going to get a lot worse."

"You want to get together?"

"Yeah. Wait for me at your apartment. I'll be there in a couple of hours."

When he hung up, he reached for a silver rosary he kept hanging in his room and fingered the beads. Just then Marilei barged in. "What's happening?" she said. "Why are the police here?"

"A girl I know is missing," he said.

"Oh," Marilei said. "Oh, that's sad." Her eyes went to the rosary, which was delicate and small, a woman's rosary.

"Take it." Robert was extending his hand. "I want you to have it."

"Oh, no. No. I couldn't. It's too beautiful." But he wanted her to have it. He thrust it at her, picked up his phone book, and started out the door.

"Where are you going?" Marilei asked.

"With the police," he said. "I'm going to help them try to find the missing girl."

THE INTERROGATION

The Central Park precinct house, erected in 1870, was built as a stable for the horses that were helping maintain the new park by pulling grass-cutting machines and wagonloads of earth and plants. Sixty years later, with animal power long replaced by gas-fueled vehicles, the Police Department inherited the stable. A handsome building, its Victorian lines are still graceful and complex, its walls made of brick and brownstone, its roofs tiled in multihued slate. Inside, however, the rooms are cramped, the floorboards rotting. Few traces of nineteenth-century splendor remain except for a tall receiving desk made of carved mahogany.

Mickey McEntee was standing beside the desk when Detective Genova and his partner arrived with Chambers in tow. McEntee saw the scratches on the young man's face, but like Genova, he didn't say anything. He just led Robert into a room off the reception area—a small room with two banged-up metal desks and a tower of chipped lockers that were plastered with stickers saying, "Police!! Don't Move!!!" He gave him a chair, perched himself informally on a desktop, and said, "I'm going to ask you some questions about this girl who's disappeared." A moment later he glanced down at the young man's hands. Like his face, they, too, were scratched. Or bitten. There was a deep gouge on the middle finger of his right hand.

Maybe he shouldn't question Chambers just yet, McEntee decided. Maybe he'd better read him his rights first. Retrieving a copy of the Miranda warnings from the room next door, he began reciting them. "You have the right to remain silent and to refuse to answer questions," he said. "Do you understand?"

Chambers nodded yes.

"You have the right to an attorney if you want one now, or in the future. Do you understand?"

Chambers nodded yes again.

McEntee finished the warnings, then asked about the girl.

Yes, he knew her, Chambers said. They'd had sex together earlier in the summer. And he'd seen her at Dorrian's last night. But he hadn't spent much time with her. She'd been circulating through the bar, talking to a lot of different people. "Floating around" was the phrase he used.

"Did you leave with her?" McEntee, taking notes, asked.

"No. She was in the vestibule of Dorrian's when I left. She said she was going across the street to the Korean deli. To buy cigarettes. I don't know where she went after that. Maybe to her boyfriend Brock Pernice's."

"What did you do?"

"Went to a doughnut shop on Eighty-sixth Street and Lexington. Then went home. Watched *The Price Is Right* on television, and a movie, I forget its name, about some kid who was all fucked up."

"How'd you get those scratches on your face?"

"My cat scratched me."

"What happened to your hand?"

"I was sanding floors for a woman who lives upstairs from me, and the sanding machine jumped around and cut my fingers."

This guy's really cool, McEntee thought. So cool that even though he's clearly been in a hell of a serious struggle, he's not even the least bit nervous. McEntee kept at him, but he felt his first homicide investigation was going nowhere, that even if Robert had killed Jennifer, he wasn't going to crack.

• • •

An hour or so after Robert's departure for the precinct house, Phyllis grew concerned about his absence. She'd expected when he left the apartment with the two detectives that he'd be back soon or, failing that, would call. Why hadn't she heard from him? Dialing Dorrian's Red Hand, she asked Jack Dorrian, the proprietor, whom she had occasionally telephoned in the past when she was looking for Robert, if he knew anything about what was going on.

"Phyllis, haven't you heard?" Dorrian said to her cautiously. A police officer was standing at his elbow.

"Heard what?" she asked.

"Didn't you hear the news?"

"No, I did not."

"Well, a girl has been found dead in Central Park."

She didn't see the connection at first. "What has Robert got to do with that?" she asked.

"I hope to God nothing," Dorrian said.

Around four in the afternoon, Jennifer's grandfather Arnold Domenitz and her uncle Dan Levin entered the lobby of the morgue and were assigned what the medical examiner's office ceremoniously calls a death counselor, a case worker whose job it is to shepherd the relatives of the dead through the identification process. Jennifer's body had just reached the building. All afternoon it had been in the ambulance, one of several bodies the driver had had to pick up, each in its turn, from various locations around the city.

The death counselor asked Domenitz and Levin about their relationship to the dead girl and how well they had known her, then gave them reassurances about what they would be seeing, promising there'd be no other bodies in view and that they wouldn't be exposed to unnecessary gore. The counselor also promised that the identification process would be quick and easy. "You will be taken down a set of stairs," the counselor explained. "You will be shown the face of the deceased. We will try to minimize the amount of whatever else you must see. There will be a doctor present. There will be a mortuary assistant with you. And I'll be with you."

The routine assurances never altogether calmed the relatives of the deceased, and consequently the medical examiner's office frequently got complaints from people who felt they'd been treated insensitively.

They hadn't been, morgue staffers believed. That was just their *perception*. The problem was *Quincy*. On *Quincy*, people identified their dead relatives on a closed-circuit televison screen. The Manhattan ME's office didn't have closed-circuit television. It was too expensive, and the identification wasn't very good. People were always not recognizing bodies they knew very well, or thinking a perfect stranger was a friend. Manhattan didn't even have a glassed-in viewing area, the way Brooklyn and Queens did. Manhattan just took the families to a window first and showed them through the glass what they were about to see, so that when they actually saw the dead bodies of their relatives, it wasn't really so much of a shock.

It worked out that way with Levin. The grandfather and uncle looked at the body, said who she was, and left. There were no complaints.

Balding John Lafferty of the Manhattan North Homicide Squad and silver-haired Lieutenant John Doyle, the squad's commanding officer, had, between them, more than forty years' experience in the arcane labor of crime detection. Hearing of McEntee's travails with Robert, they decided as the afternoon was drawing to a close to talk to Robert. They'd use a technique young McEntee couldn't. They'd be avuncular. It might relax Robert, make him let his guard down. Together, they went into the room in which he was sitting.

Doyle spoke first. "Where'd you go to school?" he asked.

Robert mentioned Choate.

"I had a niece who went there," Doyle said. "She started around three years ago. Maybe you knew her?"

Robert said he hadn't.

Lafferty thought Choate was in Vermont, so he asked how the skiing up in Vermont was.

He'd enjoyed it very much, Robert said.

Doyle asked him about his other schools. "How'd you like Boston University? What kind of a school is it?"

"Very Jewish," Robert commented. Then he said he'd partied a lot while he was up there and received poor grades.

The conversation rambled on. The detectives didn't record it. Robert wasn't a suspect. Not officially. "What kind of a name is Chambers?" Doyle asked.

"Irish."

"Really? I always thought it sounded more English."

"No, it's Irish."

"Are your mother and father from Ireland?"

"No. But my grandmother is."

"What part of Ireland?" Lafferty interjected.

"Donegal, I think," Robert said. He pronounced it with the emphasis on the first syllable.

Doyle's ear was offended. "Donneygaal," he said. "*Donneygaal.*"

"Donegal is where my father comes from," Lafferty said. "Maybe we're related. What town did your grandmother come from?"

"I don't remember."

"You ever been to Ireland?" Doyle asked.

"No," Robert said, the senseless lie leaping to his lips.

Lafferty, finding no mutual interest in the subject of Ireland, switched the topic. "How long ya been goin' to Dorrian's?" he asked.

"About a year and a half."

"Dorrian's Red Hand." Now Lafferty had found a good subject. "That's the Red Hand of Ulster," he said. "Ya know how the name came about?"

"No."

"Well, back in the old days in Ireland, there was a king who was in charge of Ulster County. And what happened was, he had two sons. One was a good son, and the other was a bad son. The king was getting on in years, and he had to make a choice on which son was going to be the next king." Lafferty liked telling stories, and he spun this one out, talking for about fifteen minutes until he reached the part where the king makes his two sons compete for their inheritance by seeing who can swim fastest to a distant shore, and one son lops off his hand with a sword and heaves the bloody member onto the shore in order to have at least a portion of himself touch shore first. "That was the good son," Lafferty said.

By that time, Doyle had left. He was in charge of the investigation and he couldn't waste all day listening to Lafferty's stories. Besides, Lafferty knew what to do next.

A few minutes later, Lafferty gave up the chitchat and slipped into asking Robert questions—the same questions McEntee had. When had he left Dorrian's? With whom? And what had he done after he left?

Robert wasn't forthcoming. Despite the softening-up period, he continued to maintain that he hadn't been with Jennifer and that his wounds had been caused by his cat.

No detective had as yet told Robert that he was being questioned about a dead girl, not a missing one. They hadn't told him this, because they wanted to keep him talking, wanted to find out as much about his movements last night as they could. And they were afraid that if they dropped their pretense, let him know they'd brought him to the precinct not to help them find somebody but to explain why she was dead, he'd clam up. Maybe even ask for a lawyer.

It wasn't honest. But it wasn't illegal.

McEntee didn't like the idea, but not because he was against playing tricks on people who may have killed others. He just felt talking turkey to Robert might bring him around. Make him come out with the truth, not run for cover. "Lemme confront him," he begged Doyle after Lafferty's efforts had failed. "Lemme tell him the girl is dead."

The older man restrained the novice's impatience. "Not yet," Doyle said. "Maybe later."

At 5 P.M. a crowd of reporters jostled into one of the rooms at the precinct house for a press conference on the killing in the park. The room was only a few feet away from where Robert was being questioned. But the reporters didn't know about Robert. They knew only that a girl was dead and the police were looking for suspects.

A bemedaled captain filled the reporters in on facts about the dead girl. She'd been a waitress at Fluties until two weeks ago, he said. She'd lived on Mercer Street in SoHo. She'd been about to enter a college in Boston. She was last seen leaving an East Side bar.

"Could this be a 'Mr. Goodbar' killing?" one reporter called out. "Could she have picked up her killer in the bar?"

"Could be," the police captain said.

Several reporters began scribbling leads right on the spot. From the start, what with the girl's being white and young, the story had been sexy in the sense that editors used that word. Now, with the Mr. Goodbar angle, it would be *really* sexy.

At times the police left Robert alone, at times as many as half a dozen detectives crowded around him. They continued to question him; and he, apparently believing that they would never dream of connecting him to a killing if he acted polite and cooperative, answered their questions pleasantly as often as they were asked.

But he wasn't altogether calm. Once while several detectives were in the room with him, he went to the little barred window that looked out onto the park and peered longingly outside. Traffic was snaking through the crosstown drive. "I'd better not stick my head out too far," he murmured. "The buses come so close they could smash it right off."

• • •

"Whatsa matter with you?" John Cotter shouted at a photographer. The photographer had just returned to Newsday empty-handed. At Fluties he'd asked a barman with a picture of Jennifer at a party if he could shoot the picture. While he'd waited for an answer, a TV reporter had made an exclusive deal for it.

Cotter was furious. Why had the photographer *asked* if he could shoot the picture, instead of clicking away instinctively? Didn't the guy know the three rules of photojournalism? Number one was get the picture. Number two was get the picture. Number three was get the picture. If *Newsday* was going to compete with the other, better-established tabloids, it had to have pictures that could break your heart. The dead girl when she was alive and at a party, that would have done it. But now it looked as if the paper would have to run instead with a shot of paramedics loading her draped body into an ambulance.

Tomorrow, Cotter planned, he'd get in there and teach the photographers their job. Politeness? In journalism? That wasn't what the work was all about. Especially with a story like this one, which was getting bigger by the hour. It was the kind of story that the middle-class reader could relate to. Something that could happen to any kid running around the pubs. The kind of story that would make people worry about their own kids. In a way, the identity of the girl wasn't even important. It didn't matter that her name was Jennifer Levin. She could have been Maggie Jones or Debbie Smith. Anybody. Identities were wood. You had to stack the wood, give the details. That was journalism. But what really mattered was what the story said about kids and bars and late hours.

He checked with his staff to make sure they were stacking up the wood. They were, and he got over his pique. Even without a mug of the dead girl, the story would probably make the front page tomorrow. For one thing, there wasn't much else going on. There'd been a gas eruption in Cameroon, which had killed a thousand people. And a congress of international scientists in Vienna was theorizing that 24,000 people might die as a result of the recent nuclear accident at Chernobyl. But none of that sold papers. One murdered girl sold papers.

Toward evening, two detectives went to the home of Betsy Shankin. One was a chunky young blond detective named John Mullally. The other was a rugged-faced older man named Martin Gill.

"*When* was the last time you saw Jennifer?" Mullally said to Betsy when they'd gotten her in a car and were heading uptown to the Central Park precinct house.

"Early this morning."

"Where?"

"Leaving Dorrian's."

"Who was she with?"

"Robert Chambers."

"Did they go in separate directions?"

"No. They went together. Toward Eighty-sixth Street."

"Is it possible that she left him and went for a pack of cigarettes?"

"Jen?" Betsy asked, incredulous. "No. She didn't smoke."

Gill listened, his eyes on the tangled rush-hour traffic.

"Do you know what's going on?" Bob Chambers was asking a heavy-set police officer in a building adjacent to the precinct house in Central Park at around the time Betsy was traveling uptown. As soon as he'd gotten home from work, Bob had learned from Phyllis that Robert had been taken to the precinct. But although he'd come directly over, he hadn't been allowed to see Robert or even to wait in the building where he was being questioned. He'd been sent to an annex, which was empty except for the corpulent officer. "I'm Mr. Chambers," Bob went on. "My son, Robert, is next door, and I haven't been able to see him."

The man he was speaking to wasn't very interested in his plight. "Well, the detectives over there are handling this, and they should be with you shortly," he said. Then he started making small talk, asking Bob if he

knew anything about hunting and telling him about a shooting trip he
was planning.

Bob couldn't have cared less. "Do you think my son needs a lawyer?"
he asked.

"You could hold off and see how things develop," the officer said, then
returned to the subject of hunting.

He was still talking about it when a few minutes before seven o'clock
the phone rang. It was Phyllis. "Have you seen Robert?" she asked Bob.

"I've tried to," he said. "But I haven't been able." He would have continued, would have told her how they were keeping him away from Robert, if he hadn't been speaking to her on the precinct-house phone. It
wasn't private. "I'll call you back," he said abruptly and, hanging up, went
out of the park to search out a pay phone.

On Central Park West he found one. But he didn't call Phyllis right
away. Instead he dug from his wallet the business card of Henry Putzel,
the lawyer she'd hired back in April to represent Robert in the burglary
affair. But whether it was because his eyes were tearing or just because it
was growing dark, he couldn't make out the numerals on the card. He
had to ask a doorman to decipher the numbers and write them down in
larger print.

When he returned to the phone booth and dialed the lawyer, all he
got was an answering machine. Disappointed, Bob reported his efforts to
Phyllis, then headed back to the park.

By seven o'clock Jennifer's death had appeared in a late edition of the New
York Post and been broadcast on radio and TV. Doyle decided it was time
to step up the pressure on Robert, time to stop pretending to him that
he was being questioned about a missing, not a dead girl. He'd been at
the precinct more than four hours without changing his original story—
that he hadn't seen Jennifer since he left Dorrian's. Maybe if he knew the
police knew she was dead, he'd start talking. In any event, it would be
interesting to see how he reacted.

Detective Lafferty, who had earlier tried to relax Robert with the story of how Dorrian's Red Hand had gotten its name, was the one sent in to deliver the information. "I have some bad news for you," he said bluntly to Robert. "I have to tell you that Jennifer Levin is dead."

"Oh, no!" Robert cried out. Then he covered his eyes with his hands and asked, "How did she die?"

Lafferty measured his responses with a practiced eye. "I don't know," he said. "They're doing the autopsy right now."

Robert took his hands from his eyes. Lafferty saw that they were misty. "Try to relax," he directed. "Try to relax, but try to think of anything that might be able to help us in this investigation. It's that much more important now."

Joan Huey was one of the first of Jennifer's close friends to hear that she was dead. Joan was at her summer house in Southampton, where she and Jennifer had summered two years earlier. When a girlfriend called her with the news, she refused to believe it and accused her girlfriend of playing some kind of grisly practical joke on her. But when she heard the news on television, she flew into a rage. She began kicking and punching the walls. And all the time she kicked and punched, she kept thinking about Jennifer and how she used to fly into tantrums after fights with her family and bang her fists so hard against walls that her hands would get bruised.

The memory of Jennifer's excitability made her own seem safe, and she went on punching until at last she stopped, stumbled out of the house, and sobbed in the gathering dusk.

It was nearly dark when Bob Chambers re-entered the grounds of the police precinct. The cars in the parking lot wore shrouds of shadows, and the trees overhead loomed like ominous giants. "God grant me the serenity to accept the things I cannot change," Bob thought, "the courage to change the things I can, and the wisdom to know the difference." The simple lines—they were known as the serenity prayer in the AA groups to which he belonged—had given him comfort in the past. Now he really needed comfort, needed to be able to think straight. Suddenly he bent his knees right there in the roughly paved parking lot, clasped his hands, rested his elbows against a car fender, and, head bowed, said the poem.

Manhattan North Detective Mike Sheehan, whose family had owned the bar on Third Avenue where Bob used to drink, had been working on the Levin case all day but hadn't yet met Robert. He'd been at the park all morning and at the medical examiner's office all afternoon. When he was briefed about the progress of the investigation at the precinct house in the early evening, he wanted to try his hand at doing some questioning. In his dozen years as a detective, he'd taken hundreds of confessions, become adept at gaining the confidence of suspects. The reason, in his opinion, was that he didn't act superior to the suspects. He tried to make them think he liked and understood them, and sometimes he even tried to make them think that if he'd been in their shoes he'd have done the same rotten things they had. That's how he'd gotten Manny Torres to confess. Manny had taken a girl up on a roof, stabbed her, and tossed her down into the street like so much garbage. When Manny started to break and said the reason he'd pulled his knife on the girl was because she'd suggested sex and then reneged on the offer, Sheehan hadn't said what he was thinking, which was *You little asshole, you're full of shit.* No, he'd acted as if stabbing a girl who said no was a perfectly reasonable thing to do, and murmured, "Yeah, I'd probably have done the same thing." Guys like Manny, Sheehan always said, believed they were acting within their God-given rights as men when they killed a rejecting girl. So he went along with them, acted friendly, made them think he shared their attitudes.

He was pretty sure he could make Robert Chambers think he shared his attitudes. They even had some things in common. The East Side? He'd grown up there himself, over on 96th and Madison. Dorrian's? Jeez, he couldn't say how many times he'd stopped in there. One of his sisters lived right across the street. Of course, according to all his fellow detectives, this Chambers was a rich kid, a preppie. Whereas he himself was just the son of a barkeep. But he was familiar with the Upper East Side rich kids. Knew how to talk to them. His sisters had dated nothing but. And he even knew the town house Chambers had given as his address. Once when he'd been a high school kid, his hair slicked back and his cheeks slathered with Old Spice, he'd gone to that very building to deliver a pair of shoes from the shoemaker he worked for after school. Yeah, maybe he and Chambers would find some things to talk about.

At eight he went in to see Robert. He introduced himself, gave Robert his card with its blue and gold Police Department shield, and said, "How'd you get those scratches?"

"My cat scratched me," Robert explained patiently.

"Jeez," Sheehan joked. "I have a cat. It's like a regular house cat. Whadda you have? A mountain lion?"

Robert laughed, and, encouraged, Sheehan kept up the chatter. "You went to St. David's?" he said. "I went to St. Francis Xavier. You ever heard of Xavier?"

"Yeah. That was a pretty tough school."

"Damn right. I wore a uniform every day till I graduated."

"I wore uniforms, too. I was in the Greys."

"The *Knickerbocker* Greys? Jesus! We used to kick their ass."

Again Robert laughed, so Sheehan went on with the banter, telling stories about the crack Boy Scout unit he'd belonged to as a kid and about growing up Catholic on the WASPy East Side. He shot the breeze for a long time, then turned once again to the subject of the dead girl. "You last saw her when you were leaving Dorrian's?" he asked.

"Yeah," Robert said. He sounded calm and relaxed.

Sheehan studied his sapphire eyes. "You know, some of her friends are saying you walked toward Eighty-sixth Street with her," he said.

Robert was silent for a while. Then he said, "Yeah, well I did leave the bar with her, I guess."

Sheehan was astonished. It was the first time all day there'd been any deviation in the story. "Come on, Rob," he pressed ahead familiarly. "Those scratches on your face. The girl got no panties on. All her girlfriends are telling us she wanted to make it with you. Tell me what happened. Maybe she was coming on too strong. Maybe you weren't in your proper frame of mind. Maybe it was an accident."

Robert began rubbing his hands together. Then his breathing changed, became audible and irregular.

I did it, Sheehan told himself excitedly. He's gonna change his story. Self-destruct. But although he'd gotten one new piece of information out of Robert, he couldn't get anything else. Would the kid break? Or would he just sit tight all night?

Sweaty and hungry, Steve Saracco, an assistant district attorney at the Manhattan DA's office, arrived home after a ten-hour workday and sank into a dining-room chair, too tired to shower before eating. He revived a little after downing a plate of his wife's gusty macaroni and meatballs, but he still didn't feel like stirring, so he stayed where he was and, pushing the dishes aside, spread the late edition of the Post out on the table. He was on page five when his eye lit on a headline that blazoned, WOMAN FOUND RAPED AND SLAIN IN CENTRAL PARK. "It is not known whether the woman was killed in a vehicle or somewhere else," he read. "Police today are trying to find witnesses."

Saracco felt a touch of energy returning to him. Although he'd been with the district attorney's office for ten years and had tried over a hundred felonies, his adrenaline never failed to pump when he heard about a new homicide. An ex-Marine, he was the kind of assistant DA who acted as if each criminal he cross-examined had committed an act that affronted him not merely professionally but personally. In court, his steely face taut and his wiry body tense inside rumpled inexpensive suits, he was shortspoken. Out of court he was expansive, a man as ready to denounce the city's thugs and muggers, creeps and killers, as any cop. Which was

why, he figured, he got on well with cops. He talked their language, wasn't
uptight around them like the new breed of mealymouthed Harvard and
Columbia Law ADA's in the office. No, he was a Villanova Law grad and
proud of it. That and his Marine stories went over big with the cops, and
sometimes brought him advantages—tips about new cases, gossip about
ongoing investigations—that other ADA's would have given their right
arms for.

Reading the story about the dead girl, he wished the cops well. New
York had an annual crop of hundreds of unsolved homicides, but it wasn't
the cops' fault, he thought. It was just that there were too few of them and
too many of the lowlifes.

He had just finished the *Post* story when the phone rang and he picked
it up to hear Mike Sheehan's bluff voice. He knew it at once. He and the
burly Irish detective were drinking buddies. "You read that thing in the
paper about a girl killed in the park?" Sheehan asked.

"Yeah, sure," Saracco said. "You got something?"

"Yeah, we got the kid over here."

"No shit!"

"Yeah. And he looks good. He's got scratches all over him."

Saracco wasn't tired at all anymore. If the kid Mike has really *is* good,
he thought, and I go up to the precinct and take his confession, chances
are the case will end up on my plate. And that's exactly where Saracco
wanted it. It already had media. Media cases were manna to ADA's, no
matter how long they'd been around. "You figure it's him?" he asked eagerly.

"Yeah. But he's maintaining he didn't do it. The boss wants a medical
examiner to come up and check out the scratches. See if he was raked by
a cat. Or a girl. Can you get us someone?"

Saracco said he'd get right on it, and he worked it out for Sheehan in
no time. A woman on night duty at the ME's office promised she'd stand
by to go up to the precinct. He called Sheehan back and told him the

mission was accomplished. Sheehan said, "Great. How about you? Can you come up?"

Just what Saracco had been hoping for—only there was a problem. He wasn't on tonight's chart, the list of ADA's delegated to report to the precincts. He couldn't bypass the chart's red tape on his own, and if he asked his supervisor for the case he could end up looking bad to his colleagues, looking as if he had tried to steal someone else's stuff. Still, for a good case like this, it was worth making enemies. "I'll see if I can clear it through channels," he told Sheehan. "I'll get back to you."

A moment later he was on the phone with his supervisor. He outlined the situation, explained that he'd already done a little work for Manhattan North, and said that while he didn't want to step on anybody's toes, he'd sure like to go up to Central Park.

The red tape didn't snap right there and then. His supervisor called *his* supervisor. But after a while Saracco got the go-ahead.

"Come and get me," he reported happily back to Sheehan and, hanging up, jumped in the shower.

Joel Coles, who was a Dorrian's regular—he'd taken part in the fistfight that had erupted in the bar the night before—and who knew Robert from Hunter College, had been up in Boston all day. He'd driven there after Dorrian's closed last night. Hot and weary, he'd just returned to his New York apartment, poured himself a cool drink, and stripped down to his undershorts when a friend of his telephoned. "Hey, Joel, didja do her?" his friend asked.

Do her? Assuming his friend wanted to know if he'd scored with the girl he'd been with at Dorrian's last night, Joel gave a macho "Yeah," even though it wasn't true. She'd turned him down at the end.

A moment later he was damn sorry he lied. His friend said disdainfully, "Come on! It couldn't have been you. It must've been Robert."

Robert? Scoring with *his* girl? "Whaddya mean Robert?" Joel asked, confused. Then his friend told him that Jennifer was dead and that the cops had picked up Robert and had been holding him all day.

Joel didn't have time to digest the information or even to react to it. Before he could get a word out, he heard a loud knock on the door and a loud voice saying, "Police!" He hung up, went to the door, and opened it to two cops. "We just want to ask you a few questions," one of them said.

As soon as Joel let them in, the other cop said, "Didja hear about Jennifer Levin's death?"

"Yeah, yeah," Joel said. But he couldn't figure out why the cop was mentioning Jennifer. All he could think was Hey, Joel, whaddid ya do? Whaddid ya do *this* month that coulda got ya in trouble?

Then gradually he understood, because the cops kept asking how well he knew Robert and what he was like. One of the cops was real nice. He acted friendly and even agreed to show off his gun. The other one was tough. He just kept glowering. They were playing good cop, bad cop. Just like in the movies.

Joel answered their questions, but he felt funny talking to them in his undershorts. "Hey, fellas, lemme get dressed," he said. They told him it was okay but they wouldn't let him out of their sight. They followed him right into his bedroom. "Hey, fellas!" he said again as he went to his bureau, but they kept on standing there and eyeballing him. Then the bad cop said, "Hey, Joel, you look like a pretty big guy. Whaddya, play football?"

It scared him. Whadda *they*, he thought. Trying to implicate me? He pulled open his shirt drawer and then quickly slammed it closed. In the back of the drawer was this copy of *Playboy* he'd stashed in there, and he just knew that if they saw it they'd think he was some sort of sex fiend or worse.

He was still edgy when they put him in their car and started driving to the Central Park Precinct. But he felt even worse when he arrived. The place was jammed with cops, and as soon as he walked in the door they all stopped what they were doing and stared at him. Like I did it! Joel worried. But then he was taken into a little room and a detective started asking him questions, and the questions were not about his movements after he let Dorrian's last night but about what the scene had been like at the bar, and he knew he wasn't under suspicion.

He told the detective everything he remembered about Dorrian's. Told him how everyone had been partying and that he'd seen both Robert and Jennifer there. Then he was asked to write his statement down. He started to write, but as he was doing it the detective said, "This kid Robert was kind of horny, wasn't he? Whyn't ya write that down?"

Joel shook his head. Jennifer had struck him as the horny one.

"He wanted to meet a woman, right?" the cop went on.

Joel put down his pen. "I'm not gonna write that," he said.

The detective let it go, but Joel felt upset after that. And he would have gone on feeling upset except that afterward, when he was done with the statement, they let him sit out in a corridor, and there he saw a whole bunch of kids he knew from Dorrian's, even the girl who'd turned him down last night. Everyone was crying. At least the girls were. It was sad. But it was sort of fun, too. The girl who'd turned him down was blushing and giggling and saying, "Hey, Joel, does everyone here know I was fooling around with you last night?" and he talked to her and his friends and in the end decided that the whole thing was, when you got right down to it, sort of an adventure. Just like in the movies.

Unaware of the crowd from Dorrian's in the corridor, Robert was being questioned anew, this time by Detective Gill, who had escorted Betsy to the precinct. "Did you leave Dorrian's with Jennifer?" the rugged-faced Gill inquired.

"Yes," Robert said. He'd said as much to Sheehan.

Gill was extremely relaxed. Unlike McEntee, who was also in the room. And unlike, for that matter, nearly all the other detectives who had been in and out all afternoon and evening. They'd hedged their questions, fear-ing that if they were too confrontational with Robert they might blow the whole investigation. Make Robert demand an attorney. Gill seemed to have no such fears. Maybe it was because he was due to retire in a couple of weeks. So maybe for him it didn't matter if the investigation fizzled out and the bosses looked bad. That's what McEntee thought as he watched the older man, trying to pick up a few tips. "What did you do when you left Dorrian's?" Gill was asking Robert.

"I went one way. She went the other way," Robert said. "To get a pack of cigarettes."

Gill gave Robert a skeptical look. "What would you say if I told you that we had witnesses who saw you and Jennifer going off together in the same direction?" he asked. "And that one of them says that Jennifer didn't smoke?"

It made Robert amend his previous statement. "Well, we walked away from Dorrian's heading toward Eighty-sixth Street," he said.

"How'd you get that wound on your hand?" Gill asked him next.

"Same way I got these," Robert said, indicating the scratches on his face. "I was playing with my cat. I threw her up in the air. And as she came down she clawed me."

"Well, you realize," Gill said slowly, "that there are people who can tell the difference between wounds caused by animals and wounds caused by humans."

McEntee, who was perched on the edge of a desk, followed Gill's lead. "Yeah. Like a medical examiner," he said ominously.

Robert hesitated. Then he said in a low voice, "I got the wounds from Jennifer."

Confrontation! McEntee thought. He'd wanted to try it hours ago.

Gill wasn't blinking an eye. "How did you get the wounds from Jennifer?" he asked.

Robert began talking animatedly. He and Jen had walked together up to 86th Street, he explained, but there on a corner they'd gotten into an argument because he told her he no longer wanted to see her. "She got very annoyed over this and she scratched my face," he said.

"Where on Eighty-sixth Street did this occur?" Gill said.

"In front of the doughnut shop on the corner of Eighty-sixth and Lexington."

"Well," Gill said, his expression bland and his tone matter-of-fact. "There's a Spanish fellow I know who works in the doughnut shop. What happens if I interview him and he tells me that he don't remember any incident or he didn't see anything like that."

"It wasn't Eighty-sixth and Lexington," Robert said swiftly. "It was Eighty-sixth and Park."

A few moments later Gill went out to tell Lieutenant Doyle that Robert was now admitting he'd been wounded by the dead girl.

Gill's really something, McEntee was thinking. I could learn a lot from him. Like that line about knowing someone in the doughnut shop. I gotta use a line like that myself. It was bullshit but it worked. He was sitting opposite Robert, and the room, vacant now of Gill's commanding presence, had a silent, empty quality. McEntee concentrated on his own thoughts and ignored Robert, who also seemed preoccupied. Then suddenly, shattering the stillness, McEntee heard a round of high-pitched weeping from beyond the door.

Robert heard it, too. "Is that Jen's friends?" he asked.

"Yeah." McEntee nodded. "We're talking to everybody." Then he said, feeling a little like Gill, "You know. *Everybody.*"

"They're outside?" Robert asked.

Robert's question has a subtext, McEntee, nodding yes, thought. He's starting to feel sorry for himself, starting to think of himself as inside and other people as outside. He gave Robert a stare, and when he did, noticed that the young man was breathing heavily and pressing clasped hands to the back of his head, as if to relieve some intense pressure in his skull.

He'd better tell Doyle about this, McEntee decided, but just then the door swung open and in Doyle walked. Behind him was Gill. The two of them strode up to Robert, and Doyle burst out, "Why'd you change the story you told us all afternoon?"

Robert shrugged.

"The story you're telling now is farfetched," Doyle said. "I don't believe it." Still Robert didn't reply. "I liked you," Doyle went on. "I trusted you. I kind of pride myself at being a judge of human nature. But you had me completely fooled. And now I'm plain shocked. And thoroughly disappointed in you."

Robert hung his head.

Doyle had berated Robert as a father might, and now he took a father's prerogative and offered him redemption. Placing a muscular hand on his shoulder in a gesture of man-to-boy intimacy, he said, "Listen, I can understand you're very nervous. I have sons of my own. But why don't you get this off your chest."

It was a classic interrogatory technique, this urging of confession as a means to solace a guilty conscience and silence a pounding heart. Both Gill and McEntee recognized it and joined in with it. "Yeah, you'll feel better," McEntee said. "Yeah, this is only going to keep bothering you," Gill said.

Robert remained silent. But once again he began taking harsh deep breaths. McEntee, some sixth sense telling him a line was about to be crossed, moved closer to Robert. He had learned in the police academy that an interrogator's physical closeness can still incipient panic.

Robert didn't look at him. He didn't look at any of them. Then he murmured: "I went into Central Park with Jennifer."

Robert's eyes were glassy, Gill noticed. Doyle and McEntee had slipped from the room, and he'd been left to dig the rest of the story from the young man. He waited a moment before he started his questions, and during that moment Robert's eyes filled with tears. Then the young man said, his voice thick with self-pity, "What's my mother going to think?"

"*You* won't have to tell her. She'll *know* what happened," Gill said, implying he himself would convey the news to Phyllis and that would make it easier on her. Then he got going. "Where did you go in Central Park?" he asked.

"We sat on a bench," Robert said.

"What happened?"

"She had an argument with me. She wanted to still go out with me. And I didn't want to see her anymore. She got very angry. She scratched me on the face."

"What happened then?"

"I got up to leave. She said, 'Can't we just stay here and talk?' I said, 'Okay but don't sit next to me. Sit away from me.' Then she said, 'Before we start talking, I have to go to the bathroom.' And she went behind me and went to the bathroom."

"What do you mean, she went to the bathroom?" Gill interrupted. "Are there restrooms there?"

"I don't know. She just went behind me in the bushes."

"Then what happened?"

"The next thing I recall is she grabbed me from behind and tied my arms up behind my back with her panties."

"How did she tie your arms up from behind your back? You being as big as you are?"

"Well, I was leaning back resting. My arms were behind me, and she just grabbed them and tied me up."

"What happened then?"

"Well, she sort of, like, tackled me, knocked me down on the ground."

"Were you complaining? Were you yelling?"

"No, I thought she was just fooling at first."

"What happened at that point?"

"She sat on my chest."

"How was she sitting on your chest? Was she facing you or facing away from you?"

"She had her ass on my chest with her back toward me. She started to open my pants. She got my pants open and she started to play with my groin."

"What do you mean, play with your groin?"

"She had hold of my dick and she was stroking me."

"What do you mean, she was stroking you?"

"She was stroking me very hard. It was hurting, and then she was grabbing me by my balls and scratching my balls."

"Did you tell her to stop?"

"Yes. I was yelling for her to stop. It really hurt. It got to the point where it hurt so bad that I got one of my hands loose, and I just grabbed her and pulled her off me. And she went back over my shoulder. I got up, I slipped my pants up, I turned around to her and said, 'Jennifer, come on, let's go.' She didn't answer me."

Gill didn't ask any more questions after that. He went outside and informed Doyle that he'd been successful. He'd gotten a confession. Of sorts.

Jennifer's friends didn't know Robert had confessed. All they knew was that Jennifer was dead.

Leilia Van Baker, who was up in Vermont, heard the news from her father when she called home to say hello. As soon as she heard it, she began trembling and the phone shook. It virtually rattled in her hand. Jennifer *couldn't* be dead. Death didn't claim people her own age. Death was what happened to old people. But then the news sank in. And when it did, she had a vision of Jennifer's last moments, of her struggling helplessly against some unknown feral assailant. Begging for her life.

New York was shit, Leilia decided. New York was filled with psychopaths, strangers who lived by codes totally unlike those she and everyone else she knew had been raised to uphold. New York birthed them by the thousands, nursed them, turned them loose. Jennifer had never quite understood that you had to guard yourself against strangers. No one in their age group really did. Jennifer had trusted strangers, had tried out her halting Spanish on Hispanic workmen and flattered cab drivers by asking them for driving lessons. Probably that's why she'd gotten killed. She'd been accosted by some stranger, some creep. God, how she hoped the police caught the bastard. If they did, she'd like to see him strung up. Not that it would bring Jennifer back. If only she hadn't been so trusting. If only she'd stuck to their own kind.

Carl Morgera, the boy who had given Jennifer piggy-back rides in the park in the days she'd been a newcomer to Manhattan, heard the news from his mother. She called him while he was over at a friend's house. After he heard it, tears flowed from his eyes and he went into what seemed to him like a coma. But then, to get out of the state he was in, he went to the movies with his friend and a bunch of other guys. Being in the movie theater made him feel worse. It didn't seem right to be there. And besides, the guys he was with hadn't known Jennifer. He didn't want to be with them, Carl realized suddenly. He wanted to be with people who'd known and liked Jennifer as much as he had. Rising, he pushed out to the aisle, went to the lobby, and called his friend Joe. Joe had gone to Baldwin. He'd been Jennifer's friend, too.

In a few minutes Joe picked up Carl. They bought a bottle of liquor and drove to Joe's house. But everything was weird, and Carl kept saying to Joe, "How are we supposed to feel? I don't know how to feel."

"I don't know either," Joe said.

"Should we feel sad? I mean, should we cry?" Carl asked him. "Or shouldn't we?"

"I don't know."

Then Joe's girlfriend Fuzzi came over, and they drank the liquor and talked about Jen and the funny things she used to say, and Carl wanted to laugh; but he wasn't sure he should, and after a while he said to Joe, "You know what? Someday I'm gonna write a play and it's gonna be just three characters, just you, me, and Fuzzi, and I'm gonna call it *When Do We Laugh?*"

"What do you mean, *When Do We Laugh?*"

"You know," Carl said. "It's, like, what do we do? Can we laugh? Are we allowed to?"

Outside the Central Park precinct house, television cameras were illuminating the darkness with their floodlights. Someone from Manhattan North had broken protocol and tipped off the press that a suspect was being questioned inside. Annoyed, Steve Saracco pushed his way past the journalists and hurried into Doyle's office.

"It's all over," Doyle greeted him. "The kid just gave it all up. McEntee's taking down his statement."

"No shit!" Saracco's bad mood evaporated. "The guy's saying he did it?"

"Yeah. The scratches are from her. He did it."

Saracco reached for a phone and called his office's videotape unit. "We need a camera up here," he shouted.

Closeted with Robert and trying to write down his statement, McEntee thought, This guy is confessing, but he isn't giving much. He's saying he killed the girl, but that in a way her death was her own damn fault because she hurt him during sex, hurt him so hard that he strangled her accidentally out of an instinctive reaction to pain. McEntee knew about strangling. It was hard to strangle someone accidentally, because to cut off their air supply you had to hold on to their throat for a long time. Robert Chambers, McEntee told himself, is giving us what he feels we're gonna accept, but he isn't telling everything. He's still lying.

McEntee knew about lying, too. When he'd been in Bronx Narcotics, he'd been in numerous situations where he'd had to hide the truth. He'd told falsehoods about the phony needle tracks on his arms, he'd pretended to overly curious pushers that he was a foreigner who spoke no English, he'd set up a shooting gallery bust and then fled into the street along with the terrified addicts, shaking and panting with feigned fear. But if I'd ever gotten caught, if my life and my future were on the line, McEntee said to himself, I'd have broken. And if I did, I'd have gone all the way. Told the whole story. Got it out. Not this guy. He's putting on an act.

"She forced my pants down," Robert was saying. "She sat on my face and began to play with me. Then she began to hit my dick with a stick. And she slapped me and squeezed my balls."

McEntee, listening, put on an act of his own. "G'head," he nodded, as wide-eyed as if he believed every word. But to himself he was saying, This guy either made this up while he was sitting here all day, or he made it up last night, got so coked up that he got paranoid and hallucinated being beaten.

"I was in incredible pain," Robert went on. "I reached down with my left arm, put it around her neck, and pulled back as hard as I could. Jennifer landed behind me."

There was more, but McEntee didn't get it all down. He made notes, then rose to go outside and tell Doyle what he'd gotten. As he stood, Robert's eyes once again filled with tears, and he murmured, as he had to Gill, "Wha 's my mother going to think?"

His mother! McEntee said to himself. What a character. He's not upset over the fact that he killed a girl. He's upset his momma's gonna find out. Myself, I wouldn't be worried about what my momma was gonna think, I'd be worried about what the girl's father was gonna think. And do. To me. Shrugging, he ignored Robert's question and hurried outside.

Standing in Mrs. Hammerstein's laundry room, Marilei sorted through Robert's dirty clothes, separating the light from the dark. Phyllis had asked her to wash Robert's clothes tonight and had helped her carry his laundry to their employer's apartment so that she could use capacious washing machine there. So much laundry! Marilei had lugged a big bag of underwear and T-shirts, and Phyllis had hefted a shopping bag with a heavy pair of jeans crammed into it. Where was the shopping bag? Not here with the rest of the laundry. Well, never mind. She could get it from Phyllis later. She wasn't going to wash the dark clothes now anyway. Just the underwear and light-colored T-shirts.

She was tossing a handful of them into the machine when a short-sleeved white mesh baseball shirt caught her eye. It was filthy. Covered with earth stains. And with bloodstains, too.

She extricated it from the pyramid of other shirts and held it up to the light. How did Hrobert manage to get it so messed up? she wondered. But it doesn't matter, she decided. It'll come clean in the wash. And, measuring out soap powder, she dropped the shirt back into the machine, poured in the white crystals, and started the cycle.

"I want to see my son," Bob Chambers, tired of sitting in the auxiliary building, demanded at the high mahogany front desk of the precinct house. Several detectives were standing nearby, but as soon as he spoke, they scattered.

"Just stay a few minutes more," a man behind the desk said.

Bob wanted to pound his fist down on the wood and say, Damn it, I want to see my son! But it wasn't his nature. His upbringing had taught him to respect police, be polite in their presence. Meekly he returned to the auxiliary building and continued his solitary wait.

He was sitting there, feeling useless and impotent, when Phyllis called him again. "Listen, I'm at work," she said. "I can't come over. I can't leave my patient. But Marilei wants to come."

"Okay."

"She'll be over shortly."

He hung up, and just then the door opened and a silver-haired man came in. "I'm Lieutenant Doyle," the man said. "May I speak to you outside?"

Bob went outside with him, and out there on a roadway the lieutenant started saying that his son had a problem and would have to stay with the police that night. Bob heard him, but he didn't understand what he was hearing. "I'm a father myself," the lieutenant was saying.

Bob was listening hard, but he still didn't get it. Didn't react. And then Doyle said, "Robert has made some statements. And we're going to have to arrest him. Book him on murder charges."

Suddenly, the breath drained out of Bob. "Would you mind if we walked over to a lamppost?" he said, struggling for air. "I want to read a prayer."

When Doyle escorted him to the lamppost, he fumbled for a copy of the serenity prayer that he kept in his wallet. For some reason he didn't want just to recite it from memory as he'd done earlier. His fingers shaking, he at last found the copy and, standing in the cold glare of the lamppost, read the prayer.

He felt better after that and asked to see Robert.

He'd have to wait, Doyle told him.

A moment later Marilei arrived. "Who's she?" Doyle asked.

"My wife's maid," he said, though in fact she was Mrs. Hammerstein's. When she did chores for Phyllis, she always insisted she was doing them just out of friendship. He didn't explain all this, just went on asking to see Robert.

"Maybe in forty-five minutes," Doyle said. "Or an hour. He's busy with Detective Sheehan right now."

Sheehan? He knew Detective Sheehan. Used to see him at his parents' bar. Hearing his name made him feel hopeful, gave him something to go on. "I'll go tell Robert's mother," he said to Doyle. "Then I'll come back and see Sheehan."

"A girl wantsa sit on my face, you bet I'm not gonna stop her."

"A girl wantsa fuck *me* in the park, yeah, all right."

Inside the precinct house, detectives joked about their newly confessed suspect. They were passing the time as Sheehan finished getting a written statement from Robert. "Altar boy," one of them said.

"Faggot."

"Yeah, well, he don't like women. That's for damn sure."

"Oh, are we in trouble," Bob Chambers said to Marilei in the cab they took to Mrs. Hammerstein's. "We need a lawyer. You tell Phyllis."

Marilei knew what had happened. As she'd arrived at the precinct, a photographer had tried to take her picture, and she'd put her hands over her face and run away and then asked a policeman what was going on and he told her that a boy named Robert Chambers had been accused of killing a girl. She hadn't believed it, but when she'd found Mr. Chambers, he'd said it was true.

"I can't tell Phyllis," she insisted to Mr. Chambers in the cab. "You have to be the one." Then they reached Mrs. Hammerstein's, and she led him into the kitchen, and Phyllis was there in her bathrobe. Marilei went away and left them alone, and when she came back Mr. Chambers was gone and Phyllis started to cry, cry, cry, cry. Marilei made her a cup of tea, but it didn't do any good. Phyllis just went on crying.

Videotaping the confessions of criminals was a relatively new phenomenon. Until the early 1980s, stenographers took confessions down in dictation. The videotapes were better because they were unchallengingly accurate. But they took a lot longer to set up. Saracco, waiting restlessly for his technicians to unpack their equipment, chain-smoked and thought about what to say during the videotaping. He didn't have much leeway. Mostly the thing was just boilerplate. You introduced yourself casually, like it was no big deal that you were from the DA's office, so the suspect didn't turn skittish when the tape started rolling. You read him his rights on camera, so no defense attorney could claim you'd tricked him into confessing. You got him to tell his story, speaking to him guy-to-guy, not lawyer-to-client or priest-to-penitent, so he felt relaxed. You got him to put some fine-tuning on the details so you could check out the story. And then, if you didn't believe it, you took your run. Got confrontational. It was in the last two areas that strategy came in. Some ADA's spent three to five hours on the details. Not him. That wasn't his style. And some went light on confrontation. Not him. He hadn't been a Marine for nothing.

He was probably going to have to take a hard run at this Chambers, he figured. Because one, he's a liar. He told Jennifer's girlfriends he wasn't even with her. Because two, he's a *calculated* liar. He didn't just say to the cops that he went home, but he gave them the name of TV shows he'd supposedly watched, shows he'd have had to have researched to know what was on. And because three, he's telling lies. This story he's been giving out lately makes no sense. I've seen the pictures of the girl. She wasn't killed in any accident.

Four cigarettes into the ashtray, he was done with his planning, and he went into Chambers's room to eyeball him for the first time.

What he saw surprised him. Sheehan had told him the kid was a preppie and not the kind of Frankie So-and-So from uptown they were used to dealing with. Given that, Saracco expected to see some fear or at least nervousness. But there wasn't any. Chambers was just sitting there, not crying, not wringing his hands. And when they were introduced, he didn't act worried, didn't recoil or even seem scared. He just looked blank.

When the cameraman was ready, Robert rotated his shoulders as if he were preparing for a strenuous exercise, groomed himself by pushing back his hair, and began talking clearly to Saracco, Sheehan, and McEntee, who sat opposite him across a big desk. Jennifer had gotten insane with rage because he told her he didn't want to see her anymore, he said sincerely. "She freaked out. And she just—she like got up and—knelt in front of me and scratched my face. I have these marks here." Touching his cheek, he showed the scratches on his face to the assistant district attorney. "I got all upset and I stood up and I was saying, 'I'm going to go. I'm going to go. This is crazy.'"

The ADA maintained an interested, sympathetic look on his face. Robert saw it and mentioned that, while he'd been pissed off at Jennifer for laughing at him when Jo Perry chewed him out at Dorrian's, he'd gotten *really* pissed off at her after she scratched him in the park. But he forgave her, he went on, because once she'd scratched him, she calmed down and got really nice. "She came up behind me and started to give me a massage, and she said, You look cute, but you'd look cuter tied up."

"Your face is scratched at this point, right?" Saracco asked.

"Right," Robert said patiently. The camera was whirring softly. He launched into what he'd already told Gill and McEntee and Sheehan, explained how she'd tied his hands behind his back with her panties, pushed him flat onto the earth, and seated herself on his chest. "She started to take off my pants," he said. "She started to play with me. She started jerking me off." As he spoke, he rubbed his right hand up and down along an imaginary penis, indicating to the ADA what she'd done. But he wanted him to know this was no ordinary jerk-off. "She was doing it really hard," he said, the camera catching him in a masturbatory gesture. "It really hurt me. And I—you know—I started to say, 'Stop it! Stop it! It hurts.'"

His entreaties hadn't softened her, he went on a moment later. "She kind of laughed in a weird way, like more like a cackle or something. And then she sat up and she like sat on my face and then she dug her nails into my chest and I have scratches right here."

The assistant district attorney made him show his ravaged flesh to the camera and kept interrupting his account, but after a while he was able to get back to the story. He concentrated on his pain and anguish. "It was nonstop," he said. "She was just having her way. And then she squeezed my balls and I just could not take it. So I was wiggling around, wiggling around, and she was leaning forward, jerking me off and squeezing my balls and laughing, and I managed to get my left hand free. So I kind of sat up a little and just grabbed at her."

It was as a result of that single grab that she had died, he continued, and pointed out that when she landed he, too, got hurt, injured a bone in his right hand. The hand was paining him badly. "It—it was just really quick," he said, "she just flipped over and then landed, and she was kind of twisted on the tree. On her side."

He had done nothing to help her, he admitted. But that was because he thought she was just trying to frighten him. "I just, I stood there for like ten minutes waiting. Maybe five minutes. I don't know how long. Trying to see if she'd move. If she's just trying to, you know, scare me." Then after a pause he described his inertia further. "I was in shock," he explained. "I didn't know what was going on."

"What were you in shock about?" the assistant district attorney asked, as if he hadn't understood *anything*.

"That this girl that I knew and I left the bar with and just wanted to talk to was—did what she did to me." Almost as an afterthought he added, "And that now she's not moving."

A few minutes later he described how he'd gone home, gotten undressed, and fallen asleep, and how when he'd awakened this morning the whole thing had seemed like a dream. Then he was done, completely drained. He'd said everything there was to say.

As Robert talked, frustration kept gnawing at Steve Saracco. The tape had been rolling for God knows how many minutes and still, so far, he hadn't gotten the young man to deviate one iota from the story he'd told earlier. I'm going to have to give him a couple of Jack Webbs, Saracco thought. Hit him hard with the fact that the girl is dead and he's alive. And I'm also going to have to hedge my bets. There's a good chance this guy won't crack no matter what I ask him, that he's gonna stick like glue to this accident bullshit. And if he does and we indict him for murder, which from the look of the girl's neck is what he ought to be indicted for, this videotape is gonna be played in court someday. I want the jury that sees the tape to know I don't give his bullshit any credence. That you could do that on a tape was the beauty of the thing. When you cross-examined a guy on the stand, you weren't allowed to communicate your personal beliefs and disbeliefs. But you could on a videotape. "I wasn't there," he said to Robert. "The detectives weren't there. But there are certain things that don't lie. The condition of the body. The condition of your face and chest." That stated, he paused and then, as if he were asking a very casual question, said, "How tall are you?' Six-four?"

Chambers saw where he was going. *"Three.* Six-three," he said.

"How much do you weigh?"

"One ninety."

"What is she? About five-eight? Five-seven?"

"Five-nine," Chambers said. "Probably weighs like one twenty or something." But then, as if to prove that despite her height and weight the girl had been a match for him, he added, "But she was strong. I mean, she would just burst into these fits and freak out."

Saracco back-pedaled. Chambers was growing defensive, and he didn't want him to clam up. Not before he established how well he'd known the girl. He began asking about their relationship and the nature of their sexual encounters. "When you had sex with her," he inquired, "did she use any protection or did you use any prophylactics?"

"It never even entered our minds at all," Chambers told him.

Never entered their minds? Middle-class kids? Saracco hurried on to the next question.

"You had sex with her three times. Was there anything out of the ordinary? Any tying up? Or was it just regular sex?"

"Just regular sex. Except for the third time. On a roof. She took pictures of me while I was asleep?"

"How did you know she took pictures of you?"

"Because she woke me up and showed them to me. She said, 'I thought you looked cute like that.'"

"You fell asleep on the roof naked?" Saracco couldn't keep a note of surprise out of his voice.

"Yeah. I was exhausted."

"What was your reaction?"

"I was shocked," Chambers replied primly. "I thought it was odd. It was out of the ordinary. I'd never come across somebody that did that."

Saracco wasn't satisfied with what he'd gotten. What I need now is to weave in a motive for the killing, he thought, and he let the past go and moved back to what had happened in the park. He had a theory about the motive. Chambers looked to him like the kind of guy whose whole ballgame was his face, and it seemed to him that once the girl scratched him—messed up his *looks*, for Christ's sake—he'd flipped out. "You were mad at her," he began, heading toward weaving in the motive. "For laughing at you in the bar."

"Right," Chambers said. Then he went right where Saracco wanted him to go, adding, "And for scratching me."

"Saracco was pleased. "And for spitting at you," he pointed out.

"Right," Chambers acknowledged.

Saracco was almost home. "That certainly would have upset you," he commented agreeably. Then he waited for another "Right."

He didn't get it. "I was upset," Chambers said. But he went on to explain, as he'd done before, that after the girl scratched him she was so apologetic and full of sweet talk that he'd made up with her and only then let her tie him up.

Saracco kept pressing him. "You just told me that she'd gone nuts on you," he said.

"She did go nuts. And then she came back and started to massage my back."

He was failing at weaving in his motive, Saracco realized. But he still believed in it, still felt that a pretty boy like Chambers wouldn't have let a girl tie him up once she'd scratched his face. Probably no man would have. Which made him wonder if there was any truth at all to the sex story. Maybe they never even had sex. "Did you ejaculate at any time?" he asked.

"No. I never did. Never did."

"Were you erect at any time?"

"Yes. I was."

Erect even though she was hurting his genitals? Saracco found this idea unlikely. "You became erect?" he repeated dubiously.

To his surprise, Chambers seemed to take his words as an affront to his masculinity and responded as if the question had been designed to explore not how come he'd been erect if she was hurting him, but how come if he *had* been erect he hadn't climaxed. "I was in too much pain," he answered. "I wasn't even thinking about it."

He'd better get into a new area, Saracco decided. This was getting no place. He'd better go for something to shake Chambers up. If he got shook up, the truth might come out. The photographs of the dead girl might do the trick. Grasping them, he slid them across the desk.

It started to work. Chambers got uneasy at once. "Please, I really don't want to see," he murmured, and put a hand across his eyes.

"Let me just describe them to you," Saracco persisted. "Her neck area depicts markings of a degree a lot more severe than could have been inflicted by the way you describe it. Do you see how discolored and even bleeding her neck is? Is there any way you can account for this?"

"Yeah." Chambers said. He had given the pictures a hasty glance. "Because when I pulled her back, she landed against the tree and just laid there like this." He put up an arm and demonstrated how the girl had landed, the camera capturing him mimicking her open, glazed eyes.

The pictures had gotten him nowhere, Saracco concluded. He was going to have to try another tack. Come right out and let the guy know, no holds barred, that he thought he was full of shit. "Your story just doesn't make any sense to me," he began. Then he added, "I'm not saying this was something premeditated on your part. I'm not saying that you were walking out of that bar and saying to yourself, I'm going to kill this girl in Central Park. I'm sure it didn't happen that way. But something triggered you."

Chambers didn't like being challenged. He waved a hand in the air, as if to brush the unpleasant words away. And when he spoke, anger made his voice shake. "She molested me in the park," he said. "She hit me with—"

Bingo! Saracco thought. Even if he couldn't get Chambers to tell the truth, if he got him angry enough maybe he'd blow his cool and reveal on tape the violent side of himself that surely had been in evidence in the park. That too would be useful in front of a jury. "How could *she* molest you?" he plunged forward. "We're talking about what?"

"What?" Chambers, a hint in his face of the fury Saracco was after, took the bait. "Girls cannot do it to a guy?"

Saracco kept going. "Wait! Are you telling me she's trying to rape you in the park? Come on, Robert!"

But Chambers had regained control of himself and now stiffly, his vocabulary stilted and Victorian, he announced, "She was having her way with me. Without my consent. With my hands behind my back."

"Wait a minute!" Saracco said. "What are we? From Iowa or someplace?"

"I don't know where you're from." Chambers's voice was icy. "That really doesn't concern me. But you see, a jogger heard me scream. The jogger even asked, 'What's wrong?'"

"Just continue that."

Chambers's face turned indignant. "I'm hurt," he said.

"You're hurt from what?"

"From *her!*"

"I know you're *angry*. From her scratching you."

This time Chambers made a guttural sound in the back of his throat.

"Look, if I were here telling you this story," Saracco said, "you'd be laughing."

"No. I doubt I'd be laughing."

"And I don't mean laughing because it's funny. But laughing because it doesn't make any sense."

"It makes no sense?" Chambers seemed at last on the verge of a true rage. "It makes no sense that somebody could put your hands behind your back and push you down and then get on top of your chest?"

"*Exactly!*" Saracco said. "You're exactly right."

But although he'd made Chambers hopping mad, made him come to the verge of exploding, no explosion occurred. Nor did his story change. He just kept petulantly repeating it. Disappointed, and needing time to formulate a new plan, Saracco turned the questioning over to Sheehan.

"Did there come a time when after she spit at you and everything else," Sheehan said, "you slapped her in the face or shoved her away from you or punched her in the eye or something?"

"I never slapped her or punched her or anything," Chambers said. He sounded utterly convincing.

"You just let her scratch you?"

"What am I going to do? Hit her with a stick?" Under Sheehan's questioning, Chambers had grown calm, even casual, once again. Time for a Jack Webb, Saracco decided, and broke in. "She's dead. You're not. Something happened. That's a fact, isn't it, Rob?"

But Chambers merely grunted, "Yeah," and held firm.

A short while later Saracco took a parting shot for the sake of the trial that he now felt was an inevitability. "It seems to me," he intoned in his best summation style, "that it wasn't her that freaked out. That it was you. You that lost your temper to some degree. That you killed her. That you *knew* you killed her. That you *intended* to kill her. That you left her there dead. You went home. You went to sleep. And through good police investigation, they found you. The account you give is just an accommodation."

When he was finished, he gave Chambers one last chance to change his story.

Chambers didn't want it. "I've told you exactly what happened," he said. "I'm sorry if you can't see it. I'm sure that I've heard of other men being raped, other men being tied up."

"Well, I'll tell you one thing," Saracco snapped. "I haven't."

"Well, good. You're lucky."

"I've been in this business for a while, and you're the first man I've seen raped in Central Park."

"Good. That really makes no difference to me. But it happens. It can *happen*. It *did* happen."

Saracco delivered a final Jack Webb. "You didn't wind up raped," he said. "And she wound up dead. That's all I know." But Chambers wanted the last word. "I didn't mean to hurt her," he said. "I *liked* her very much. She was a very nice person. Easy to get along with. Easy to talk to. She was just too pushy. And she liked me more than I thought. More than anyone actually thought."

See you in court, Saracco thought, and a moment later announced that the taping was finished. Although Chambers hadn't budged from his story, and although he himself had failed at weaving in a motive, he'd taken a pretty good statement, he told himself. One that no defense attorney would be happy with. And that made *him* happy.

He was leaving the room when Detective McEntee, who had been silent throughout the taping, spoke up and said to Chambers, "You're under arrest."

Sheehan was exhausted. All he wanted was a shower and a beer, or a beer and a shower. He was trying to make up his mind which of them he wanted first when Lieutenant Doyle beckoned to him and said, "Hey, did you know Robert Chambers from before?"

"No," Sheehan said.

"What about his father? You know him?"

"No."

"Well, the old man knows you. He mentioned your name to me."

"You're kidding."

"No. He said something about Is this Detective Sheehan the one from Sheehan's bar on Third Avenue?"

Unhappily Sheehan breathed, "Oh, boy," and just then Bob Chambers entered the precinct-house door.

"There he is," Doyle said, and Sheehan stared. He didn't recognize Bob right away. The man he was looking at was clean-shaven and trim, and the Bob Chambers he'd known had always worn thick muttonchop whiskers and seemed a little sloppy. But a moment later, when he saw Bob shrugging his shoulders at him familiarly, he realized with a start that of course it was Bobby Chambers. Holy Christ, he thought. So the intelligentsia was Robert Chambers's dad! I didn't know the guy had a son. Then he thought, Jeez, the poor guy. This stuff with his son is all he needs. Even back when he used to come into the bar, he was having tough times, talking about how bad his marriage was, and now look what's about to happen to him. Concerned, he walked up to Bob, shook his hand, and said, "Jeez, Bobby, it's been a long time, eh?" Then he added, "I didn't know Robert was your son. If I'd've known, I wouldn't've continued on the case. But the kid didn't say anything. I even gave him my card. He never said his father knew me. Never said, Hey, did your family own Sheehan's bar?"

Bob just shrugged again. Then he asked, "How's your mom?"

"Mom's great."

"I hope your family's not mad at me. I mean, because I haven't been by in five years."

Sheehan couldn't believe his ears. Here the guy's son has just been arrested for murder, and he's shooting How's mom? "It's okay," he murmured. "It's all right."

"Mike, I want to apologize for not coming by these past five years," Bob persisted.

"Forget it. It's nothing," Sheehan assured him. But Bob wouldn't let the matter go. "It's not because of the bar or your family," he said. "It's because I have a problem. I'm an alcoholic."

Holy Christ, he hadn't known that either, Sheehan thought. Damn, if only the guy had opened up about it back in the old days, maybe I could've helped him. But there was no point in crying over spilt milk. It was now that the guy really needed help. "What are you going to do?" he asked. "I mean, What are you going to do now?"

Bob's voice was glum. "I was going to ask you that. What the hell should I do?"

"You gotta get a good lawyer."

"Yeah, but the whole thing is, I haven't got the dough. I don't know if I can afford one."

"Yeah, well. You could wait, I guess. They'd give you a guy. A public defender."

"Yeah." Bob sounded resigned. But a few moments later he said, "Who's a good lawyer?"

"There's lots of guys," Sheehan said. Then he rattled off a few names. One of them, Bob would later tell a friend, was Jack Litman, who had just that past June won an acquittal for a Brooklyn cop accused of shooting an unarmed black man.

Inside, in the precinct house, the videotape technicians were packing up their equipment and Saracco was preparing to leave. Robert seemed almost forgotten. He was alone except for young Detective Mullally, who had been asked by Sheehan to keep an eye on him. The two were sitting quietly on opposite sides of the room when suddenly the door opened and Bob Chambers walked in. Mullally saw Robert start, stand up, and throw his arms around his father. Then he heard him say in an excited voice, "That fucking bitch, why didn't she leave me alone?"

Bob Chambers didn't hear the remark. Or if he did, he managed to deny its passage from his ears to his brain. He heard not a rush of angry, accusatory words but the sound of sobbing. And he saw in front of him, not an angry young man but a distraught boy, one whose eyes were watery with tears. "I'm here," he said at once. "I've been trying to see you. But I'm here now, and that's the important point."

Robert put his head down in his hands.

"I'm with you all the way," Bob said. "Your mother is with you. And we'll do everything we have to do to take care of you." But although he put his arm around his boy's shoulder and continued to speak in a soothing voice, Robert didn't pull himself together. He went on crying.

About an hour later—it was 2 A.M.—Robert was taken on "The Walk." The Walk is a courtesy the police department generally grants the press, a chance to photograph a criminal before he leaves the precinct in which he has been arrested and disappears into the bowels of Central Booking. The Walk gives photographers the opportunity to get enough mugs to last them from the day of arrest to the day of bail—or right through a criminal's trial if he isn't granted bail. Robert, his hands cuffed and his body surrounded by police, did The Walk from the precinct house to a nearby van along a route jammed with jostling newspeople.

He tried to ignore them. But their cameras were pointing at him like guns, their lights were so bright that the roadway seemed illuminated by a brilliant dawn, and the newspeople kept calling out to him as familiarly as if he and they were intimates.

"Hey, Robert! I'm over here," a voice rang out.

"Yo, Rob!" another one sounded. "Why'dja do her?"

He turned several times, lights exploding in his eyes. Sheehan was with him. Sheehan who had a few minutes earlier taken him into a men's room and made him drop his pants, examining his genitals for what proved to be nonexistent traces of squeezing and scratching. He'd suffered passively through that indignity. But this one, the surge and onslaught of the press, made him angry. The press was like a pack of wild dogs hot for his blood.

While Robert was departing the precinct in police custody, Brock Pernice, still out in the Hamptons, was startled by the sound of a telephone piercing the nighttime silence. He picked the phone up and heard his mother's voice. She was crying.

It's my grandfather, Brock thought. He's died. It has to be that, because the last time my mom sounded this tearful was when someone else in the family died. "What is it?" he asked at once. "Is it Grandpa?" His mother said, "No," and the next thing Brock knew, he was saying, "Is it Jen?" He didn't know why he said that. But somehow he just knew that something had happened to Jen.

When his mother told him yes, and said that Jennifer was dead, he threw the phone down, flung it from him as if it were a messenger of evil tidings whose destruction he could effect. He broke into a sweat, began perspiring all over, and he couldn't stop.

The holding cells at Central Booking in lower Manhattan were jammed when McEntee and Robert arrived at about three-thirty in the morning. The place had the look of a zoo, with herds of men, most of them dark-skinned, standing upright in a crowded pen. It smelled like a zoo, too, because there were no toilets in the pens. If a prisoner wanted to go to the toilet, he had to ask a cop or a corrections officer to take him to it, and some didn't bother to ask. They relieved themselves right on the cement floor. Robert, his eyes dazed, took in the sights and smells that greeted him and stayed close to McEntee.

His fingers were bandaged, and he had with him antibiotic pills for his scratches and a small ice pack for his aching hand. On the way to Central Booking, he'd been taken to a hospital, where his bites, scratches, and hand injury had been examined and prescribed for. McEntee told him he'd probably be able to keep his ice pack once he was booked, but not the pills. Jail was funny about pills.

They went first to photography, so he could get his mug shot taken. He stood in front of a Polaroid camera on a tripod, and a female police officer pressed the shutter. But nothing happened. The camera was broken. The officer sent for another, but it, too, was broken. She sent for a third, but when it arrived it turned out to be unable to expose color film, which was the only kind of film she had. Each time a new camera appeared,

Robert wiped perspiration from his forehead and combed his bandaged fingers through his hair. Finally a working camera that could expose color film arrived, and four views of his face were recorded. The pictures that resulted were unlike any for which he had posed in the days when he had hoped to be a model. Despite his efforts to tidy himself, he appeared as disheveled as any common criminal—his hair unruly, his face dirty, his chin stubbled. But what was most striking about his appearance were the brownish-red scratches that streaked across his pallid cheeks like the warpaint on a movie Indian.

Once his pictures had been taken, McEntee led him to a counter where he was asked to relinquish any money he had with him. He had none. Then he was asked for his sneaker laces. "They don't want you hanging yourself inside," McEntee said. Stooping, Robert undid the laces and handed them over. Then he started to move forward, his sneakers suddenly gaping on his feet and the metal grommets into which the laces had tongued looking like tiny empty mouths. "That string, too," McEntee said and pointed at the waistband of his sweatpants. Robert untied the pants, removed the string, and laid it on the counter. As soon as he did, the pants began to crawl down his hips. He clutched at them with a gauze-wrapped hand and held them up as best he could. Then McEntee took him to get his prisoner number and have his fingerprints taken.

That process should have gone smoothly but didn't. The computer that assigned numbers and fed the prints to a central clearinghouse in Albany was down. There was no telling when it would be working again, a corrections officer informed McEntee. In the meanwhile his prisoner would have to wait in one of the pens.

McEntee was distressed at the news. He had been feeling great for the past few hours. His first homicide had not only been solved but the culprit apprehended, a confession obtained, and the booking nearly completed. Everything, give or take a couple of broken cameras, had gone smoothly. But now the whole thing threatened to come to a bad end. The fact of the matter was, he didn't want Robert in a pen and had planned to get a private cell for him once he was booked. There were three or four such cells, and although they were generally reserved for transvestites, who fared poorly in the big pen, prisoners who were considered suicidal and therefore in need of close watch could be assigned to them. In McEntee's estimation, Robert wasn't suicidal. But he wouldn't know how to look after himself with the animals he'd be meeting in the pen. Not with those bandaged hands. All *he* knew how to do was defend himself with girls. But there was nothing McEntee could do about a private cell now. He'd just have to hope for the best. He turned to Robert and said, "You gotta go in there with the rest of them."

Robert looked frightened, but McEntee told him not to worry. "Just don't get into any fights in there," he cautioned. But he couldn't put out of his mind the time not long ago when he'd seen a guy locked up for having thrown his baby daughter off a roof. The guy had been in one of the pens only ten minutes before he'd had to be pulled out and rushed to a hospital. Prisoners had a code. They didn't like guys who killed kids. Maybe they wouldn't like what Robert had done either. "Listen, whatever you do," he warned Robert, "don't tell anybody why you're here. If anyone in there asks you, just say we booked you on assault or robbery."

When Robert was led away and placed in a pen, McEntee got himself coffee and talked to some fellow officers. The radio was on—someone had tuned it loudly to News 88—and the officers were listening to it and guffawing at Robert's story, which they found hilarious. "Tell me, you think this guy is attractive?" one of the listeners, a male officer, demanded of a female one. "Well, yeah," the woman replied. "Yeah, he's cute."

"*Very* cute?"

"Yeah, very cute."

"Well, just don't squeeze his balls."

The female officer giggled, and all the men cracked up. But McEntee couldn't relax. Even if Robert doesn't say why he's here, he kept thinking, those guys in there will figure it out pronto. Because the damn radio's on.

Worried, he quit the group he was standing with and hurried to the pen to check up on his prisoner.

What he saw amazed him. Robert had managed to clear a few feet of space for himself amid the roiling, shoving mass, and he was curled up on the dirty cement floor. His eyes were closed and he appeared to have shut out his surroundings and fallen soundly asleep.

He still seemed to be sleeping when, an hour or two later, the computer at last came on line. McEntee did a first set of prints, squeezing the thick ink that looked like black toothpaste onto a Lucite pad and pressing Robert's fingers down on the pad as firmly as he could, given the bandages. But he wasn't an experienced fingerprinter, and the prints came out smudged. A fingerprint specialist tried the process over again. But he was reluctant to do the printing the way he usually did, which involved grabbing the prisoner's fingers and plunging them into the swirl of ink as if they were anchors being heaved into the sea. Robert's gauze-wrapped fingers made the specialist nervous, and he pressed them down so lightly that he got only a partial set of prints. McEntee tried again, and managed to print nine fingers. It was enough. The booking was over.

By now it was 8 A.M. McEntee got ready to go. But he was still feeling uneasy, still worrying that some harm might befall his first homicide collar. He knew that Robert had managed to make out all right when surrounded by other prisoners for an hour or two, but wasn't certain he'd go on managing if he had to hang around with them for another eight hours, or however long it took till he was arraigned. Leaving, McEntee arranged a private cell for him. Then he said goodbye to Robert. "I hadda lie for you a little," he said. "I hadda tell 'em you were suicidal."

Robert looked grateful, but McEntee shrugged the look away. He'd done what he'd done for himself, not for the preppie. "The last thing I need is for you to get killed in there," he said grudgingly.

A few moments later Robert, holding up his sweatpants with his bandaged hands and pushing his feet slowly in front of him in their gaping sneakers, shuffled off with a corrections officer.

ROUGH SEX

Jack Litman of Litman, Asche, Lupkin and Gioiella was one of the most sought-after criminal defense attorneys in New York. His very posture radiated that fact. Chest forward, shoulder blades so taut they looked starched, he stood like a man who had never known a moment of less than complete self-confidence. He'd always had that look, even back in the days when he was starting out as a lowly assistant in the Manhattan district attorney's office. Even then he'd known he was going places. And so had most people who met him. He'd had the kind of smarts that set him off from his fellows, and few had been surprised when within four years he'd become the star of the office's elite Homicide Squad.

By the time he was thirty-one years old, he'd struck out on his own. Gone to the other side. The place where the money was. It had been time to go. In his handful of years in the DA's office, he'd tried close to forty cases and lost only one.

On the morning of August 27, 1986, Litman was at the height of his career. He'd been in private practice for twelve years, handled everything from securities fraud to murder, and had a string of dramatic wins. There'd been the Brooklyn policeman who'd shot the unarmed black man. Acquittal. A Bronx policeman who'd shot two unarmed Hispanics. Acquittal. A business magnate accused of insider trading. Charges dismissed. A bank robber caught only moments after he fled the teller's counter, a clutch of stolen money and even a hand-it-over note still in his possession. Acquittal.

Litman had also had a couple of clients accused of murder for whom he'd gotten convictions on lesser charges. One had been a seventeen-year-old boy who according to the police had repeatedly bashed his girlfriend's head with a rock. Litman persuaded the boy's jury that his client had merely pushed the girl away from him and that in falling she'd hit her head on the rock. Another client—his most famous to date—had been Richard Herrin, a Mexican-American who won a scholarship to Yale and subsequently hammered to death Bonnie Garland, a fellow Yalie with whom he'd fallen in love. Herrin had confessed to killing Garland; he'd even told police he'd begun thinking about doing her in hours before he actually did. But Litman convinced Herrin's jury that the young man had been suffering from extreme emotional disturbance, and got him convicted of manslaughter rather than murder.

Many people condemned Litman for his victories. Called him a soulless man. But he let the condemnation run off his back like water down a granite wall. The public didn't understand the Constitution, he often said. The rights of the accused. Spelled out by our Founding Fathers. Those were sacred rights. Holy. He believed ardently in the Constitution and frequently spoke on panels explaining and defending it. He also believed ardently in the family. Had a secret side hidden beneath his arrogant stance and razorsharp observations. He could be domineering and scene-stealing with his wife, a French-born talented lawyer in her own right, but he loved her, and he adored his two young sons. Good boys who excelled at school and could be counted on never to get into trouble. *Mensches.*

Not long after he first heard about the Chambers case and the teenagers who drank and caroused at Dorrian's until all hours of the night, the thought crossed Litman's mind that his own children and those of his

friends could never have been part of a scene like that. Because he and
his friends controlled their children, didn't say to them, You can go out
into the jungle now. You're strong enough. You've got claws. You've got
muscles. He and his friends didn't treat their children the way an animal
society treats its young.

But that was after August 27, 1986. On that morning, when he first
heard about the case over the radio, he merely shrugged and continued
dressing for work. He had just finished, was just ready to leave his spacious Central Park West apartment for his spacious lower Broadway office, when the phone rang and a man who identified himself as a friend of
the Chambers family started rattling off a whole *megillah* to him. The gist
of it was that the Chamberses wanted to know if he would be interested
in handling their boy's predicament.

Maybe, Litman thought. Aloud, he said, "Well, I'll meet with the parents to discuss it." Then he took Bob Chambers's phone number from the
caller, spoke to Chambers briefly, learned he had an apartment nearby,
and drove over and picked him up in his Cadillac De Ville.

He interviewed him in the car. He didn't waste time asking him how
he felt. People in Bob Chambers's situation, he had long ago learned,
were often inarticulate or confused. There was no point in dwelling on
the emotional aspects of the matter. So he just zeroed in on information
that might help in the defense of his son, like what had happened to Bob
in the police station last night.

By nine o'clock he had met Phyllis, too, and by nine thirty, having
agreed to take the case, he was gunning the Cadillac downtown.

He arrived at Central Booking just as the cops were leading Robert
onto the street in order to transfer him to a detention cell in the Criminal
Courts Building. Reporters were thronging the sidewalks, and TV vans
were poking the sky with their periscopes. Litman raced toward his new
client, introduced himself, and explained that he'd been retained by Bob
and Phyllis.

He wasn't sure how much the boy understood. He's petrified, he thought. "Try to be calm," he cautioned him. Then he glanced at the wall of cameras and lights. "Please be calm," he said. "And don't talk to anyone."

．　．　．

Mickey McEntee was at the medical examiner's office waiting for the Filipino doctor who had examined Jennifer in the park the previous morning to start the autopsy. They were down in the photography room in the bowels of the building, where the photographer was leaping around the body and snapping pictures with a monster zoom lens. McEntee got the creeps just watching the guy, who had a long ponytail, a Harley-Davidson T-shirt and belt buckle, and big black motorcycle boots with silver ornaments. A weirdo. But probably you had to be a weirdo to work in the ME's office. Even the doctor seemed a little bizarre. When he told her he thought the marks he'd seen on the girl's nipples were bite marks, she giggled and blushed like an embarrassed virgin. Then she said she didn't agree.

"Why not?" he asked her.

"Because there's no hemorrhaging."

"But suppose the killer bit her after she was dead? Her heart would have stopped pumping, so there'd be no blood going to the skin. She wouldn't get a hemorrhage if he bit her after she was dead."

The doctor giggled and blushed again. Then she tittered. "You Americans, you're such a kinky people." Unbelievable, McEntee thought. He wanted to say, Jesus Christ, Doc. This is a homicide, not a sociology lesson. But he held his tongue. She wasn't an experienced ME. No point in aggravating her.

Not that he didn't want to. Especially when they got to talking about the police theory that the dead girl had been dragged through earth and twigs. The doctor didn't believe that either, even though there were linear scratches all over the back of the girl's buttocks and thighs. "That's her tan peeling," she said.

Her tan peeling! Peeling skin doesn't make a linear pattern, McEntee steamed. When you peel, it looks like a mosaic. Like alligator hide. This medical examiner is hopeless. She's probably never gotten a sunburn in her life.

He watched her for a while as she began her job, washing Jennifer's body with a huge sponge and sealing her clothes in plastic bags. But he took off right after that. He wanted to be well out of the way when the doctor started cutting into the body. He didn't mind dead bodies. He didn't mind seeing people shot and stabbed and lying on the ground with their arms sliced off or their guts hanging open. But when it came to doctors sticking their hands inside skin and pulling things out and weighing and measuring them, well, that kind of thing made him sick.

After McEntee left, Dr. Alandy went calmly on with her work, examining and making notes about all the bruises on the skin.

There were plenty of them. Not just the big band-shaped abrasion at the neck and the marks McEntee had been asking about earlier. There was a contusion above the right eyebrow. There was an irregular abrasion just below that. There was another abrasion on the ear. Another at the left side of the chin. More on the elbows, stomach, and insides of the thighs. And there were small vertical markings on the left cheek.

These interested Dr. Alandy. Probably the girl made those marks herself, she thought. Scratched herself because she was trying to remove something the assailant placed around her face. A gag most likely. Because there was also a laceration inside the upper lip, the kind of laceration a gag made of rough cloth might have caused. Though she couldn't be sure of that. The laceration could have been caused by a punch in the mouth, too.

Alandy kept going, noting her external findings into a tape recorder.

While Alandy began her autopsy, Litman had his first real talk with his new client. They talked at the Criminal Courts Building, where Robert was in a cell with a crush of other prisoners. Litman didn't ask to have him brought out to the lawyer-client conference room, a topsy-turvy Alice in Wonderland place where the floors were bare and the walls carpeted. He just stood outside Robert's cell with his hands on the bars and asked him quietly what had happened in the park. He got the same story the police had gotten.

"Is there any reason that the police could point to that would indicate you didn't like Jennifer?" he asked once he'd heard the story. "Was there any hostility between you?"

Robert told him there wasn't and that their relationship had been so casual and uneventful it hadn't really been much of anything.

Litman didn't linger. He said, "Take it easy," and hurried to his office. There was a lot more he could do for the kid from there than from here.

Back at the precinct, Mickey McEntee was dealing with the public. The public always had to be dealt with once a crime got into the papers and onto TV. People called up to say they'd seen the crime in a vision or knew all its details from radio signals they'd picked up through the metal fillings in their teeth, or the police had the wrong guy, because the right one was following them right now even as they spoke. Crazy stuff. But you had to be polite. Because you never knew when someone who really knew something might call up. When a man named Alan Garber got through to him, McEntee expected just another nut call, but he heard the man out patiently. He was a doctor, the guy began explaining, and every day he went running in Central Park. Sometimes he noticed strange things there. Like the night before last, when he'd seen two people lying on the ground.

"Whereabouts?" McEntee asked.

The doctor went into a long-winded story about his jogging route, and how he'd been heading south on the east drive just north of the Museum when he'd spotted the couple under a tree to his right.

"To your right?" McEntee's brain went on alert. The man had certainly been in the correct area. "Tell me what you saw."

"The couple was on the grass and they were rocking."

"Rocking? What do you mean 'rocking'?"

"Well, you know. Humping. I mean, I couldn't tell if they were actually humping. It was too gray. But I thought it was humping. Or rocking. Something sexual."

McEntee was making notes. He wrote down "rocking." Then he asked, "What did you do?"

"Just kept running. I didn't stop or anything. I just finished out my loop. But then about twenty minutes later I passed the same spot again, and the couple was still there."

"Still there?" McEntee's heart skipped a beat. Maybe the guy had actually seen the killing.

"Yeah. They were still there. Still rocking."

McEntee shook his head. Dead end. He thanked the doctor for calling and said he'd report the information to the district attorney.

Twenty-seven-year-old Roger Stavis had just started working for Litman's firm. Before that, although he came from Queens, he'd been a prosecutor in the Bronx district attorney's office. When he joined Litman, Asche a week ago, he'd been looking forward to interesting work. But he'd never expected to be involved with a juicy case like Chambers. So when he got to the office this morning and learned the firm would be handling it, he felt terrific, sure he'd made the right career move.

By eleven o'clock he was actively engaged on the case. Go over and see Robert, Litman told him. Find out who was in Dorrian's the night of the killing. Find out who his friends are. So we can check out his story. And him.

Despite having been an ADA, Stavis had never been to the hidden world that snaked through Manhattan's Criminal Courts Building, the gloomy skeleton of cells that occupied whole floors and twisted behind every courtroom. He'd seen only the courthouses's looming polished portals and the inspirational words about justice that soared above them, carved in marble. But he made his way eagerly into the labyrinth and located Robert, who had been moved to a private cell. When he saw the kid in there, sitting on a hard bench that jutted out from the wall, his heart went out to him. Because there wasn't that big an age difference between them. Just eight years. But look where he was, and look where Robert was.

Later Stavis would think that the difference in their circumstances said something important—and rather self-congratulatory—about social expectations. Because Robert, who had gone to expensive prep schools, had come out a loser while he himself, who had gone to public schools all his life, was a winner. But that morning at the detention cell he concentrated on his similarities to Robert. Their youth. Their inexperience. And because of their similarities he felt he and Robert related well to each other. They struck up a rapport and Robert supplied him with all the information he needed, including the names of friends of his who had seen him with Jennifer at Dorrian's.

.   .   .

In front of 11 East 90th Street, dozens of reporters and photographers were ringing Phyllis Chambers's doorbell, hoping to be able to snag an interview with her. But Phyllis wasn't in her apartment. She was in a coffee shop on Madison Avenue with her old friend Barbara Dermont, where, terrified of being recognized, she was sitting far in the back and facing away from the entrance.

She looked, Barbara fretted, crushed. Her lips were trembling and her eyes were red. The last time she'd seen Phyllis's face show even a vestige of emotion had been back when she'd broken up with Bob. Now, as they talked about what had happened in the park—"the terrible accident," Phyllis kept calling it—she looked devastated. And it wasn't just Robert she was worried about. It was money.

Litman didn't come cheap. He charged between $250 and $350 an hour, depending on the case. If it was a long one, he billed at the lower end of the scale. But he also charged separately for the services of associates like Stavis—$100 to $150 an hour. And he charged for the services of private investigators and scientific experts. And for their travel expenses.

Phyllis and Bob didn't have the kind of money a big Litman-run case would cost. Nor would they ever have it. Eventually, Litman would end up receiving considerably less money from the Chamberses than he customarily got from clients. (He would never say how much.) And eventually Phyllis would raise money for Robert's defense from various people she had worked for. Dorothy Hammerstein would contribute $20,000. But on this morning in August 1986, the money that was worrying Phyllis was not money with which to pay Litman but money with which to bail Robert out of jail.

"Come with me to Litman's office," she said to Barbara, and explained that she was going down there to start organizing a letter-writing campaign and a fund-raising drive to ensure Robert's bail.

Barbara agreed to come. When they reached Litman's office, Phyllis tore into action. She made a list of friends and contacts who might write character references for Robert. She made a list of people like Barbara who could serve as her delegates and do the actual legwork of getting the letters. And she made a list of people who might contribute money. "My friends will come through," she told Barbara. "Even those who don't have much money. They can take loans against their life insurance policies. Or even utilize the cash surrender clauses."

Barbara was impressed by her nerve. And by the fact that now that she was planning strategy, Phyllis no longer appeared devastated. Whatever she was feeling before, Barbara thought with a certain amount of awe, she's over it now. She's pushed it aside.

Later that afternoon, Litman asked Barbara to come into his private office and have a chat with him. "How long have you known Phyllis Chambers?" he asked her once she sat down. The room was spacious and airy, with a view of the Statue of Liberty. Litman's desk was a huge slab of thick glass, and in a corner was a chess set carved of green and white jade. "Several years," Barbara said.

"Are there people who will stand behind her?"

"Yes, she has a small group of close friends who will stick by her even if the sky falls in."

Litman nodded. Then he said, concern spreading over his face, "Things could really get rough. From what you know of Phyllis, do you think she's going to be able to survive all this?"

"Phyllis can survive anything," Barbara said.

Litman looked surprised at her response. "I don't think," he said, "that she knows what's hit her yet."

"She'll be all right," Barbara reassured him. But to herself she said, It's you that may not survive. You don't know what's hit *you* yet.

About four-thirty in the afternoon, Dr. Alandy put a block behind Jennifer's back to elevate her torso, made a Y-shaped incision from the top of the shoulders to the mid-portion of the abdomen, and commenced her internal examination. She had discovered by then that one thing Robert had said in his confession was true. He hadn't raped the girl. There was no trace of semen in—or even on—her body. Now she discovered that something else he'd said was also true. The girl had voided before being killed. There was no urine in her bladder. Still, not everything he'd said was true. In a short while she learned something that gave the lie to his story. It happened when she finished studying the abdominal organs and beganexamining the head. Sectioning Jennifer's tongue and temples, Alandy found hemorrhages.

They were different from the hemorrhages she had observed in the girl's eyelids when she had examined her in the park. Those indicated that the blood flow to the brain had been curtailed. These were more substantial and suggested that the girl's mouth and the sides of her head had been punched.

The girl she was autopsying, Alandy concluded when her work was finished, had not just been strangled but beaten as well.

In the early evening, Leilia Van Baker, who had left Vermont after learning that Jennifer was dead and returned to her home in New York, paid a condolence call on Steve and Arlene Levin. She arrived at their loft bearing a big turkey her mother had thoughtfully roasted for them. She sat with Steve and Arlene. She watched them eat some of the turkey. And she listened, pained, as they asked her why Jennifer had gone to the park with Robert.

"Because she trusted him," she said. "Because they already had a relationship."

The Levins asked, too, why Jennifer had had so many friends. The phone hadn't stopped ringing all day.

Leilia didn't want to tell them what she really thought. It was that Jennifer had been desperate for attention and affection. Attention and affection she hadn't gotten enough of at home. She let the question slide.

While Leilia was visiting the Levins, Roger Stavis was outside Dorrian's interviewing some of Robert's friends. He was outside because the friends didn't want to talk to him inside. There was too much press in there, they said. So he spoke to them on the sidewalk or took them around the corner for coffee.

He didn't get much from them. A lot of the kids said they hadn't noticed anything at all, even though they'd been at Dorrian's the night of the killing, and some said they just hadn't been there. Maybe Jennifer's friends would be more forthcoming. But they weren't around yet. They always arrived late, he'd been told, and if he wanted to see them he'd have to hang around till midnight or so. He hated to do that after a grueling day. But he knew that the first twenty-four hours of a case were generally the most productive, so he went inside and waited.

Fortunately he didn't have to wait at the noisy bar itself. Jack Dorrian offered him his private office for his interviews, and he went and sat in there. And then after a while Dorrian came in and brought a couple of girls. Friends of Jennifer's. And yes, they'd been at the bar with her on Monday night.

Stavis spoke to them consolingly. Then he began asking them questions about how Jennifer had behaved that night. The girls said she'd been drinking and that she'd been pursuing Robert.

Stavis had them sign written statements.

He felt relaxed after that, pleased because Jennifer's friends had not only confirmed Robert's story about her having been hot to trot with him, but even said nice things about Robert. Said he was gentle. Said *Jennifer* said he was gentle. Which proves, Stavis thought as he cheerfully headed home to Queens with the statements tucked safely into his briefcase, how important it is to do your interviewing early. Later on the kids at the bar may break up into enemy camps—a camp for Robert, a camp for Jennifer—but tonight no partisan lines have as yet been drawn.

Jack Litman had also worked late. He'd gone to night court and, with Robert at his side, argued in front of an arraignment judge that his client should be released from jail immediately, as he was guilty of nothing but an accident. "Mr. Chambers didn't mean to hurt Miss Levin," Litman said, and explained that he had killed her while reacting to the sexual pain she had caused him.

Reporters who were listening to the argument were delighted. Litman was giving the story a whole new push. They leaned eagerly forward and whispered among themselves that if the case ever came to trial it would be a dandy. The defense wouldn't be the run-of-the-mill self-defense in which a defendant argues he killed his victim because he was reacting to the fear of annihilation. It would be something new. Self-defense in reaction to sex. Rough sex. The notion gripped the imagination of the newspeople.

They were out in force. So were Robert's preppie friends. Stylishly dressed, they sat on the edge of their seats, cheek-by-jowl with friends and relatives of night court's usual catch of woebegone mostly dark-skinned hookers, pushers, and thieves, and seemed to be enjoying the atmosphere, as if night court were but a variation on the slumming that had drawn them to clubs like Area and the Palladium. Robert saw them and tossed them a thumbs-up sign.

But the arraignment didn't go well. "Far more than one blow was land-ed," a prosecutor from the district attorney's office told the judge. "We have reports that there were bruises and bite marks on the body."

The judge ordered Robert back to jail pending a grand jury investiga-tion of the charges.

"JENNY KILLED IN WILD SEX" and "SEX 'GOT ROUGH'" screamed headlines in the New York Post and the Daily News the next morning. The Levin family was furious. But so was Jack Litman. He'd never used the words "rough" or "wild" sex, he shouted at a Post editor, demanding to know why the words had appeared in quotes and been attributed to him. The editor tried to calm him down. "My headline writer just took a bit of literary license," he said.

Litman wasn't assuaged. The grand jury was about to meet to decide whether or not to indict Robert, and he was afraid they might be nega-tively swayed by the newspaper stories. Moving fast, he filed a request that the grand jury not be allowed to read about the Chambers case while they were sitting. But if granted, what good would the request do?—even if the jurors didn't read *about* the case, how could they miss the headlines?

New York, perhaps more than any other city in America, was a town where headlines were inescapable. Every major corner had at least one newsstand, sometimes two, side streets had coin-operated newspaper ma-chines, and the subways were filled with riders clinging to poles with one hand and turning tabloid pages with the other.

Mickey McEntee entered the grand jury room and immediately became self-conscious. There were three tiers of jurors staring down at him, and the room was so quiet that he feared the sound of his own voice would startle him.

The quiet was unusual. He'd gone before grand juries often before. But he'd never encountered this kind of pervasive stillness. Probably it was because all the other times he'd been testifying about drug deals and the jurors couldn't have cared less. They'd sat there rifling through their newspapers while he faced them, or even taking little naps, their eyes closed and tiny snores coming out of their mouths. He wished this grand jury was a bit more like the ones he was used to. Not that he liked disrespect. But he sure didn't like the way the people out there looked ready to hang on his every word. Because he was worried about the words he was going to have to say. The words Robert had used and which he'd written down when he was taking his statement. Dick. Stick. Lick. How come so many of the words rhymed? And how was he ever going to be able to say them in front of those rows of neatly dressed middle-aged men and women?

It was the women who bothered him most, he decided. He could say Robert's words in front of men all right. But in front of *women*? When Steve Saracco, who was conducting the inquiry for the district attorney's office, started to question him, McEntee avoided the eyes of the women and, directing his gaze toward a handful of distant male faces, began edgily to deliver his testimony.

He got the words out. And he kept a straight face, too. Even though half the time he was talking he wanted to burst out laughing because the story was so preposterous. At the same time, it was crucial to be expressionless. "Chambers said that after Jennifer scratched him," he said, trying to keep his tone even, "they made up, and she licked his dick. Kissed it." The men he was staring at seemed mesmerized. "Then she hit his dick," he continued, his face a deadpan. "Whacked it with a stick."

Those were the hard parts for him. After he'd said those parts, he relaxed.

That wasn't the end of his ordeal, though. When he was finished testifying, the jurors were shown the crime scene photos, and, to McEntee's fury, one man snickered at them. Snickered and smiled to himself, as if Jennifer's naked body was turning him on. The jurors' questions were unbelievable, too. "Are there sticks in the park?" one man wanted to know, as if he'd never been in a park. "What did the panties look like?" another guy asked. "What style were they?"

What's he want me to say? McEntee wondered. Teeny-tiny? Lacy with a cotton crotch? This guy must be a panty freak. Shrugging his shoulders, he evaded the question. "White," he said. "White panties."

When he left the room, McEntee felt wrung out, and all he could think was thank God the public doesn't get to hear what goes on in grand jury proceedings.

While the grand jury was sitting, members of the Dorrian's set began to rally around Robert, who had been moved from his courthouse cell to Rikers Island. They worried about his treatment. "There's nothing we can do for Jennifer," said Nora Bray, in whose apartment Jennifer and Robert had made love. "We have to fight now for Robert's rights." They worried, too, about his accommodations. "I can't imagine Robert on Rikers," said Madelaine Hogue, the girl who had years ago dubbed him Romeo. "I can't imagine anyone I know there. Our world just doesn't go that far; it doesn't go east of First Avenue or north of Ninety-sixth Street."

At first Robert's supporters concentrated on praising him, telling one another what a great guy he was. How considerate. How generous. How slow to anger. But in a short while standing up for Robert took the form of putting down Jennifer, and hostile rumors about her began to circulate. She was wild, one Dorrian's regular said, so wild that her father used to lock her in a closet to control her. She was exhibitionistic, another remarked, so exhibitionistic that she'd posed for photographs in the nude, surrounded by a group of clothed boys. She was provocative, a third sniffed, so provocative that she'd carried handcuffs with her on dates. And several of the college-bound chic who had been at Dorrian's the night of the killing insisted that at least some of the marks that had been found on Jennifer's body—in particular the marks on her breasts that the police had termed bites—would prove to have been made not by Robert but by other boys with whom she'd indulged in fierce sexual play.

There was a wake for Jennifer on the evening the rumors began to fly. The Levin family and some of Jennifer's closest friends went to view her body at a West Side chapel and tried to console one another. But their efforts were hopeless. The coffin was open from the waist up, and although Jennifer was dressed prettily in a mint-green cardigan and her lips and face were painted to give her a semblance of life, her family and friends could see bruises through the thick mortician's makeup.

Steve Levin wore dark glasses to the wake. Perhaps he was trying to shield himself from the sight of Jennifer's mauled face, perhaps just to shield the rest of the family from his own tear-ravaged eyes, for he had been crying a lot. Indeed, he had been suffering in a new way today, suffering not only from the grief of losing his daughter but from the grief of reading about her in the newspapers. Later he would tell a reporter that having to read about her had been just about the worst experience he'd had since learning of her death, because reading about her had made him doubt his perceptions of his own child. In his perceptions Jennifer had been the kind of girl who'd had such a good self-image that she not only wouldn't have engaged in kinky sex but she wouldn't even have pursued a boy who didn't want to be with her. She'd have simply walked away. The press coverage made Jennifer sound altogether different and made him have to ask himself if he'd gotten things wrong, seen his daughter wrong, and the self-doubt was devastating.

The wake anguished Jennifer's friends. Betsy Shankin, who had served as go-between for Jennifer and Robert, shivered and screamed at the sight of the body. Margaret Trahill, who had gone to the party in East Hampton with Jennifer the weekend before she died, kept imagining that at any moment Jennifer might sit up and begin talking. If she did, Margaret thought, Jennifer would say, Get this ugly sweater and this horrible lipstick off me! Because Jennifer had had wonderful taste. She'd never have worn such an awful sweater or that hideous lipstick. But the worst thing for Margaret was seeing Jennifer's swollen eye. It made her realize that the story Robert had told about not laying a hand on her except for his sudden accidental choke hold couldn't be true. Jennifer's eye looked as if it had been socked.

When she got home from the wake, Margaret called up Nora Bray, who'd been quoted in the newspapers about getting their set together to fight for Robert now, and she screamed at Nora in language she blushed to recall. "You bitch," she screamed. "You cunt!"

Julia Zapata, the Colombian cook who had years ago longed to be Phyllis Chambers, had been thinking all day about calling her, but she hadn't known what to say. At last she picked up the phone and made the effort anyway. It was a terrible experience. Phyllis sounded agitated and kept saying she didn't know how she would be able to get through her calamity.

"You have to accept it," Julia soothed. "You cannot stop it. It's like the water when it's a storm. You just have to hold on and take one day at a time."

"I can't. I can't."

"You have to. And you have to count your blessings. The other parents, the girl's parents, it's worse for them. Their child is dead."

"God give them peace," Phyllis said. "Give us all peace." Then she started to cry.

Julia tried to comfort her. "You're lucky," she said. "You're lucky. Those other parents, their child is dead. But you're lucky. You have your boy alive."

"I suppose so," Phyllis said. "I suppose so."

Litman was gloomy that night. He'd sent his own pathologist over to the ME's office to examine Jennifer's body, and his pathologist had confirmed what the district attorney's office was claiming: There were other marks on the girl besides strangulation marks. When the phone rang and a reporter he knew told him she was thinking about writing a magazine article on the case, Litman couldn't keep despondency out of his voice. "Getting this one off on manslaughter will be a triumph," he said.

Then he became gloomier still. "I might even lose," he murmured. "I hate to lose."

In the morning there were funeral services for Jennifer. Eight hundred people attended. "Jennifer would enter a room and your heart would leap at the sight of her," her uncle, Dan Levin, said in a heartfelt eulogy. "She was passionately alive and she had style. Her only flaw was that she was too innocent. She never had any idea that anyone could hurt you." Then he exhorted the mourners to think of one of Jennifer's many qualities—something that would not only remind them of her but help them to lead their own lives better—and treasure it. Some of her friends took Jennifer's vitality as the quality they would treasure. Some took her humor. Some her warmth.

Sasha Forsythe, a classmate from Baldwin, took Jennifer's risk-taking. Jennifer had always been daring, Sasha remembered. But that wasn't a bad thing. It was a sign of her courage. Something she herself had always wanted more of in order to lead her life well.

The funeral was weird, Brock Pernice thought afterward. The weirdest event of his life.

He had been supposed to read some of Jennifer's poetry from the podium. But when he got up to the front of the crowded chapel, he realized that many of the people facing him had hardly known Jennifer, had just run into her at Dorrian's a couple of times. *They're just here because they* want to see and be seen, he thought resentfully. This funeral is just based on the Dorrian's scene.

After that he couldn't speak. And he didn't read the poetry.

But he felt better after the burial. On the way back from the cemetery he went to a restaurant with Edwina and William and Alexandra LaGatta. They talked and laughed and felt very close. It reminded him of *The Big Chill.*

Leilia Van Baker went to another restaurant with another group of friends, and there she kept thinking of how wonderful Jennifer had been and trying to make sense of what had happened to her. She didn't feel guilty about having introduced Jennifer to Robert. Who could have anticipated the relationship would end this way? But why had it ended this way? What had really happened?

"I don't trust Robert's story," Leilia said to her friends. "Jennifer would never have had sex in the park. Fooled around, yes. No big deal. But nothing more. No, knowing Robert, something else must have happened."

"But what?" one of Leilia's friends said.

"I figure he wanted more. And she went, like no. And he went, What do you mean, no? And he was probably buzzed from alcohol. Or high on something. And he had this rage. Because he'd just been dumped by his girlfriend and here he was, getting nothing."

The scenario sounded right to her, and the more she talked about it the more Leilia felt rage building inside herself. That bastard, she seethed about Robert. He murdered one of the greatest friends I ever had. And one of these days I'm going to let him know that I know he's a murderer.

All over the city and its environs that Labor Day weekend, the death of Jennifer Levin was on people's lips; and many people, men and women alike, seemed to be blaming the girl for her own death. "She was wild," a guest at an East Hampton party told her friends. "My kids knew her, and you should hear the things they say about her."

"Believe it," a man chimed in. "She was into S and M. That's why she tied this guy up and tortured him."

A third guest was skeptical. "The guy *says* he was tied up. Does that mean it's what actually happened."

"Sure it does," the woman whose kids had known Jennifer said. "Who could make up a story like that?"

"But she had bruises," the skeptic pointed out. "Bruises all over her."

"Because they were having rough sex," an authoritative fourth guest said. He was certain Robert's story was true, certain that today's young people were capable of any sort of depravity. "That's what's so astonishing about all this," he went on, a hint of envy in his voice. "The way kids today are doing things we never even dreamed of doing when we were their age. And right out in the open. In the park!"

What was Robert feeling? It was difficult to know. He was tucked away on Rikers Island, where he saw only his parents and a few priests and, abiding by Litman's instructions, was giving no interviews to the press.

But on the Tuesday after Labor Day weekend, while the grand jury was still considering whether to indict him, and if so for what, a young *New York Post* reporter named David Colby managed to trick him into breaking his silence. Pretending to be a close friend and not a journalist, the preppie-looking Colby gained admission to his presence and asked him how he was.

"I'm really strung out," Robert said. "I'm dazed and confused about everything. And I can't believe Jennifer isn't alive."

The room was empty, but through a high-up window guards and doctors sat peering down at the two young men. "I liked Jennifer," Robert went on. "I liked her very much."

"Tell me your side of the story," Colby suggested. "I'll get it into the paper."

"I'm completely innocent," Robert said. "It was a total accident."

Colby believed him. He sounded so sincere, so trustworthy. But he also sounded disconsolate, depressed. During their forty-five-minute interview he rarely raised his voice above a low monotone.

"Tell me about your life here," Colby pressed him.

"It isn't so bad," Robert said. "The guards treat me okay. And I get to shoot baskets. And to lay on my bunk and think about my future."

HOPES AND PRAYERS

On September 10, two weeks after Jennifer died, Robert was indicted on two different counts of murder. One was intentional murder. The other was murder committed "under circumstances evincing a depraved indifference to human life."

Manhattan's district attorney, Robert M. Morgenthau, was pleased by the indictment. But two days later the man who had won it, Steve Saracco, was asked to step down from the Chambers case. There could be problems at the trial if he stayed on, Saracco's supervisor told him. "Litman might make a motion to have you removed. Because of some of the things you said on the videotape."

Saracco was ticked off. He'd expressed himself strongly on videotapes often before, and not once had he had to be removed from a case as a result of doing so. Besides, Litman might *not* make the motion his supervisor was talking about. "Let's give it a couple of weeks," Saracco suggested. "See what Litman's going to do."

But his supervisor just shook his head. "Linda Fairstein's taking over."

Saracco wasn't surprised. All afternoon he'd been hearing rumors that the thirty-nine-year-old Fairstein, head of the office's Sex Crimes Unit, might be getting Chambers. People were saying she'd been lobbying for the case—she and the man she was dating, Justin Feldman. Feldman, who was nearly thirty years older than the chief of the Sex Crimes Unit, was not only a prominent lawyer but a close friend of both the mayor and the district attorney.

"Strictly a business decision," Saracco's supervisor told him. "Politics has nothing to do with it."

Linda Fairstein was exceedingly happy to get Chambers. For one thing, she'd never yet tried a homicide. For another, Chambers promised to be a high publicity case, and she enjoyed being in the limelight.

The press, in its turn, enjoyed putting her there. She was glamorous, a tall, statuesque woman who dressed stylishly, had thick, flowing blond hair, and wore four-inch heels to court. She was also witty and more open than many of her colleagues—an ADA who liked to joke with reporters and who was willing to tell her side of a story not just with cold facts but with color and anecdote.

She had been in the DA's office since the early 1970s. In those days there had been an unofficial quota of one female assistant DA per year, and the man who had hired her, then District Attorney Frank Hogan, had tried to discourage her from applying, saying the job was "too tawdry" for a woman. In those days when a female assistant tried a case, the men in the office used to run down to watch her as if they wanted nothing more than to see her fall flat on her face, and Fairstein had had to struggle to get any sort of trial work. But she hadn't let the chauvinism that plagued the office back then get her down. She kept on plugging and eventually made her mark: prosecuted some thirty rape cases and lost only two. Earned a reputation for having an almost uncanny ability to communicate to juries the sufferings of victims. Lived down the day a supervisor had reprimanded her for crying over a case, telling her, "Why don't you just go throw up like a man." Won the respect of the police. On a wall in her office hung her proud proof: a plaque from the men of Midtown North. The plaque cited her legal boldness and displayed two halved walnut shells, the symbolic embodiment of what the cops were honoring her for: "A Pair of Balls."

Still, she didn't feel very ballsy the afternoon Morgenthau told her she could have Chambers. Start right away, he'd said. The Levin family is coming in shortly for their first meeting.

Fairstein panicked. Couldn't she have time to prepare? No—and an hour or two later the family arrived. There were so many of them. Jennifer's mother, father, stepmother, sister, and brother-in-law. It made Fairstein nervous just seeing them pile into her tiny cluttered office. But she made room, found them chairs, and began talking to them. "I want you to know that your daughter didn't just die," she said. "She fought for her life. There's evidence all over her body."

She'd meant to make them feel better. But they looked at her with such drawn and desperate faces that she feared she had said the wrong thing and for a moment was sorry she'd taken the case. After all, it was living victims that she was used to. She knew how to comfort them, and giving comfort was something she valued. Perhaps it had to do with her father's having been a doctor, and her mother a nurse. Whatever the reason, she was a nurturer. That's why she often took calls from her rape-victim clients on weekends or even in the middle of the night, when memories of their traumas kept them from sleeping. Giving comfort to the Levins was going to be a more complicated matter.

In her crowded office, her desk piled high with papers, her aged file cabinets looming like metal monsters waiting to be fed with fat files, she couldn't figure out what to say to make the family feel better. Other worries began to haunt her, too. She suspected the family had already been told this was her first homicide case, and that they doubted her abilities. She suspected, besides, that Jennifer's father was a controlling person—he was doing most of the talking for the family—and that he mightn't relinquish control to her, let her make the decisions. Her worries made her lose her usual poise, and she found herself playing with her hair, gesticulating wildly with her hands, and talking a blue streak.

But despite the blue streak, she didn't tell the Levins everything she knew. She didn't tell them, when they complained that the press was making Jennifer sound wild, that if the case came to trial there might be much worse in store for them. There'd be time enough for that later. And she didn't tell them all the police had already discovered about Jennifer's activities on the night she was killed. She got the feeling they didn't want to know. But she did mention warningly that Jack Litman was a formidable opponent.

She knew him well. He'd been the brightest light in the Homicide Bureau when she'd first joined the DA's office, and he'd once asked to have her second-seat him at a celebrated murder trial involving a cop who'd killed a prostitute. She'd been flattered, and even though the old boss had scotched the arrangement, saying a female prosecutor had no business handling a prostitute's death, she and Litman had become buddies. They'd had a lot in common, not the least of which was the fact that the man Fairstein was seeing at the time—André Surmain, the former owner of the restaurant Lutèce—was, like Litman's wife, French. The four of them had found pleasure in one another's company and shared any number of Lupercalian dinners together. But even when the French connection was over, once Fairstein had broken up with Surmain and starting dating Feldman, she and Litman had remained good friends.

The friendship with Litman would have to go, Fairstein decided shortly after the Levins left. When Litman tried a case, he left no stone unturned. And if he was going to turn up stones and search beneath them to expose all he could of Jennifer's past, she wanted no part of him. She couldn't bear the thought of seeing the drawn-faced family that had sat opposite her become any more stunned and miserable than they already were.

John Cotter met with Jennifer's grandfather, Arnold Domenitz, that week. Newsday had run the first column to state unequivocally that Robert's story was just that. A story. And the columnist, Pulitzer prize-winner Murray Kempton, had even indicted the police for leaking Robert's story to the press. They'd done it, Kempton had suggested in his usual eloquent style, because they were male chauvinists, "entrapped in our too-common assumption that these days no girl is virtuous." Jennifer's grandfather had felt grateful to Newsday after Kempton's column and allowed one of the paper's reporters to interview him. Cotter had been overjoyed. Newsday was new on the Manhattan press scene. It was fighting for readers, battling the two other tabloids in an out-and-out newpaper war. And with the Domenitz interview, the paper had gotten a leg up. Now, if he could persuade Domenitz to go on talking, Newsday might keep climbing.

At the grandfather's office—Domenitz was an insurance agent with New York Life—Cotter urged Domenitz to keep the lines of communication open. "Tell your story," he said. "If you do, you can beat this guy Litman. Because public sympathy will be with you. But otherwise, Litman will wipe the floor with you."

Domenitz said he didn't want to give *Newsday* another interview. He'd been advised by a lawyer to stop talking to the press. Some lawyer, Cotter thought, who didn't know the way things worked.

He was disappointed. Levin-Chambers was the biggest, juiciest story to have hit New York in years. In fact, he couldn't remember a bigger one. The story had been on the front page of the tabloids day after day, and had even appeared twice on the front page of the one paper that generally didn't treat murder up front—the *New York Times*.

Why had Robert strangled Jennifer? Even after she'd been working on the case for several days, the motive eluded Linda Fairstein. But the motive might reveal itself later, she thought. For the present what she needed to do was become an expert on strangulation, even the kind that was supposed to enhance sexual pleasure, for it was possible that Litman might decide to abandon Robert's accident story and claim instead that Jennifer's strangulation had been part of the couple's sex play.

Fairstein had first learned about erotic strangulation from some of her rape victims. He put me to sleep, they'd say. At first she'd thought the victims meant that the men had drugged them. But she'd come to understand that they meant that their partners had used on them what forensic specialists called "the carotid sleeper"—applied pressure to their carotid arteries just as they were on the verge of orgasm. The pressure, which caused dizziness and even blackouts, was supposed to induce a sexual climax that went beyond the natural euphoria and feeling of blacking out that accompanies orgasm.

The practice had grown more widespread in recent years. And it could kill. It had killed a Manhattan homosexual whose partner had insisted he'd been begged to try the sleeper. It had killed a Westchester boy who had strangled himself during masturbation.

By her second weekend on the case, Fairstein had digested all the technical material on the carotid sleeper that was available at the New York Academy of Medicine. But she was curious to see what young people like Robert and Jennifer might have known about it. After dinner in a restaurant with Feldman, she went with him to a popular bookstore and began combing the shelves.

She saw nothing and realized she'd have to ask the clerk. Embarrassment flooded her. She couldn't speak up. Not even with all her years of handling the most sordid and hideous sex crimes. She stopped silent in her tracks.

Feldman came to her rescue. "Do you have anything on sexual strangulation?" he murmured to the clerk.

The clerk shook his head and glanced at Fairstein worriedly.

"You get a choice. You can use the regular wheel or the 'P' wheel," Judge George Roberts said on the day that Litman and Fairstein came to have their trial judge selected. Roberts was no great believer in the wheels, which contained the names of available judges and, working on the same principle as a lottery drum, ensured that justice was selected at random.

Roberts didn't like the system, because not all judges were suited to all cases. Some trials were simple. Others were long and complex. To pull a judge's name out of a hat—or in this case a wheel—could throw the courts into utter confusion, could put a judicial monkey at the controls of a legal moon shot.

Of course, the court's administrators had recognized this, too. That's why there were two wheels. The regular wheel, which had the names of geniuses and lamebrains alike, and the "P" wheel, named for the fact that the judges in it were skilled at handling protracted trials. Lawyers with complex cases were urged to use the "P" wheel.

Roberts proposed to Litman that he use it. But Litman shook his head. The judges in the "P" wheel were formidable. Hammers who socked defendants with stiff sentences. Stones who were inured to courtroom razzle-dazzle. "The regular wheel," he said.

Roberts let him have it. He spun the wooden box, pulled out a name, and it was Judge Howard E. Bell, a black judge held in disdain by some of the men and women with whom he worked. Ding-Dong Bell, he was called behind his back.

Judge Jeffrey Atlas, who had helped set up the wheel system, was in his courtroom when, about twenty minutes after Judge Bell's name had been drawn, Litman and Fairstein came barging toward his bench. Atlas got a knot in his stomach. Could he have been selected for Chambers? Well, if he had been, it would make the court reporters happy, even if it gave him a stomachache. His court reporters loved a big trial. The minute they heard he was on one, they started seeing the cash registers going, started dreaming about all the movie producers who would be asking to buy extra copies of the trial record. At three dollars a page, a big trial could net these guys fifty grand or more.

Alas, his court reporters were going to be disappointed. Bell had been chosen as the trial judge, Fairstein and Litman said. But if that was the case, why were they here? Just to find out about Bell? "Bell's a very nice man," Atlas told the two lawyers. "A very gentle man."

They shrugged and asked if they could speak to him in private. He led them into his jury room. And there they astonished him. They asked, "Would you consider taking the Chambers case?"

"I'm not going to break the rules I helped create." Atlas was getting irritable.

Litman did most of the talking. "We can understand your reluctance," he said. "You're worried how it might affect your relationship with your colleagues."

"I'm not talking about jealousy," Atlas snapped. "I'm talking about principle."

But Litman went on arguing. "Suppose Mr. Morgenthau spoke to the administrative judge? Then would you take it?"

Atlas was tempted. Of course it was flattering to know he was wanted. And Chambers was going to be a big, juicy case. But he conquered the temptation, kept on saying no. Bell's name had come out of the wheel, and it was Bell who should try the case no matter what the two lawyers thought or felt.

•   •   •

Judge Howard E. Bell had no idea about the lawyers' reaction. Even if he had known, it probably would have made no difference to him. He was a man who had long ago learned that life was heavy with rejections and hardships.

Bell had been born some sixty years ago in segregated Norfolk, Virginia. He'd been the youngest of six children. His mother had had only a high school education. His father had quit school after the third grade. The prospect of Bell's becoming an educated man, let alone a judge, was remote indeed when he was a boy. But the Bell family, despite lack of schooling, placed great emphasis on education and encouraged Bell to do the same. He still felt grateful to his parents for that. To his father in particular. The old man—who had made his living as a building contractor—had taught himself to read by buying a nine-volume set of books called *The History of the World* and devouring every single word in the set. When his father died, Bell wanted those books more than anything in the world, but the family house caught on fire. The books went up in smoke.

Pushed by his parents, Bell went to Virginia Union University in Richmond. And while he didn't feel he'd gotten the best schooling in the world—to this day he often made self-deprecatory remarks about his knowledge and ability to comprehend complexities—he'd learned enough by the time he was nearly through college to realize he was capable of law school. So he'd come north and gone to Brooklyn Law.

It was during his law school years that he'd faced some of his most painful rebuffs and difficulties. And learned at firsthand that racism wasn't restricted to the South. In order to keep body and soul together while studying law in Brooklyn, he tried to find a decent-paying part-time clerical job. Every night before he went to sleep in his tiny room in Harlem's YMCA, he read the want ads in the *New York Times*, and every morning he got up at the crack of dawn and visited the employment agencies that had placed the ads. But no matter how early he arrived, the jobs he applied for were already filled.

New York had a Fair Employment Practices code, so the employment agents he spoke with were polite and gave him lengthy applications to fill out. But they didn't send him out on interviews. And sometimes they told him, Howard, if you'll take a dishwasher's job, we can accommodate you.

Ultimately, however, he found work. Not in a white company, of course. The NAACP hired him as a mail clerk. In their offices he met men like Roy Wilkins and Walter White, Thurgood Marshall and W. E. B. DuBois. Giants: men he would never forget and whose achievements filled him with awe. Inspired by their examples, he eventually made it through law school, worked for the city's Housing and Redevelopment Board, made political connections, got appointed to the Civil Court, and ultimately was elected to the State Supreme Court.

But even by the time he was selected to try the Chambers case, he still knew what it was like to be scorned. One day just a few weeks earlier he had boarded a Central Park West bus, his eggshellcolored fedora tilted nattily over his forehead and a sleek black umbrella tucked under his arm, only to hear the driver slam on the brakes and see two police officers scrambling up the bus steps. There must be a thief on the bus, he'd thought, and then suddenly one of the cops began pushing him toward the back of the vehicle and shouting at him to get off.

"Tell me what this is all about," he demanded as soon as he'd been herded off the bus.

"A woman across the street saw a man with a knife in his hand get on the bus," one of the cops said coldly. "A man wearing an eggshell-colored hat."

Bell grew indignant. "My umbrella," he said. "She must have thought the handle was a knife." Then he said, "I'm a Supreme Court justice."

The officers didn't believe him. "You got any identification?"

He had nearly blown up. But he'd realized the cops were within their rights to ask him for ID. He produced it, they were chagrined, and that was the end of the incident. Except for his anger. And his embarrassment. Those didn't go away. And he couldn't help thinking how ironic it was—not just that a Supreme Court justice had been dragged off a bus like a common thief, but that the man the police had gone for was the only person on the bus wearing a jacket and tie, let alone a hat.

• • •

By Wednesday, September 24, two days after Bell had been selected as trial judge, Litman and Fairstein were reconciled to the draw. They had made inquiries about Bell, learned that although he had many detractors he also had admirers, people in the judicial system who viewed him as fair and hardworking. And on that Wednesday they came before him for the first of hundreds of appearances—this time for a hearing on whether or not Robert should be granted bail.

Litman had prepared elaborately for the hearing. He had submitted to Bell a lengthy bail application motion and forty letters gathered by the Chamberses, attesting to Robert's character. Some of the letters were from friends of Robert's. A girl named Francesca Coloma wrote that Robert was "a sweet and sensitive young man. An example of his sensitivity is reflected in a conversation I had with him two weeks ago. He said he was very upset because he had just seen a man run over a cat. As he said this, he had tears in his eyes."

A girl named Nicole Breck wrote that Robert had always helped her with personal and family problems. "Twice he has waited outside my school for me in order to walk me to work because he knew otherwise I might have called in sick. I have called him repeatedly very late at night with certain problems. Not once has he told me to call back at a reasonable hour. He simply woke up and talked to me until I felt that everything was worked out."

Some of the letters were from friends of the Chambers family. John Dermont wrote somewhat frivolously that, "if possible, I would substitute myself for incarceration in Robert's stead should the court see fit to release him on any grounds pending court appearances."

Eve Murphy, the neighbor whose apartment Robert had agreed to paint during the summer, wrote that she had given him a set of keys to her place. "He was aware of my financial situation, knew where my stocks, bonds, credit cards, and sometimes large sums of money were kept," she remarked, but "at no time was anything missing from my apartment."

There were letters, too, from teachers who had known Robert when he was a boy at St. David's. He had been a "dream student" when he was in the seventh grade, wrote Michael A. Imbelli, his home-room teacher at the time, and "a first-rate photographer, skilled in the darkroom." "While at St. David's," wrote Frank Mahoney, who'd taught Robert in seventh and eighth grades, Robert "helped organize a fund drive at Thanksgiving to help the poor of a parish in Harlem." The school's headmaster, David D. Hume, wrote that Robert had been put in charge of the school's soda vending machine. "This required handling a reasonable amount of money," he explained, yet Robert had done so in an impeccably trustworthy fashion.

There were also letters from people who had known Robert when he was in the Knickerbocker Greys. Robert had had "a high Esprit de Corps," wrote the organization's former commandant, Thomas J. Hayes.

Robert had given him extra instruction in pivots and rifle maneuvers, wrote Daren Jaime, the first black member of the Greys.

Robert had asked to borrow her husband's tuxedo, wrote Elizabeth Kratovil, a former board member, and "not only returned the tuxedo promptly and in good shape, but also had thought to have it professionally cleaned."

In addition, there were letters from priests. Robert had often been "around collection money and altar wine," wrote Monsignor James Wilders, who had known him when he was an altar boy at St. Thomas More. Yet he'd "proved to be most trustworthy and reliable."

"I have always judged Robert to be a responsible person," wrote the Reverend Charles McDonald, assistant pastor of St. Anthony of Padua in Lancaster, Pennsylvania, and a cousin of Phyllis Chambers. "In November 1985 I was in town for a few days and was willing to let him use my car. . . . He said, 'Thanks anyway, Father Charlie, but I'd rather have things like that on my own head.'"

Above all, there was a letter from Theodore E. McCarrick, the archbishop of Newark. Robert possessed "a true respect for his neighbor and an unwillingness to cause pain," he wrote, and expressed the hope that the court would find his letter of recommendation helpful.

McCarrick was a heavy gun. It wasn't often that a judge received a letter from such a high dignitary as an archbishop. Bell was impressed. "When I receive letters from a person of that stature," he announced at the bail hearing, "I do give them consideration. It's hard for me to believe that an archbishop may not know what he's talking about."

Litman, princely in a European-tailored suit, leaned back in his chair, a small smile playing about his lips. He had packed his side of the courtroom with friends and relatives of Robert's, including a priest in full clerical garb and, for ethnic balance, two dark-skinned young men who had known Robert in the Greys. The priest was Monsignor Leonard, who had taught him religion when he'd been in the second grade. Litman had personally supervised the monsignor's seating, placing him in a front row alongside one of the black youths, and he had proposed to Bell that if he granted bail the kindly-looking priest would make himself personally responsible for Robert's future court appearances. Bell seemed interested in the idea.

Fairstein was ardently opposed to it. As far as she was concerned, Robert was bad news. She'd been checking into his background, and she'd discovered he'd been a longtime drug user and petty thief. She'd also discovered that the police file on the burglaries he'd committed with David Fillyaw was still open—and that since his having been booked and fingerprinted for killing Jennifer, sufficient evidence to indict him for the burglaries had turned up. One of his fingerprints matched a print that had been lifted at one of the buglarized apartments. "Robert Chambers is a thug and a murderer," she declared. And she said that she strongly suspected that many of the letter-writers didn't know Robert well, or hadn't town him since he was a boy.

Bell listened to her arguments. But he kept coming back to the archbishop's letter. "Of course, we all can make mistakes," he said, musing over the document. "When letters like this one from the archbishop come in, you read and you say, 'Does he really know the man he's writing about?'"

"Your Honor," Fairstein called out. "I'd like to ask the archbishop the same question."

Bell told her he'd give her until Monday. But, he said, "As of this moment, I'm inclined to grant bail."

•   •   •

Fairstein wanted to fly out of the courtroom to get to the archbishop before Litman did. But her progress down the crowded aisle was impeded by her rapier-like high heels, and for a moment she cursed the vanity that had made her wear them. Remembered how her father, whom she had adored above all men until his death the year before, used to tease her about her footgear and tell her, "Linda, sometimes I think you've got more shoes than you've got brains." But she put the memory out of her mind and pushed her way forward. And in what seemed like only seconds she was at her desk and on the phone. "May I speak to the archbishop?" she was saying to a secretary at the archdiocese in Newark.

"He's in a meeting," the secretary said.

"Can you get him out of the meeting?" Fairstein asked. "It's important."

"I'll try." The secretary put the phone on hold and disappeared. Two minutes later she was back on the wire. "I can't find him," she said.

Fairstein was annoyed. "I thought you said he was at a meeting."

"He is," the secretary replied testily. "But it's somewhere in this building, and I don't know where."

Fairstein didn't hear from the archbishop until several hours later, and then only in a message. The archbishop knew about Robert's drug use and the burglary charges, the message said, and his position hadn't changed.

Litman got to him first, Fairstein was sure. She was descendent.

Still, she kept after the archbishop, called him first thing the next morning and insisted on speaking with him in person. She got him. He told her that he hadn't seen Robert in three or four years, except for the day of his installation in July.

Just as she'd suspected. "At your installation?" she asked. "When there were hundreds of other people around?"

"Yes," said the archbishop. But he still refused to withdraw his support of Robert and his statement that the boy had "a true respect for his neighbor."

It was a difficult weekend for Bell. On Monday he would have to deliver a decision about Robert's bail, and he knew that whichever way he ruled he risked making himself vastly unpopular. The eyes of the city were upon the Chambers case. On Sunday he sought strength from God, going to the Bethel African Methodist Episcopal Church on 132nd Street in Harlem where he always worshipped and where for many years he had been a trustee. He went upstairs to the gallery where he always sat. It had been in the gallery of a Methodist church in Philadelphia that the idea of the African Methodist Church had been born over a hundred and fifty years ago. The founder, Richard Allen, had helped renovate the church in Philadelphia, but when the work was done and he came to services, an usher made him leave the church proper and go upstairs. He did, but even in the balcony they wouldn't let a black man worship. As soon as he knelt down, another usher told him he couldn't pray there. It didn't matter that he'd built the gallery they were in. Allen had left the white men's Methodist church and in a little blacksmith's shop had started the A.M.E.C.

Perhaps it was to commemorate Allen that Bell always chose to sit in the gallery. Or perhaps it was just because, as he told worshippers who asked him why he bothered climbing the stairs, "Upstairs is where religion is." Whatever the reason, he was sitting in his familiar upstairs pew when the minister, an old friend of his, told the congregation in a booming voice, "When you come to the altar this morning, I want you to mention someone's name in your prayers. He's a very religious man. He comes from a deeply religious family. He's got trouble and needs your prayers."

Bell hook his head. Poor man. Who was he? And what were his troubles? Then suddenly the minister boomed, "The man is Howard Bell. How many of you know his name?"

Two-thirds of the congregants' hands went up.

"Don't worry," the minister said. "Nothing's happened to him. He hasn't done anything bad. But he's involved in a very difficult case, and he has some hard decisions to make. I want you all to pray for him."

That night Bell called the minister to thank him for the prayers.

"I hope I didn't embarrass you, Howard," the minister said. "I don't know why I did that, except that I woke up in the middle of the night last night thinking about you, and I just wanted to pray for you."

Bell reassured him. "It was fine. Who doesn't need prayers?"

. . .

There were prayers for Robert that weekend, too. On the East Side of Manhattan a Catholic charismatic church at which Phyllis had sometimes worshipped held a candlelight vigil, and across the river the pastor of the nondenominational Brooklyn Tabernacle Church directed his congregation to beseech God to help Robert. The pastor had read about Robert in the papers, where he often learned about people who needed God's help. And he'd said to himself, Let's pray for this young boy in trouble. We have a lot of young people in our congregation.

On Monday morning, over Fairstein's continued objections, Bell granted Robert bail, setting the sum at $150,000 and making his second-grade religion teacher responsible for his court appearances. "Monsignor Leonard must know where you are at all times," he said. "You must report to him."

Litman jumped to his feet. "The bail is too high," he began arguing. "I'm not even sure the family can come up with it."

Jack Dorrian visited Phyllis at her apartment the next afternoon. He found her crying. "I don't have enough money," she said. "For the bail."

Dorrian felt sorry for her. He couldn't help picturing what it would be like to have his own two sons in trouble the way hers was.

He knew a bit about jail. Back in the 1970s he'd been falsely accused of possessing stolen merchandise certificates from Gimbels and using them to make a purchase. He'd been tried and acquitted, but before he was cleared he'd spent a night in the Tombs. They'd put him in a room with maybe a hundred people standing up. You couldn't sit down. There was no toilet paper. There were flies and cockroaches. And there was one big

animal there. The guard. A kid gave the guard five dollars to get him
cigarettes, but when he asked for his cigarettes the guard said, "What five
dollars?" Dorrian had felt like a creep when he got out of there, overcome
by disgust for mankind.

Maybe it was that experience that made him decide that afternoon to
help Robert out. Or maybe it was just Phyllis Chambers's tears. Whatever
the reason, by the time he left her apartment he'd decided to put up his
$600,000 East Side town house as partial collateral for the bail.

That night he telephoned Steve Levin to prepare him for the news.
He'd offer his condolences, too, he planned. Tell Levin that death is really
just a continuation of life and that everyone has to go over that way sometime. Most religions saw death that way, he'd say. Judaism. Catholicism.
Whatever. We're all just preparing to see God later on.

But he didn't get to deliver his philosophical ruminations. Levin cut
the conversation off as soon as he heard about the bail.

Robert was at Litman's office, where he'd just given a press conference.
"Get him and his folks out of here," Litman told Roger Stavis right after
the conference. "And don't let the media see where you're taking them.
They need some private time before Robert goes to Monsignor Leonard's
rectory."

Stavis got Robert and his parents down to the building's garage and
into his car without their being observed by the press. But as soon as he
pulled the car onto the street, he saw camera lights flashing. He threw a
blanket over Robert's head, told him to slump down, and sped the car
through the crowd. But a moment later he realized he was being tailed. A
TV van was right behind him.

Stavis was confident he could shake them. He'd take the FDR Drive,
get a few car lengths in front of them, and that would be that. His mind
made up, he sailed onto the drive and immediately swerved and changed
lanes. It didn't help. The van was still behind him.

Had his passengers noticed? Not yet probably. "Now don't you worry," he said. "It's just I'm in a hurry," and he changed lanes again.

He wasn't a very brave driver. His friends teased him about his caution, called him Mr. Safe. But now he stepped on the gas and zigzagged crazily from lane to lane. His new boldness paid off. The van fell behind. But then it zoomed right up behind him again.

All right, I'll fix 'em. I'll get off the drive and I'll head to Queens, Stavis decided. They'll never be able to find me there, because I know Queens like the back of my hand and Queens doesn't exist for the media. These guys have probably never been to Queens once in their whole lives.

He followed his plan, gunning across the Queensboro Bridge, and with the van still hot on his trail suddenly swerved to the right at the Long Island City exit. Did it!

Off the exit, he turned down a deserted street, made a quick turn onto another, and, heart pounding, pulled the car over. There was no one behind him. Whooping with pleasure, he turned off the lights and parked.

"I don't think they'll find us here," he said to the Chamberses.

He stayed where he was for fifteen minutes. Then he drove the family to a nearby Italian restaurant. He was as excited by winning the car chase as he'd ever been about winning a legal battle.

At the restaurant he communicated his excitement to Litman over the telephone. "Bet you didn't know when you hired me that you were hiring a wheelman, didja?" he said exuberantly.

Litman had no time for small talk. "The press is swarming around Monsignor Leonard's church," he said. "You can't take Robert there. We've got to find someplace else."

Monsignor Wilders, Phyllis's old friend from the church of St. Thomas More, found a church-run home in Brooklyn in which Robert could stay until the coast was clear at Leonard's rectory. Wilders had been helpful to Robert's cause in another way, too. He had given the family $21,000 of his personal savings for bail money. He considered doing so an act of mercy. Hadn't the Lord said, "Come you, blessed of my Father, inherit the kingdom prepared for you since the foundation of the world because I was hungry and you gave me to eat, I was thirsty and you gave me to drink, I was sick and you came to see me, I was in prison and you visited me."

Besides, he believed Robert's story, believed that, although the sex Robert had described having with Jennifer was sordid and shocking, it was a mutually agreed upon activity. The kind of thing that kids today did, because kids today were always after new thrills.

The problem with Kids today was, parents didn't discipline them. Not properly, not the way they did when he was a youngster. Take his mother. When he was growing up in the north Bronx, he and his brother used to play stickball in the street before dinner and one night they dawdled and their mother came to the door and called out, "You better come home, it's six o'clock, time for dinner," and his brother called out, "Wait, I have to get my licks," and his mother said, "If you don't get in here in one second you'll really be getting your licks."

That's what parents were like in the old days. They gave discipline. And kids respected them for it. Not anymore.

John Cardinal O'Connor, New York's highest prelate, wasn't altogether happy about the role some of his priests had played in getting Robert out of jail. It was true there was a Gospel basis for aiding prisoners. But Archbishop McCarrick and Monsignors Leonard and Wilders had received hate mail from Jews because of their activities on behalf of Robert. And the cardinal himself had received an angry letter from the Levin family— Jennifer's Jewish mother and father and her Catholic stepmother. In the cardinal's view, the priests' intercession had the potential for inflaming the city. It was being perceived as a move on the part of the Catholic Church to exert pressure on behalf of a Jew-killer.

A week after Robert was freed from jail, O'Connor attempted to avert incipient religious strife by anticipating it. "I am worried," he wrote in an open letter to a Catholic newsweekly. "I am worried that mercy toward a Catholic boy could be*perceived* as callousness toward a Jewish girl. I am worried that the Catholic 'Establishment' will be seen as rallying around its 'own,' seeming to protect and defend its own, while a Jewish girl lies dead and her family is shattered with grief. . . . I worry that some Catholics will fail to recognize the potential for resentment on the part of some Jews. I worry even more that some other Catholics will recognize the potential for resentment, but attribute it to Jewish 'paranoia.' Either reaction would be unfortunate."

Jack Litman was stunned by the cardinal's open letter. Why had he written it? he wondered. And why was he suggesting that the case might divide the city along religious lines? There was no such issue—but now there might be. He put the letter down with sadness and apprehension.

. . .

"People are going nuts," a Catholic reporter said to a Jewish colleague the day after the cardinal's letter appeared. "The radio stations have been getting calls all day saying Jewish girls are whores and the Catholic Church loves murderers."

"It's the cardinal's fault," the Jewish reporter said. "He shouldn't have mixed in."

"He was just trying to calm the waters," the Catholic reporter said.

"No. He stirred them up. Talking about 'Jewish paranoia.' I resent that 'Jewish paranoia.'"

"Maybe the Levins wrote him a paranoid letter," the Catholic reporter said. "Maybe they said the Church was being anti-Semitic."

"So he rebukes his priests?" The Jewish reporter whistled. "Now that's what I call *Catholic* paranoia."

District Attorney Robert M. Morgenthau wasn't known for his expansiveness. A reserved man, he found small talk tedious. But on the morning of

October 15 he held a press conference in his paneled, flag-draped office and engaged in a bit of banter with the reporters and camera people who were milling around him. "Don't get too carried away by what I'm going to tell you," he said. "Don't go rushing off for the phones. Because the phones are down. And no, it isn't because we haven't paid the bill."

The newspeople laughed, and he laughed too, a thin smile playing on his austere face. He was in good spirits. He was about to reveal that his office had just won the burglary indictment against Robert. The indictment would give his staff good leverage in Robert's murder trial. And it would go a long way toward molding public opinion about the so-called preppie. Litman would have a hard time passing Chambers off as an altar boy after this.

When the newspeople stopped jostling each other and jockeying for better positions, Morgenthau got down to business. He read them the indictment and explained that David Fillyaw, who was under indictment for attempted murder, was Chambers's co-defendant in the burglaries.

"Why'd it take a year to get this indictment?" a reporter asked.

"These are difficult cases to solve," Morgenthau said.

"How did you solve them? What evidence do you have?"

"I don't want to discuss the evidence," Morgenthau snapped. Then he relented. "Well, I'll tell you this," he said. "The media attention paid to Chambers for the killing of Jennifer Levin made some people more willing to cooperate in this investigation." He looked around the room and smiled his thin but happy smile again. "So I guess," he said, "that the press isn't so bad after all."

Pat Fillyaw was in a rotten mood that night. For hours the press had been ringing her up and banging on her door, trying to get her to talk to them about her son. How had he met Robert Chambers? they wanted to know. How close was their relationship?

She didn't tell them anything. Why should she? The press hadn't been the least bit interested in talking to her when David had been arrested for stabbing Sarah. They hadn't wanted to hear what it was like trying to raise a child drug-free in coke-ridden New York. They hadn't wanted to know that she'd sent David to private school or that once upon a time he'd been talented and full of promise. No, they'd simply called him an "ex-con" in their headlines, and implied that he hadn't been reared but just thrown up. Hatched. Well, now they could go to hell. They and that assistant district attorney Linda Fairstein, too. Pat had heard her quoted on the radio. She'd heard Linda Fairstein say David represented the evil side of Robert, or proved that he had an evil side.

That wasn't the way Pat looked at it. To her it was clear that Robert was the evil one. Because David hadn't blamed Sarah for making him stab her, the way Robert blamed Jennifer for making him kill her. It wasn't her son who'd said, "A girl hurt me, did nasty things to me, raped me, so I had to get her."

David had known better. He'd been raised better. He knew if he blamed the girl for what he'd done to her, his mother wouldn't have stuck by him the way Robert's mother was sticking by Robert. He'd known that if he said the kind of garbage Robert was saying, *his* mother would have cut him out of her life.

A week passed. And then another. The two lawyers buckled down to familiarizing themselves with the case, investigating witnesses, and inquiring about the lives that Robert and Jennifer had led. They were shocked by some of the things they discovered, appalled by the extent to which flippancy, promiscuity, and drugs marked the Dorrian's crowd. Litman blamed the crowd's problems on the tendency of upper-class parents to want to satisfy their offspring's every desire. "In this country," he told a French friend one night, "l'enfant est roi. But you know, when you're a king, you can also be abandoned."

Linda Fairstein was equally critical. She had talked to Jennifer's friends and found herself singularly unimpressed: there were girls who were giddy and given to hysteria, boys who were ignorant and arrogant. One had come down to see her and, trying to explain the atmosphere at Dorrian's, boasted that all the guys who hung out at the bar, himself included, were rich and good-looking, and consequently able to have sex with a different girl every night if they chose to do so. Then he'd asked her to reimburse his taxi fare and handed her a cab receipt from the week before. Trying to rip off the district attorney! "This kid, he's just like Chambers," she told a reporter privately. "Grows up with all the advantages life can afford. Goes to the fanciest schools. But what was he *taught?*"

Late that autumn Leilia Van Baker, who had been thinking steadily about Jennifer's last hours, at last telephoned Robert from Vermont to tell him what she thought of him. She dialed him at home and got his mother.

"Robert's not here," Phyllis said. "But I'll get your message to him."

Not long afterward Leilia's phone rang and she picked it up to hear Robert. At the sound of his voice, she got frightened. But she started speaking at once. "I want to know *why* you killed Jennifer," she said.

"Do you think I did it intentionally?" Robert asked.

"Damn right I do. You murdered her."

Robert said nothing for a while. Then he asked, "Why'd you call me then?"

Why had she? The whole idea seemed stupid now.

"Because we used to be friends," she said. "Because you once told me you wanted to come stay with me up here. Because I wanted you to know that I'm totally glad you're not here."

But somehow it wasn't enough, wasn't what she'd meant to say at all. She decided to end the conversation. Decided she'd never speak to him again. "Well, listen man," she said, "like, good luck, but I'm glad you're not in my life."

Over on Roosevelt Island, Pat Fillyaw was having second thoughts about the man she and her husband had hired to represent David. He was Alan Friess, a lawyer who had been a judge until he'd been barred from the bench for frivolous conduct, including deciding the length of a defendant's sentence by tossing a coin. Friess had been advising David to plead guilty to the various charges against him. And he'd persuaded Pat it was a good idea. But ever since Robert had received bail, she'd begun to have doubts. And recently she'd called the fiery black activist lawyer C. Vernon Mason for advice. He'd suggested letting Friess go and hiring a different lawyer. One who might take the case to trial. He knew of one such fellow, he said, and recommended him. He was smart and sharp. But very expensive.

"Maybe we should do it," Pat said to her husband.

"It'll cost," he said.

"I know. We're talking life savings."

"And the little one's college fund," her husband said, alluding to their younger son, who would be graduating high school next year. "Still, do it if you want. Take the money out of the bank. Take *all* the money."

Pat thought she would. And then she thought, No, better not. How could she risk the family's entire assets on what, according to Friess at any rate, was a terrible gamble. Sure, David *could* win a trial, he'd said. But he also could lose. Probably *would* lose. And if he loses, he'll go to jail for a helluva longer time than he will if he pleads.

She didn't want that to happen, and she decided to stick with Friess.

Marilei, agitated, scurried around Phyllis's apartment and laid out wine and sandwiches. Phyllis had invited a group of ladies to have lunch with her and get their fortunes told for twenty dollars a head.

A soothsayer was coming, and Marilei wasn't altogether sure she approved of soothsaying. Phyllis was clutching at straws, she fretted. She was looking for someone, something, anything that would make her feel good. Of course, she'd always been that way. Once, she'd even dragged Marilei off to some woman in Queens who diagnosed people's diseases by looking into their eyes and cured them by administering vitamins. But now Phyllis seemed even more needy than before. She was even con-

sidering worshipping at that Tabernacle Church where they'd prayed for
Robert. And her a good Catholic!

When the soothsayer arrived, Marilei went to have a look at him. He
didn't seem like a fortuneteller at all. He was a big man, and he was wearing a well-tailored expensive suit.

Phyllis's guests liked him. He told them wonderful, positive things.
Your future looks bright. You're going to have good luck. Your wishes will
come true.

He had spoken similarly to Phyllis, too, on another occasion. That's
why she'd asked him over. He'd told her that everything was going to be
all right, and that Robert was going to be a great and famous man. He
said the same sort of things to her today, too.

Downtown, about that time, Linda Fairstein hung up a picture of Robert
in her office. A Post photographer had snapped it while Robert was off
guard. It showed him leaving the place he was living in now—Monsignor
Leonard's rectory in Washington Heights—a gym bag over his shoulder,
a Walkman around his neck, and an open-mouthed smile stretching his
lips. No one who's killed someone else has the right to look this relaxed,
Fairstein steamed. She tacked up the photo and said to herself, I'm going
to look at this every day to remind me how unfair the world is, and I'm
going to keep it hanging here till I put this guy back in jail.

THE LONG WAIT

By the time they had been working hard on The People v. Robert Chambers for several weeks, both Litman and Fairstein were aware that their respective cases would not be easy to win. Fairstein knew by then that Litman wasn't going to introduce the idea that Jennifer had asked Robert to compress her neck in order to heighten her sexual pleasure. He was planning to stick by Robert's own explanation of what had happened—that he'd strangled Jennifer while reacting to pain. Not that that made Fairstein's job any easier. There were no witnesses to what had happened in the park so the only way to prove that Robert had intended to kill Jennifer would be to show, through medical testimony, that he'd choked her for enough time, whether minutes or seconds, to have considered his act and yet kept on with it.

Litman faced a similar yet altogether different task. To see Robert go free, he'd have to prove that Robert had held on to Jennifer's neck for only a few brief seconds.

The problem for both lawyers was that there was no absolute way to establish the amount of time Jennifer had been throttled. Even skilled medical experts were offering not proof but merely opinion. And in the

233

courtroom, Fairstein and Litman knew, one expert's opinion might easily cancel out another's.

The lawyers had other difficulties, too. Fairstein had no motive. Litman had no witnesses to verify Robert's contention that Jennifer was sexually aggressive either in the park or in general.

One morning in October, Litman decided to see if he could get Fairstein to reduce the charges against Robert to manslaughter. He stopped by her office and said briskly, "C'mon, you know this isn't a murder case!"

Fairstein didn't bite. She realized she was going to have a hard time proving murder, but she believed that in the end she would succeed. The pictures of Jennifer lying dead in the park gave her that feeling. Whenever she thought about them, she could see them in front of her. Jennifer's face puffy and smeared with dirt. Her breasts and her pubis left uncovered, disdained. Her neck blazing with scarlet bruises. She knew, whenever she thought about the pictures, that Robert had murdered Jennifer, and she was hopeful a jury would react the same way.

Litman was waging psychological warfare with her, Fairstein decided. Ignoring his remark, she changed the subject.

"Dear Ms. Fairstein," Litman wrote to his opponent on October 21. "Pursuant to Article 240 and Section 200.95 of the Criminal Procedure Law, we respectfully request that you make available to us . . . the following 'property' without which the defendant cannot adequately prepare or conduct his defense." He listed various items he wanted to see, including Jennifer's journal. The little black spiral book in which Jennifer had written, among other things, feverish descriptions of sexual activity, had been given to the police by Alexandra LaGatta the day they came to her apartment, and they'd turned it over to the district attorney's office.

Litman had heard tantalizing rumors about the book. He'd heard it mentioned Robert twice. He'd heard that some of its pages dwelled on sexual acts that were kinky and aggressive. And he'd heard that the journal contained a list of Jennifer's lovers, a list in which she'd rated sexual prowess, drawing erotic symbols next to the names and giving exceptional performers extra symbols, in the way that critics gave stars to exceptional restaurants and movies.

He needed the book, Litman had decided. It might give him just what he was missing—the names of men who could corroborate Robert's story that Jennifer was a sexually aggressive young woman. He was entitled to use the book to look for potential witnesses, he felt. Entitled, too, to examine whatever it was that Jennifer had written about his client.

"Dear Mr. Litman," Fairstein wrote to Litman about the journal on November 7. "The requested property is beyond the scope of discovery under C.P.L. Article 240."

Fairstein's playing games, Litman thought. She's the one who told me the sex acts in the journal were kinky and aggressive. He told Judge Bell this, and although he hadn't made his initial request for the book public, a week after receiving Fairstein's turn-down, he filed a copy of that request in court papers accessible to the press.

JENNIFER KEPT SEX DIARY: LAWYER, screamed the Post the next day. "SEX DIARY" KEPT BY JEN? said the News. And television news shows repeatedly referred to Jennifer's journal as a "sex diary."

Fairstein was annoyed. "There isn't a sex diary," she announced. "There is a school datebook, but nothing chronicling [Jennifer's] sex life." She denied ever having told Litman anything about what was in the book, and continued to refuse to let him see it.

A week before Thanksgiving she went out of town. The day after she did, her assistant, Tom Kendris, telephoned her and told her that Litman had grown even more importunate. He'd come to court and demanded that Judge Bell compel her to produce the journal. "That so?" she grinned. "Well, we don't even have the book anymore. I gave it back to Jennifer's father."

She was amused at Kendris's astonishment. And sure she'd made the right move. Now if Litman wanted the journal, he'd have to subpoena it from Steve Levin, and she knew the press well enough to know that if he went after the book from a grieving father he'd probably come off looking like a coldhearted monster. A male chauvinist, too, out to suggest that because a young woman had been sexually active she'd somehow been responsible for her own death.

Litman had suggested something similar to this in the Bonnie Garland case. He had introduced testimony about an affair Garland had had with a young man other than her killer, and afterward he had told an interviewer that he had purposely soiled Garland's reputation. "It was necessary to taint her a little bit," he'd said, "so the jury would not believe, as the parents wanted them to, that she was this ingenue who fell in love for the first time [with] this wily man." Many voices had protested Litman's tainting of Garland, and that trial in 1978 had been a milestone for a new social movement—the movement for victims' rights.

Although newspaper readers and television viewers are titillated by the idea of Jennifer's diary, Fairstein thought, public opinion will probably go against Litman for demanding it. And perhaps that will scare him into thinking twice before trying to use blame-the-victim tactics in the trial.

He had to see that diary, Litman decided two days before Thanksgiving. Had to see it no matter how bad going after it from Jennifer's father was going to make him look. He spoke with Fairstein that day and mentioned he was afraid Levin might alter or destroy the book. She told him not to worry. "Mr. Levin knows the diary may be the subject of court proceedings," she said.

"Did you copy it before you handed it over?" he asked.

"I Xeroxed the relevant pages," she answered. "Including those pages on which your client's name appears."

Relevant pages? That made him furious. If Fairstein had considered some of the material in the diary so relevant that she'd gone to the trouble of Xeroxing it, then he damn well was entitled to a read.

On Thanksgiving Eve he personally delivered a subpoena for the diary into the hands of Steve Levin's lawyer, Jeffrey Newman.

"Are you sure you want to do this?" Newman said as he accepted the paper.

"*Ein breirah,*" Litman said. "I've got no choice."

Thanksgiving weekend was a confusing time for Brock Pernice. He'd been up in Boston at college, but he'd come back to New York for the holiday, and a part of him almost expected to see Jennifer. As if she hadn't died. As if the past few months without her had been just another of the many times they'd broken up.

"What was it like being with her?" an inquisitive reporter asked him over lunch at Pinocchio's, an Italian restaurant a few blocks from Dorrian's, on the Friday after Thanksgiving.

Brock remembered many things, but one of them, he explained, was something that always made him sad. "I couldn't open up with her. At least I couldn't as much as she wanted me to."

"What was *she* like?"

"Terribly attractive. And very fun-loving," Brock said. But he also criticized her. "She was hyperactive. Always jumping around. Always getting mad about something. A handful."

He's angry at Jennifer for dying and thereby abandoning him, the reporter thought. But when she asked him about his final memories of Jennifer, she began to suspect there might be another reason: that Brock was angry at Jennifer for having hurt his pride by going out with Robert the night she got killed. "I'd gone away for the summer," he was reminiscing. "And we'd broken up. But just before she died, I'd come back. I saw her out on the island. We confessed our flings. We said we were going to see each other again." His face looked deeply puzzled, his voice sounded irritable. "I was back. Everything was good between us."

A friend of Brock's named Shane Keller was at the table and he, too, seemed to detect wounded pride in Brock's words. As if trying to comfort him, to let him know that no matter whom Jennifer had gone off with, he still thought of her as Brock's girl, Shane murmured, "Yeah, but if she hadn't died that night, if she'd just fooled around with Robert, you'd have found out. It would have been just one more time you two broke up. But then you'd have gotten together again."

Brock seemed soothed after that. He spoke more positively about Jennifer and implied that he might even have married her one day. "We could have solved our problems. Or the problems could have just gone away. People change. If I was ready to change, and to change her, I could have." Then he began speculating about what had really happened in the park. "Robert must have gone temporarily insane. He's got mental problems. The scene can give them to you."

"Yeah," Shane agreed. "Also, Robert kept a lot hidden. His robberies. His drugs." He shook his head. "I can just see Jennifer trying to get to know him. You know, trying to get him to open up with her, the way she always wanted people to do. With him having so much hidden, she could have made him really mad by trying to find things out."

Brock stared at him. And suddenly his slight body went rigid and he could no longer contain or mask his anger at Jennifer. "Why the hell," he said, "did she want to find out anything about that idiot!"

Mike Pearl, who covered the courts for the New York Post, was in Atlanta that weekend. Pearl was a legendary figure among New York journalists, a man who had reported on trials for so many years that he had developed an intricate network of sources and spies and could be counted upon to sniff out a story even before its principals realized they were involved in one. Shortly before the weekend, he had stumbled on a curious piece of information: the prosecution now had a theory about why Robert had murdered Jennifer. Robert, Pearl's informants told him, had been trying to rob Jennifer. The theory had been sparked by the long-ago observation of McEntee and other detectives when they first saw Jennifer's body that her earlobes seemed recently divested of earrings. And it had been augmented by photographs newly obtained by Linda Fairstein that showed Jennifer partying at Dorrian's shortly before she went with Robert to the park. In the photographs, her ears were alight with little fake diamonds.

Pearl hadn't filed the story. He'd held back, planning to check it out further, and gone south for his holiday. Ordinarily he wouldn't have dragged his feet. But who reads the papers over Thanksgiving weekend, he'd said to himself. Why waste a scoop?

Esther Pessin of United Press International was hungrier than Mike Pearl. She, too, had stumbled on the prosecution's theft theory just before the weekend, but she didn't sit on the information. She called Jennifer's grandfather, Arnold Domenitz, to check it out, weasled a confirmation out of him, and filed her story. By Friday night it was all over the airwaves.

• • •

Linda Fairstein was livid when she learned that the theft theory had leaked. She'd meant to produce it only at the trial. And she hadn't meant actually to *say* that robbery had been Robert's motive for killing. There'd be no way to prove such an assertion. For one thing, Jennifer's money and jewelry had never been found. For another, even if they had been, and even if by some remote chance they could be traced to Robert, he might not have killed her for them. He could have killed her and *then* decided to take her possessions. So what Fairstein had planned to do was just tease the suggestion of theft into the trial. Let the jury arrive at the idea on their own by looking at the photographs of Jennifer at Dorrian's. But now, she realized, she probably wouldn't be able to rely on the photographs. Litman would make a move to have them excluded, or at least ask to have them cropped so the earrings weren't visible.

She'd lost something big, Fairstein thought. But she didn't scold the Levins. She had become very fond of them in the months since she had first met them in her crowded office. And besides, the leakage hadn't exactly been their fault. She hadn't thought of warning them to keep her theft theory under their hats. Anyway, how could she be mad at the Levins? Especially right now when they were spending the weekend trying to decide what to do about the diary subpoena.

Shortly after the weekend, the Levins decided they would fight that subpoena. There was nothing in the diary relevant to the case, as they saw it, and besides, it would be obscene for the lawyer defending their daughter's killer to paw through her private, innermost thoughts. Early in December they petitioned Judge Bell to quash the diary subpoena.

At the rectory in Washington Heights, Monsignor Leonard was trying to reform Robert. One of his efforts involved seeing to it that Robert ate dinner with him and his fellow priests every night. Meals were the beginning of civility, Monsignor Leonard reasoned. In ancient days they signified alliances. If you ate with the liege lord, you were putting yourself in his hands and he was putting his hands around you. He owed you something after you dined with him, and you in turn owed him. That's what the manna in the desert in the Old Testament was all about. And what the Eucharist was about. These things symbolized an alliance between people and God.

But although Robert took his place at the dining-room table every night, chatting with the handful of priests who made their home in the rectory and dining on the same fare—concoctions whipped up by Leonard himself out of Pierre Franey's *Sixty-Minute Gourmet*—the young man didn't seem very different now from the Robert who'd first come to live at the rectory. He did the odd jobs he was assigned—a little painting here, a little carpentry there. And he did some reading about business, a topic he claimed to be very interested in. But he didn't exactly knock down the doors of the church trying to get in. Nor did he seem to understand yet that even if he had killed Jennifer unintentionally, he still bore responsibility for her death.

This troubled Monsignor Leonard, who saw it as a sign of immaturity. But perhaps in time the young man would grow up. And perhaps the process would be speeded along by nightly exposure to the conversation and concerns of the rectory's priests.

December's days were growing colder and drearier. On one gray, sleety morning, Judge Bell shivered his way from the subway to the courthouse. He was just bypassing the gloomy facade, heading for the judges' private entrance, when he saw a group of demonstrators shouting and parading. "Justice for Jennifer!" they were calling out. "No more blame-the-victim tactics!" Bell stopped for a moment to look at the demonstration. A woman gave him a flyer. A moment later he reached the judges' entrance to the courthouse and boarded the private elevator.

People were staring at him, he noticed then. Staring at his coat. He looked down at his lapel and to his surprise saw a pin on it. The pin had a picture of Jennifer Levin and bright fuchsia lettering that read "Justice for Jennifer."

The woman who had given him the flyer must have fastened the thing onto his lapel, Bell realized, and he quickly removed the pin from his coat. But although afterward he shoved the pin into the back of a drawer in his chambers and soon lost track of it, he was unhappy about having been made to appear, however briefly, a partisan in the case. He believed it was the judiciary's job to stand between the accused and the mob. That's how he saw his role, and he didn't care if people didn't like him for it.

A few days after the incident of the pin, Bell moved to resolve the diary dispute. The Levins had no right to refuse to produce the diary, he decided, and ordered them to do so at once.

Its relevance to the case was another matter. That was something he himself would decide, he ruled, once he had read it.

By mid-December, Linda Fairstein, who had interviewed the police who had questioned Robert and many of his former teachers, employers, and neighbors, felt she had a good fix on him. He was anti-Semitic, she suspected. He'd used that buzz word "pushy" about Jennifer, and told the police that Boston University was "very Jewish." He was also, she suspected, a sociopath, the kind of youth who had no conscience and no moral rudder. That last idea made her feel better about having lost her fight to deny him bail, even though she now had a sociopath loose on the streets. Because in time, she believed, he would display his essential nature, would start using drugs again, or stealing or scamming. She looked forward to that occasion. If Robert was caught doing something illegal, she'd be able to cite his transgression when he was convicted and sentenced for killing Jennifer, and that would help see to it that he got put away for a long time.

She was thinking about this one afternoon as she shopped for Christmas gifts in Tiffany's. She couldn't help it, because as she pondered a display of golden earrings and silver cufflinks, she turned her head and saw a young man who looked surprisingly like Robert Chambers. She pondered the jewelry again. Then she looked at the young man again. And then she realized it *was* Robert Chambers.

He's probably shoplifting, she thought. That'd be just like him. And as he loped past her, she sprinted after him, to see if her hunch was correct.

She was too late. The aisles were packed with Christmas shoppers, and at the elevators she lost him. Frustrated, she returned to the jewelry counter.

A half hour later she saw him again. He was exiting the store, a small Tiffany shopping bag in his hands. She felt a moment's disappointment. He hadn't stolen anything. Then, never mind, she told herself. I know this kid. And sooner or later he's going to do something reckless and play right into our hands.

On another short December day Detective Mike Sheehan made his way along Sixth Avenue, where Salvation Army Santas were ringing their bells and the stores were ablaze with Christmas decorations. He entered the building in which Bob Chambers worked. He rode the elevator to the floor on which Bob's company was located. And there he delivered a subpoena for Bob's employment records.

Sheehan had completed his errand and was just about to leave the company's offices when he spotted Bob Chambers himself.

"Hey! Ya look fantastic!" he called out.

"You think so?" Bob asked.

"Yeah. Since we were together, you drink nothing but club soda, right?"

"Yeah."

"Good job."

Sheehan would have preferred to leave things at that. But Bob asked if he would stay and talk to him awhile. Sheehan hadn't talked to Bob since the August night Robert was arrested. But he'd seen him sitting in the courtroom during several of Robert's hearings, and Bob always looked as if he was about to burst into tears. Feeling sorry for the guy, Sheehan agreed to a chat. The two men sat down on a bench near the elevators.

"You know me, Mike," Bob said.

"Yeah," Sheehan nodded.

"Well, the kid was just starting to get his thing together. His life was just starting to work out. At least I thought."

Sheehan felt a surge of unwanted compassion.

"I had so many problems with him," Bob went on. "And then everything was just about to gel. And then this thing. There's no breaks."

Sheehan felt awful. "Bobby, that's the way life is," he murmured. "You just gotta keep on going. Tell yourself, The strong survive, and this too shall pass." But the memory of his interview with Robert in the Central Park police precinct came to his mind, and the next thing he knew he was apologizing. "I'm gonna tell you this," he said, "if I'd have known it was your son, I wouldn't have continued on the case."

The two men parted after that, but out on the street, amid the bell-ringing and the crowds, Sheehan got a choke in his throat. He couldn't stop thinking how it was Christmastime, and Bob's kid would probably be going upstate one of these days, upstate to one of those maximum security prisons, and, oh, Jesus, why do things like this happen to people, and God forgive me, but this could be me years down the line, I could have a son like that and how the hell would I deal with it. And then he went down the street and popped into a bar and, although he usually drank nothing but beer, ordered himself a scotch on the rocks.

The scotch didn't help. He was two sips into it when he began thinking about the Levins. Jesus Christ, that was a tough thing there, too. The new year coming. Without a daughter. Yeah.

He finished the drink, so troubled by the confusion of sentiments swirling through his brain that he got up and called Linda Fairstein, and only after he spoke to her, and she told him she understood his ambivalence about the case, did he begin feeling better.

Fairstein's first months on the case hadn't gone smoothly. The diary fight had consumed a lot of her time and energy, and she'd had trouble getting Robert's friends to cooperate with her investigation. Many had refused to speak with her, a few out of loyalty, others because they had things to hide. Drug use. Robberies. Credit card scams. Their parents had called her in terror when she tried to get in touch with the kids, and said they would fight her tooth and nail if she dragged their offspring into the case. She had promised the parents that their teenagers, however delinquent, would not be prosecuted. She had begged them to tell their kids to come down and see her. "My God," she had said, "a child has been murdered. And your child can help us convict the murderer." But the parents hadn't helped. Agitated parents can be adamant.

She despised the lot of them. Especially one. A psychiatrist. "Please, let me speak to your son," she'd implored him. "There are parents who are never going to see their daughter again, and your son could help us

see to it that their pain isn't made any greater." The psychiatrist hadn't
cared about other people's pain. He'd just kept saying that if the press got
wind of his son's relationship with Robert and put the family name into
the newspapers, his patients would be distressed. That's a psychiatrist?
Fairstein had said to herself. All he thinks about is what's bad for business!

She'd been discouraged. But right after the new year started, she learned
through an informant that Robert had smoked dope at a New Year's Eve
party. Her spirits soared, buoyed not just by the information, but by the
fact that a friend of Robert's had delivered it. Perhaps she was rounding
a corner, she thought, perhaps a tide was beginning to turn in her favor.

Fairstein was right. Jennifer's diary need not be turned over to the defense,
Judge Bell ruled at the end of January. He had closeted himself with the
spiral date book, read and reread its scrawled impassioned entries, and
come to the conclusion, as he wrote in a brief decision, that there was
"nothing in the document which was relevant and material to the defendant's case or which must or should be disclosed to the defendant
pursuant to his due process right to a fair trial or pursuant to any other
constitutional, statutory or common law right."

Jack Litman was disappointed. He had cited scores of legal arguments
to support his claim to the diary, had searched out precedents that went
as far back as the trial of Aaron Burr. But he had lost the fight. And not
only that, he had in the process garnered himself extraordinarily bad publicity. As Fairstein had anticipated, he had been painted as a blackguard,
out to drag Jennifer's reputation through the mud. The popular press had
roasted him, and even *The American Lawyer*magazine had taken a dim
view of his diary quest, granting him, in their first issue of the new year, a
"Now You Know Why People Hate Lawyers" award.

He could make another try for the diary during the trial, Litman realized. But he'd have to think carefully before doing that. The way public
opinion was going, any moves he made that could be construed as attack-

ing Jennifer's reputation might end up hurting Robert more than helping him.

. . .

Kitty Schoen ran into Robert at a party that February. She hadn't seen him since her Valentine's Day party the year before, the party to which she'd invited both him and Jennifer. The year before! It was hard to face, and hard to face him. She'd thought about Robert often, and seeing him standing in front of her now, she felt faint. "I can't deal with this yet," she told him.

Robert wandered away, and the party swirled around Kitty. But after a while she realized she wanted to talk to him, wanted to hear from his own lips what had happened to her friend. She approached him and pulled him away from the heart of the party into the quiet of the hostess's kitchen.

"I'm sorry I ever met Jennifer," he said when they were alone in the kitchen. "You know, she was flirting with me at Dorrian's that night. She kept on doing it. She was becoming a pain in the ass."

Kitty was surprised to hear him talk about Jennifer that way, but she didn't say anything. Just listened to his whole account. Heard that Jennifer had begged him to come visit her at school and that he'd said he wouldn't. That his refusal had made her freak out and scratch him. And that he'd killed her accidentally.

When he was done, Kitty didn't know what to think. Parts of the story sounded believable to her, but other parts didn't at all. She shook her head.

Her less than enthusiastic response to his story made Robert self-pitying. "Well, my life is over, too," he said. "I'm going to die in jail."

He's being melodramatic, Kitty thought. "No you won't," she said.

"Yes I will. But I'd rather die in jail than be raped there by a big black motherfucker."

Then Robert perked up. "I've got one thing going for me, though," he boasted. "There's this book and movie being done about me."

"Movie?" Kitty was interested.

"Yeah. Some people are making a movie about me. If I let them, should I let Rob Lowe play me?"

• • •

Winter was nearly over, Judge Bell had set a date for pretrial hearings in May, and still Linda Fairstein had settled on no motive for Jennifer's killing. She didn't have to have a motive. The law didn't require one. But jurors liked motives. Without one, they were loath to convict. Perhaps the FBI will help me determine the motive, she thought, and in the middle of March traveled to the FBI's National Center for the Analysis of Violent Crime in Quântico, Virginia. The center was known for analyzing the clues in unsolved murder cases and helping local police forces determine who the killer was. "We know who our killer is," Fairstein had said to an official at the center some months earlier, "but we don't know why he did it. Would you be willing to work backwards? Take our killer and help us analyze why he killed?"

The FBI had said yes. She'd supplied them with a packet of her evidence. Crime scene photographs. Jennifer's clothing. Background information about Robert. And at last she'd been informed that a group of experts were ready to give her the benefit of their experience.

She flew down with Tom Kendris to the futuristic-looking center—the buildings extended not skyward but many stories underground—and in a windowless room met the experts who had studied her material. There were eight of them, some of them detectives, some of them specialists in forensic pathology and psychology. She told them a bit more about the case—new information she'd received about Robert—and then listened avidly to the experts' theories.

"Robert's got the same kind of personality as that serial murderer Ted Bundy," a psychologist said. "The charm, the deceptiveness. And the emotional vacuity that makes killing easy. Given that, he might kill again."

An FBI detective argued strongly that Robert had killed Jennifer and then positioned her body and clothes in such a way that she would appear to have been raped. "He pulled up the skirt and blouse," he said. "And he tossed her jean jacket over her arm. There's no way that jacket could have landed the way it did if he flipped her off him the way he says he did."

Another detective likened Robert's remaining in the park after Jennifer was dead to the habit that arsonists had of watching the fires they set. "People who linger at the scene of their crimes get sexually aroused by what they've done," he said.

Fairstein found all of this fascinating. But what about the motive, she wanted to know.

"Maybe Jennifer refused some sexual demand," one of the experts said. "Or maybe she wanted sex, but not there, not in the park. Or maybe she wanted intercourse, and he wanted oral or anal sex. Any refusal could have triggered his rage."

"Or maybe he was impotent," another said. "We all know that impotence is common among drug and alcohol users. If he was impotent and she made fun of that, he could have become enraged."

"Maybe he was trying to rob her," said a third.

Fairstein took her leave of the experts warmly. An interesting day—but on the plane back to New York she knew she still didn't have a motive. "Let's just hope we have the kind of jury that can put two and two together," she said to Kendris. "The kind of jury that reads Elmore Leonard."

"Do you know the one about the prosecutor in the rural Tennessee court?" Jack Litman said the following day to an audience of young lawyers at the New York County Lawyers Association. He had come to the elegant building with its crystal chandeliers, thick red draperies, and portrait gallery filled with the austere faces of once-famous lawyers to lecture about his widely admired trial techniques. Like all good speakers, he began with a joke.

"The prosecutor is summing up in a hammering-to-death case," Litman said. "Dutifully he's doing what he's been taught. Repeating what each witness said. By lunchtime he's only gotten to Witness Number Seventeen. After lunch he's gotten to Witness Number Twenty-two, and suddenly the worst happens! A juror falls asleep. At that moment the prosecutor realizes he's got to liven things up. So he picks up the murder weapon and says theatrically, 'Do you remember how the deceased was on his knees, begging for his life because of his two little children? And do you remember how the defendant here cruelly paid no heed and just picked up the hammer and brought it down on the victim's head?' As he says this, the prosecutor bangs the hammer down on the jury railing. And then suddenly the head of the hammer bounces up and hits the sleeping juror on the head. 'Sir, are you okay? Are you okay?' a court officer shouts. And the juror looks at him and says, 'Hit me again! I can still hear that son-of-a-bitch lawyer a-talking.'"

When the laughter subsided, Litman at once turned tutorial. But he seemed, as he began to draw a lesson from his joke, to be speaking as much to himself as to his young audience. "Never forget," he murmured, abstracted for a moment, "that what a trial really is is a dramatic incident in the confines of a courtroom."

In April, Pat Fillyaw came to court with her father and watched David plead guilty to the burglaries he had committed with Robert and to the attempted murder of the Columbia student he had stabbed. Friess, the lawyer she'd hired and stuck with, asked the judge for leniency. "The defendant, at the time of these incidents, was not a person acting solely on the basis of his own free will," he said. "He was a narcotics abuser, and on the eve of the Columbia incident he had been drinking. That he did what he did under the influence of these substances may not have legal merit, but the court should take it into consideration. Mr. Fillyaw isn't a mean or vicious person. He's a person who would not ordinarily have committed these acts were it not for narcotics and alcohol."

The judge shrugged. "The reasons for the defendant's activities were his own responsibility," he said. "His use of drugs was self-induced. His use of alcohol was self-induced."

Then he sentenced David to ten to twenty years imprisonment on the attempted murder, five to ten years on the burglaries, and two to four years on an additional charge of attempted assault. But, he said finally—perhaps because David had cooperated with the district attorney's office and provided information about Robert—"the terms will run concurrently."

Pat heard him and began to cry. Even with the concurrent terms, David would be a grown man when he got out of prison.

When she left the courtroom, her body leaning heavily on the arm of her father, she felt torn in half. Part of her kept saying it was only right that a person who commits a crime pays for that crime. Even if it's my own son. But another part said, He's the victim of a corrections system that never tried to help him. And of racism. He didn't get bail, the way Robert Chambers did—even though his victim lived and Robert's died. And I didn't have the means that the Chamberses have, so I couldn't risk letting him go to trial. She wasn't sure she would have, even if she'd had the means. A crime shouldn't go unpunished. But maybe she could have learned to live with the idea. Mrs. Chambers lived with it. She was okay with the fact her son was walking the streets, and that he might go free.

She kept trying to reconcile her mind and her heart. And three weeks later she was hospitalized for tachycardia—a racing, pounding heart.

"Are you the prosecutor in the Chambers case?" a police captain from the 19th Precinct said to Linda Fairstein over her home telephone on the first Saturday in May. "Yes," she said impatiently. She and Feldman were going to get married that evening and her hairdresser was due to arrive any moment.

"Does the name John Flanagan mean anything to you?" the police captain pressed ahead.

"Yes. Why?" Flanagan had been one of Robert's best friends.

"Because several hours ago, there was an accident at Flanagan's apartment."

This has to be a joke, Fairstein grinned. She'd kept her wedding plan a secret from most of the people she worked with, but someone in the Police Department must have found out about it and decided to play a practical joke on her. Tease her into a little turmoil before the wedding. It must have been someone who knew how hard she'd been trying to get Flanagan to talk to her, and how firmly and constantly he'd refused. "Yes?" she said, waiting for the joke to unfold.

But it didn't. "Flanagan went out drinking with some friends," the police captain was going on. "And then he and two of the girls he'd been with went back to his apartment and climbed up the fire escape to see the view from his roof. And then one of the girls tripped. Fell four stories. Landed on her head, fractured fifteen ribs, and ruptured her spleen. She's on life support."

Life support! Fairstein was amazed at the coincidence of another tragedy striking a member of the Dorrian's crowd, and for a moment she was skeptical that the event had been an accident. "What about Flanagan?" she asked suspiciously.

"He acted right," the captain said. "He covered her with a blanket and ran to Lenox Hill Hospital to get help. But he's pretty worried. Our chief of detectives thought you might be interested."

She was interested. Terribly interested. If she could get to Flanagan now, while he was scared, he might talk to her, tell her some missing pieces of information about Robert's drug use and his scams. If anyone knew Robert, Flanagan did. "I'll call the chief of detectives," she said.

But although a part of her longed to race over to the precinct and interview Flanagan, the rest of her resisted. She had been immersed in tragedy for fifteen years. She had been eating, sleeping, breathing the Chambers case every day for nine months. She needed to be free of tragedy and of the Chambers case today. Needed to be a proper bride, with nothing but joy on her mind. Telephoning Tom Kendris, she asked him to handle the Flanagan matter for her. And that evening, standing under a tent on her mother's Westchester lawn, her blond hair styled and her body resplendent in a pale pink sequined sheath, she married Feldman. But throughout the ceremony and throughout the fleeting hours of dancing afterward, she kept expecting a ringing phone and a brusque voice telling her the girl was dead.

Pretrial hearings were scheduled to begin the week after Fairstein's wedding. They did, but Litman interrupted them by filing myriad motions. He lost most of them, including one asking to have Robert's videotaped confession suppressed, but he succeeded in getting the hearings delayed. Delay is generally desired by defense attorneys. Evidence disintegrates. Witnesses disappear. The public forgets the animus it first felt toward the defendant. There are a host of reasons why defense attorneys like to delay trials—but they especially like to delay them when their clients are out on bail. Robert, out on bail, was having a pleasant spring. He had left the rectory and moved back home.

When the hearings finally resumed in June, John Dermont attended them. He sat in a back row of the courtroom and listened intently to Litman. He heard him argue that the statements Robert had made to the police the night he was arrested should be excluded from the upcoming trial for a variety of reasons. One of the reasons he gave was that although Robert had not told the police so, he had a lawyer at the time of his arrest—a lawyer his mother had retained in May of 1986 to represent him in a burglary inquiry.

A lawyer representing Robert in a burglary inquiry back in May of 1986? Dermont was startled to hear the date. When Phyllis had asked him and Barbara to write bail letters for Robert, she hadn't mentioned that Robert had previously been questioned by police in regard to other matters. And when Robert's burglary indictment had come down several weeks later, she had implied the charge was something brand-new, something the district attorney's office had just cooked up in order to persecute Robert.

Phyllis was dishonest with me and Barbara, Dermont thought. She used us. But though angry, he forgave her. Poor woman, it wasn't her fault that Robert kept getting into trouble. It was cheap psychology to blame parents for their offsprings' failings.

Barbara Dermont disagreed. Parents did form their children, she insisted when they discussed it. And if a parent was a manipulator, his or her child was likely to become one, too. "You know the way Robert always sees himself as a victim," she said to John one night in July. "The way he says Jennifer *made* him kill her. And Fillyaw *made* him commit the burglaries. Well, he is a victim. He's Phyllis's victim."

The summer sped by. Almost a year had passed since Jennifer had died. Robert resumed doing painting and carpentry for his upstairs neighbor, Mrs. Murphy. He learned to use a computer. He played with his cat—a new one, for the Siamese that he'd claimed had scratched him the night Jennifer was killed had been put away—dressing it up with a little collar from which dangled a pair of tiny handcuffs.

He also dated girls.

They weren't the kind of girls he had favored before Jennifer's killing. They weren't elegant blondes with the tinkle of money in their Chapin or Miss Hewitt's School voices. The girls he hung around with now hadn't gone to prep schools, or if they had, they'd gone to the less elite ones. There was a whole gang of them from York Prep. A few of the gang had been friends of Jennifer's, but that didn't prevent them from wanting to spend time with the notorious Robert. He had become a celebrity; to be with him was to feel oneself a part of history.

Even Kitty Schoen succumbed to the urge one day. She visited him at his apartment, and sat on his bed and leafed through his album of news

clippings about himself. The room was tidy, decorated with religious pictures that Phyllis had hung up. Some were just little paper pictures of
saints. Others were framed portraits of priests. Kitty pondered one of
Archbishop McCarrick dressed in his fancy robes. It was autographed "To
Robert, from Uncle Ted."

Robert told Kitty he had grown more resigned to going to jail. The
film star Matthew Broderick had got himself arrested for some kind of car
accident, he pointed out. And a rock musician he liked was being sued
for statutory rape. "Maybe we'll be together in jail," he said. "Maybe we'll
have this really good cell. And we'll start a band."

He seemed still quite casual about what had happened to Jennifer. But
that didn't make Kitty angry with him. Rather, a great sadness came over
her. Robert wasn't such a bad guy, was he? Okay, he'd gotten into drugs
and all that. And yeah, he'd ended Jennifer's life. But he was going to pay
for that. He was going to jail. And that was sorrowful, too, because in
some way what had happened to Jennifer hadn't been entirely Robert's
fault. It was the fault of the way they'd all lived.

On the anniversary of Jennifer's death, Steve Levin swam out into the
surf near his summer home in Montauk and flung a bouquet of pink
roses into the sea. The New York Post ran an editorial demanding Robert
be brought to trial. "Chambers, now free on a $156,000 bond," said the
editorial, "should have gone on trial four months ago. The newest trial
date is October 4, but it won't be an enormous surprise if, at the turn of
the year, Chambers is still waiting for his date with justice." The article
blamed the delay on Jack Litman for filing a mountain of motions, each
of which had had to be argued and ruled upon, and on the inertia of the
criminal justice system. "If the wheels of justice turned any more slowly
in New York," it observed, "they'd be turning in reverse."

The *New York Post* was correct about the snail's pace at which the case
was proceeding. Summer passed. Autumn started. And still Robert did
not come to trial. But his time was running out. Judge Bell set a date

in late October for the start of jury selection. And he ruled that all of Robert's statements to the police on the night he was arrested could be admitted into evidence at the trial.

Linda Fairstein was elated. Robert's statements contained numerous remarks that he himself had eventually admitted were lies—among them that he had never gone to the park with Jennifer, and that it was not Jennifer but his cat and his neighbor's sander that had injured him. When the jury hears all the lies he told, Fairstein thought, they'll think as I do that he never came out with the whole story. That whatever he offered the police in his last statement, the videotaped confession, was just another lie.

The weekend before jury selection began, John Dermont received a disturbing phone call from Robert. "Can you come over here?" Robert said. "Come over and be with my mom?" Dermont didn't know what was wrong, but he knew that something was, and he and Barbara hurried to Phyllis's apartment.

They found her in bed. She was upset, she told them, because there was trouble brewing. The stepdaughter and son-in-law of Mrs. Murphy, for whom Robert had been working, were coming over soon, and when they got there they were going to accuse Robert of stealing from their aged relative. Phyllis didn't want them to come. She didn't want a confrontation. But Robert had insisted on it. And he'd already invited a half dozen of his friends to join him and witness it. They were out there in the kitchen now.

Barbara stayed with Phyllis, and John went out to talk to Robert. He found him drinking vodka and orange juice with his friends. "Let it go, Robert," he said to him. "Forget about it. You've got more important things to worry about right now than Mrs. Murphy's relatives."

"No!" Robert shouted. "I want to have it out. These people went to Monsignor Leonard and accused me of *stealing*! I didn't steal. I did work, and I billed Mrs. Murphy for it, and she paid me."

"Then why are they accusing you?" Dermont asked.

Robert said he didn't know. "Maybe because I went on doing work for Mrs. Murphy after they told me not to do it anymore," he suggested.

"Why'd you do that?" Dermont inquired.

Robert was indignant. "Because a lot had to be done."

When Mrs. Murphy's stepdaughter and son-in-law arrived, they began a litany of complaints against Robert. He'd bilked their aged stepmother out of $7,000, he'd presented her with extraordinary bills for work done in her apartment, and he'd forged her name on checks to pay for it. If he didn't stay away from their stepmother in the future, they'd go to the DA.

Robert got furious. "You people have one hell of a nerve saying things like that," he yelled, "especially after all my mother has done for Mrs. Murphy."

In the bedroom Phyllis grew hysterical. She was going to check herself into a psychiatric clinic, she told Barbara. No, she was going to throw herself out the window. She got as far as the balustrade.

"You people!" In the living room Robert's face was dark with rage. John Dermont was growing frightened. The boy was shouting at the top of his lungs. "I'm sick and tired!" he was shouting. "Sick and tired of people shitting on me!"

Mrs. Murphy's relatives, perhaps frightened, too, left after that.

Later Robert's friends told him he'd been terrific, just great, and he calmed down and acted pleased with himself. But Dermont, who thought there might be some substance to the charges Mrs. Murphy's relatives had made, remained uneasy and warned Robert, "You'd better do what those people said and stay away from Mrs. Murphy."

"Why?" Robert said. "I *didn't* steal from her. It's my word against theirs, and my word is as good as anybody's."

Dermont couldn't believe his ears. "Your word isn't as good as theirs," he said." Your word isn't as good as anyone's right now."

Robert shrugged. And Dermont thought, My God, this boy—he has no perception of the straits he's in!

Jury selection started three days later, October 21, 1987. Concerned about all the publicity the case had received, Judge Bell laid down some unusual ground rules. The jurors would be examined one at a time, he decided. The lawyers would go about their questions in a slow and detailed fashion. And the examination would take place not in the courtroom, where a prospective juror's remarks might be overheard by his fellows, but in the privacy of a small jury deliberation room.

All these decisions would prove of enormous significance to the final outcome of the case, but perhaps none more so than the one concerning the room. Because of its tiny size, the prospective jurors were placed cheek-by-jowl with Robert. They sat opposite him at a table, their chairs and his no farther apart than those of people about to have a friendly lunch together. He wore a preppie blue blazer, looked handsome as his photographs, and glanced at the people who might one day sit in judgment on him with polite attentiveness and, occasionally, a charming smile. By the time those people left the room, he had become for them not the kind of depersonalized defendant they saw on television trial shows, a person invariably seated distant and remote across a vast courtroom, but someone with whom they had shared hours of physical proximity, someone with whom they had experienced a closeness that bordered on intimacy.

Robert's defense picked up other advantages during the uncommon jury selection process, too. Litman had the time not just to probe jurors' reading habits, but the kinds of movies they went to and their attitudes about sex and child rearing. He also had the leisure to pursue a hidden agenda, to ask questions that laid out ideas that were essential for Robert's defense but which he mightn't be able to state directly during the trial. "You know, don't you, the pain that is caused when a man's testicles are squeezed?" he said to each and every prospective juror. "You understand, do you not, that while it may be morally wrong to tell a lie or to fail to seek help for an injured person, there is a distinction between morality and the law?"

He didn't like the jury pool. Most prospective jurors seemed already to have made up their minds that Robert was guilty of murder. That's what the press had been feeding the public for months. He didn't want anyone who'd read too much about the case. And he particularly didn't want anyone who'd read certain magazine articles that detailed Robert's past. He got Fairstein to agree that if people admitted they'd read those articles, they could be automatically excluded, and he used a psychologist to help him screen out those who might be lying. The psychologist also advised him on other matters—suggested which prospective jurors seemed overly authoritarian, which were likely to identify with Robert's plight, which had the kinds of personalities that would enable them to stand up for what they believed no matter what others told them.

Jury selection dragged on and on.

October. November. December. Hundreds of jurors were examined and hundreds turned away. The days grew shorter and out the windows of the jury selection room, a pale moon rode the skies in the middle of the afternoon. One dark December afternoon Bell insisted that the lawyers work late. He had been criticized by a court administrator for letting jury selection take too long.

Robert sighed at the new requirement. "I've got to get home so I can watch *Wheel of Fortune*," he said.

Linda Fairstein, staring at him, thought that what she was looking at was, among other things, a big baby.

The next day Litman took Tom Kendris aside and began talking to him about letting Robert plead guilty to a lesser charge than murder. "Talk to Linda," Litman urged. "Tell her to be reasonable. After all, Robert's just a kid."

When Kendris told her about the conversation, she shook her head in amazement. Litman must have seen the way I looked at Robert yesterday, she thought. He doesn't miss a trick.

Pumping Kendris, she asked him what Litman wanted. "Manslaughter Two," Kendris said. "With a three- to nine-year sentence."

"Ridiculous!" Fairstein fumed. "I won't even talk to him about it."

It took nearly eight weeks to pick the jury, but at last, on December 14, after 486 people had been examined, the panel was complete. Sitting in judgment on Robert would be a clothes buyer, two bankers, several businessmen, a mortician, a subway conductor, a typist, a project director for an insurance company, a graduate student of anthropology, and an advertising copywriter. Four of the jurors were women, eight were men. Two of the men were black. And three-fourths of the jurors were in their twenties or thirties—ages at which they might presumably still be able to remember fairly clearly what it was like to be an adolescent and thus not be too judgmental about Robert and Jennifer's behavior on the night of the killing. Both Litman and Fairstein wanted this.

Bell was anxious to get the trial under way, and as soon as a handful of alternates was also selected, he announced to the lawyers and the jurors that the case would be tried right after New Year's Day 1988. He also informed the press that he would not permit the trial to be televised. Among his reasons was concern that "audiovisual coverage . . . may induce disruptive behavior."

Nineteen-year-old Melissa Buschell gave a party that night. She invited several of her girlfriends, and she also invited Robert. He was an old acquaintance. She'd known him when she'd gone to York Prep.

Auburn-haired and lissome, Melissa had dreams of becoming a model or an actress, and she loved dressing up and having her picture taken. She also liked taking pictures, and had recently gotten a Panasonic Omnivision video camera and learned how to film home videos. Preparing for the party, she got out the camera and, when her girlfriends arrived, suggested they make a movie.

Her friends were delighted by the idea, and Melissa lent them costumes. Fancy underwear. Filmy negligees. Cute pajamas. Scantily clad,
the girls pranced around the living room, and Melissa began filming them.

The girls were rocking and rolling when Robert arrived. With him was
his newest girlfriend, Shawn Kovell, a flashy young woman with cascading
coppery red hair. Shawn slipped into one of Melissa's black nightgowns so
that she could participate in the moviemaking, and Robert decided that
he'd join in, too.

It was fun. The girls joined hands and, pretending they were still little
kids, sang, "Ring around a rosie, a pocket full of posies, ashes, ashes, all
fall down," collapsing at the end of the song into a giggling heap. Robert
lolled on the floor and let a girl in a bra and flimsy bikini underpants rub
her cushy behind up against his shoulders. He also donned a big black
wig, then pulled it off and thrust it obscenely between his legs. Between
takes, some of the group drank beer and whiskey and smoked marijuana.
And after they'd danced and mugged to their hearts' content, they began
performing little skits.

Several of the skits, some of them devised by Robert, had sadomas-
ochistic overtones, plot lines that featured a hapless boy being taunted
by, or having to obey the orders of, a cruel female. In one, Robert was
commanded to kiss a high-heeled shoe and slip it onto the foot of an
imperious girl. In another, he was threatened with a cigarette burn by a
dominatrix of a "mother" garbed in a blue corset, garter belt, and black
stockings. In a third, he played a naughty boy caught reading dirty magazines by his school librarian. "Give me your hand, mister," Melissa, playing the librarian, ordered him, a stick with which to beat him swinging in
her own hand. But then she suggested another punishment. "We're going
to the principal's office," she ordered. "Come on!"

Robert ad-libbed fast to escape her wrath. "The principal's my daddy,"
he said.

In all his scenes he managed to avoid threatened punishments. Sometimes he did so by producing lust in a would-be tormentor. He did this in

the library sequence, where instead of dragging him off to the principal's office, Melissa removed a prissy-looking outer garment, stripped down to her tights and undershirt, and tried to seduce him. But sometimes he avoided punishment by talking his way out of impending discipline. In a scene in which a girl threatened to expose something he'd done, he dissuaded her by uttering a line like many he had uttered in real life. "I'll just say you're lying," he murmured. "And people will believe *me.*"

He said and did other things for the camera that drew heavily upon his real-life experiences. Pretending to be playing a game of charades, he mimed the title *Death of a Salesman* and acted out a choking scene, clutching his throat and swooning to the floor. And grabbing one of Melissa's dolls, he held its little rubber body up to the camera and talked for the doll in the way that little children talk for toys. "My name is," he began in a falsetto hiss, and then suddenly he gave a strenuous twist to the painted rubber head. The head started to come off. "Ooops, I think I've killed it," he announced in his own voice. "Both its eyes are like . . ." Then he let his words trail creepily off.

Several of the girls at the party had been friends of Jennifer's. They weren't perturbed by this mocking allusion to their dead friend. Instead, they eyed the doll's broken neck and burst into squeals of laughter.

Melissa kept the tape under wraps at first. She gave it to a lawyer who put it in a vault. But she liked to read spiritual books, and one day—it was after Robert's trial—she read a passage in one of her books that seemed to be telling her to let the public see the tape. She knew David Colby, the reporter who had interviewed Robert on Rikers Island. Colby was working for the TV show *A Current Affair.* Melissa gave Colby the tape—receiving for it, according to a newspaper account, $10,000.

THE TRIAL

The trial began on January 4, 1988. It was a dismal morning. Snow had begun falling the evening before and continued throughout the night. Jurors, chosen when russet leaves still clung to autumn trees, picked their way to the courthouse through sidewalks dense with city-gray flakes and gutters awash with slush.

Inside, on the thirteenth floor, spectators jostled on a long queue and scores of photographers strained against wooden barricades with the ferocity of penned animals. They were struggling for the best views of the metal detector through which the trial's principals would have to pass before entering the courtroom.

When Robert arrived, flanked by his parents and Litman, flashbulbs lit the dim corridor like a night sky torn by lightning.

The bulbs flashed again for Shawn Kovell, her red hair flowing and each of her fingers adorned with a ring. They flashed, too, for the Levins. Ellen Levin, dressed in black. Jennifer's sister Danielle, seven months pregnant. Steve and Arlene, huddling close.

In the courtroom, a high-ceilinged chamber with scuffed floors and hard wooden seats coated underneath with ancient clumps of chewing gum, the Levins sat down in a row reserved for them. It was but a few feet from the reserved row in which the Chamberses had just seated themselves, but the narrow aisle between them might as well have been a broad and turbulent sea; neither family acknowledged the other. Spectators, shoving, raced for their seats like hysterical children playing musical chairs. Reporters—there were four rows of them—began scribbling obsessively even as they waited for the judge to enter. Robert was in the well of the courtroom, seated between Litman and Stavis. One of his legs jounced nervously up and down, up and down. Then at last Judge Bell arrived, striding black-robed to his bench and taking his place beside a furled American flag and beneath gilt lettering that read, "In God We Trust." The final "t" in the motto was crooked, had been that way for months.

A few moments later the jury was called and the case on trial got under way. It would follow a hallowed order. Openings—prosecution, then defense. Next, witnesses—first for the prosecution, then for the defense. Finally, summations, the judge's charge, and the jury's verdict. Linda Fairstein rose and, her generally warm brown eyes heated, fiery now, began speaking. "Keep Jennifer Levin in your mind's eye," she said to the jury. "Think of her. Let her be in this courtroom through you."

Soon she put aside her avenging angel's passion to coolly outline her case. The jury would learn, she promised, that Robert couldn't have killed Jennifer where he said he did, for police witnesses would prove that the death had occurred elsewhere—in an area where the ground was disturbed and her panties had been found. They would also learn, she continued, that Robert had beaten Jennifer and dragged her through the ground, for photographs of her dead body would bear silent witness to her body's scarring and the presence of dirt in her upturned nostrils. Then she turned eloquent once again, informing the jury that Robert had lied even about what he and Jennifer had been doing in the park. "There was no sex," she said, her voice soaring. "Only violence. Only death."

Jack Litman doubted that Fairstein would be able to prove that assertion. Indeed, he doubted she'd be able to prove any of her assertions. The initial police investigation had been less than stellar. The police could have mishandled Jennifer's body and thus scarred her skin and dirtied her face. They could have made up the story about the ground disturbance and the location of the panties. If he could get ideas like these across to the jury, there might be reasonable doubt about Robert's guilt.

Reasonable doubt. It was the pinion of the American justice system. When it was his turn to speak, he concentrated on its majesty. "The prosecution must prove its case beyond a reasonable doubt before you can convict Robert Chambers of anything," he said. "Our Constitution says the state must produce the proof. It is what makes our country different from so many places in the world, places where you are charged and told, Now *you* go prove your innocence. Robert Chambers does not have to prove his innocence. *They* have to prove his guilt." As he spoke, he wheeled and turned, bent into his statements, looked like a feline animal about to spring or a prizefighter entering the ring. "Probabilities may not amount to a conviction," he explained. "Theories may not amount to a conviction. Only proof of facts which satisfy you conscientiously and morally will suffice."

He didn't talk much about presenting witnesses, for he had few. He didn't need to put on a show. That was the state's job. All he had to do was fracture and fragment their story. Cast doubt on it through cross-examination and block it through interruptions and delays. His victory would depend on his making Fairstein's story seem both incredible and hard to follow.

"Your honor, I object to the introduction of these photographs," Litman said on the second day of the trial. He was referring to blowups of the photographs of Jennifer's dead body. "The originals of these photographs are sufficient. These blowups are lurid and inflammatory. They are an outrageous size."

Bell ruled against him, and the jury was permitted to see huge repro-
ductions of Jennifer's face and the front of her body as she lay dead in the
park.

Fairstein was pleased. Her first homicide trial—what was it of Litman's?
his thirty-sixth?—was off to a good start. Fairstein had believed from the
beginning that the photographs would speak louder and more eloquently
of murder to the jurors than would hundreds of hours of words. Blowups
were even better.

I'm going to wrest victory from defeat, Litman thought after losing the
battle of the blowups. Stéphane Mallarmé once said that a word has power if you say it once, but loses its power if it's repeated over and over again.
The same should be true for pictures.

From that time forward, he shoved the horrifying photographs at the
jury, as if they were *his* evidence. Once he even supplied the panel with
magnifying glasses so that they could examine the gore and dirt with scientific detachment.

Fairstein spent her opening days presenting Nightwatch and Crime Scene
Unit detectives, reasoning backward from the forensic traces they'd observed to the human drama that had caused them. But she kept having
difficulties, for the police investigators she was producing as witnesses
were used to working on cases that were defended by overworked public
defenders; their methods weren't standing up to Litman's extensive prepa-
ration and intense skepticism. Time after time, when she put across to the
jury a chain of inference, Litman snapped it in cross-examination.

Did she get a detective to suggest that Jennifer couldn't have been killed
where Robert claimed, because the earth there was undisturbed, whereas
fifty feet away it was raked up? Litman, cross-examining, pointed out
that the Crime Scene Unit had failed to take photographs of the ground
disturbance, and that therefore the "ground disturbance" might exist only
as a policeman's say-so.

Did she get another detective to suggest that Robert couldn't have extricated his hands from the bond of Jennifer's panties and killed her right then and there, because her panties had been found far from her body? Litman, cross-examining, showed there was no evidence to prove where the panties had been found, for they, too, had not been photographed in the park.

Did she get a whole parade of detectives to suggest that, based on their detailed observations at the crime scene, Jennifer couldn't have died in an instant, but only after a prolonged fight? Litman showed that these same diligent detectives had been so derelict in their observations at the scene that they had even allowed one of their vehicles to park virtually on top of it, leaving distinct tire tracks on the grass.

Fairstein was dismayed. Why hadn't the cops photographed everything? Why, for that matter, hadn't they used a video camera and taped the entire crime scene?

What a comedy show, juror Eliot Kornhauser, an advertising account director, thought after the Nightwatch and Crime Scene police had testified. "I'm almost embarrassed to be a tax-paying citizen of New York."

Keystone cops, thought another juror, Michael Ognibene, a young banker who was also a part-time wrestling coach.

Bunglers, thought a third juror, Sheldon Forman, a computer hardware corporation executive. Weeks later during deliberations he would laugh when a fellow juror suggested—with the black humor that often alleviates jury-room tensions—that one reason the jury was shown only frontal views of Jennifer, but never pictures of her back, was because there were tire tracks on her back.

"Do you remember telling Detective McEntee that Jennifer Levin told you she wanted to spend the night with Robert Chambers?" Litman, cross-examining, asked a nervous, lip-chewing Betsy Shankin on the seventh day of the trial.

"I don't remember."

"But you might have said that?"

"I could have. I don't remember." Betsy looked on the verge of tears.

"By the way, Ms. Shankin, Jennifer was taking diet pills that night, wasn't she?"

"Objection!" Fairstein shouted.

"Overruled," Judge Bell called out.

"Ms. Shankin, was Jennifer taking diet pills that night?" Litman said again.

"Yeah."

"There's something terrifically wrong with our legal system," a woman from the Justice for Jennifer organization said to a reporter that evening.

"What in particular?" the reporter asked.

"That Jennifer Levin's use of diet pills is allowed to come out during this trial, but Robert Chambers's use of cocaine isn't."

The reporter nodded. Where dependence on chemicals was at issue, it was far better to be a defendant than a victim—at least if the defendant didn't take the stand in his own defense, which it appeared likely that Robert wouldn't be doing. As long as he didn't testify, the jurors would be allowed to hear nothing about his past, not his drug use, his petty thefts, even the fact that there was a burglary charge pending against him. That was the law.

Alexandra LaGatta, eighteen and a sophomore at college now, testified four days later. Listening to Fairstein lead her through her memories of the night Jennifer was killed, Litman thought about what he was going to do when he cross-examined her. He was going to make her corroborate the videotape. He was going to get her to admit that—just as Robert had said—Jennifer chased him from the minute she got to Dorrian's.

When he began to cross-examine her, he said, "You knew that Jennifer wanted to stay at Dorrian's when you left because Robert Chambers was still there, isn't that right?"

"I think that was one of the reasons she wanted to stay," Alexandra said, resisting him.

"Earlier, Jennifer had mentioned that she wanted to spend the night with Robert Chambers, hadn't she?" Litman probed further.

"I don't remember her saying that," Alexandra said coolly.

Litman stepped up the pressure. "Did you ever tell anyone that at Dorrian's that night Jennifer was physically flirtatious?"

"I don't remember. I don't think so."

Litman knew this was not true. Alexandra had said exactly that to a reporter from *Mademoiselle* magazine, and the remark had appeared in print. "Well, do you remember ever describing to anyone that Jennifer was physically flirtatious?" he rephrased his question.

"Yes," Alexandra had to admit.

Litman smiled and kept going. "Had Jennifer told you that Robert was good sexually?"

"Yes," Alexandra murmured. That, too, had been in the article.

"And did she tell you that she didn't like him as a person?"

"She had told me—"

"Did she tell you that?"

"Yes, she did."

Good, Litman thought when he had wormed that final answer out of Alexandra. We have here a classic role reversal. We have Jennifer doing what guys are always accused of, viewing a member of the opposite sex as nothing but a piece of meat. That ought to tell the jury something about her.

Just before Alexandra took the stand, he had tried once again to obtain Jennifer's diary—and once again been rebuffed. Now that he'd insinuated to the jurors that Robert might have been just an ordinary guy who'd got-

ten into a bizarre situation with a strange, predatory girl, his yearning for
the diary faded.

I don't really need it, he told himself. Not anymore. In fact, I won't
have to attack Jennifer myself. Her girlfriends will do it for me.

Larissa. Edwina. They, too, had been with Jennifer in Dorrian's, and they,
too, testified about events at the bar.

"To your observation, was Jennifer drinking?" Fairstein asked Edwina
on direct examination.

"No," she said.

A few minutes later Litman took over the questioning. "Now on August 26, 1986," he said, "you were questioned by the police weren't you?
And they asked you to write out in your own words what you saw in the
bar earlier that morning?"

"Yes," Edwina said uncomfortably.

"And at that time did you tell the police you believed Jennifer was
drunk?" He looked down at a police report in his hand. *"Definitely* drunk?" he said.

Edwina squirmed, sighed, and said: "Yes."

What's the big deal? juror Cole Wallace, a social worker turned marketing
analyst, thought after hearing Jennifer's friends testify. So Jennifer and
her friends drank. I did, too, when I was college age. So did all my peers.

If I had daughters, I wouldn't let them do what those girls were doing,
thought juror Gerry Mosconi, a computer graphics specialist.

Mickey McEntee, togged out in a three-piece suit, got to court early on
the morning he was due to testify and took a seat in the witness room.
What a dump, he thought. The chairs are rows of chewed-up attached
seats from some abandoned courtroom, the windows are filthy, there's
nothing to read, and even the pictures tacked up on the walls are boring.
Just Pavarotti and a bunch of big fat sopranos. Whoever supervised this

decoration has refined taste in music. But he sure ought to make the room a little more refined.

He was growing painfully restless when at last Linda Fairstein arrived to brief him on his testimony. When she did, she threw him for a loop. "You can't talk about any of the lies Robert told you when you first interviewed him," she said. "You can only talk about his videotape confession and the story he told just before he made the tape."

"Ya gotta be kidding!" McEntee exploded. "The lies are the meat and potatoes of this thing. If Robert hadn't told us all those lies before the final story, we might almost have believed him. What the hell's going on?"

"The judge," Fairstein said. Just before the trial began, Bell had overturned his previous decision and informed her that Robert's statements to the police would not be admissible. "He said we didn't notify Litman about the lies in time," she explained to McEntee. "It's a defendant's rights issue."

Judges, McEntee thought. Don't they care what's right? Or just about rights?

When he took the stand, he obeyed Fairstein's instructions in the main. He was a cop. He knew how to take orders. But several times, a mischievous grin playing on his lips, he snuck into his testimony indirect allusions to the fact that Robert had told a different story before his final one.

Litman came down on him hard whenever he tried it. "Objection!" he shouted. "This is an outrage!"

In the afternoon a television screen was wheeled in front of the jury. Robert's videotaped confession was about to be played. It had been edited slightly. Litman had succeeded in persuading Bell that certain portions ought to be removed. Among them were several of Steve Saracco's most intemperate remarks—the remarks he had inserted on the tape in the hopes of letting the jury that would someday hear the case know just how preposterous he'd thought Robert's story.

Also excluded was an allusion Saracco had made to the police having seen bite marks on Jennifer's breasts. McEntee and other detectives had insisted the breasts had been bitten, but bite marks had not been detected by Dr. Alandy when she examined Jennifer's body, nor by subsequent medical examiners—whether hired by prosecution or defense—who had studied the autopsy slides and pictures.

Litman was happy as the courtroom's lights were dimmed. Back in May he had tried to have the tape suppressed. But he had since come to the conclusion that the tape, at least the edited version, wasn't harmful to Robert's case and in fact might even be helpful. After all, Robert had stuck to his story despite Saracco's cynicism. And he'd never lost his temper, erupted into rage. At worst, the tape showed him as petulant, irritated at not having his word taken for granted. At best, it showed him as a frightened, candid teenager. The jury would see him that way, Litman believed. Just as groups of friends to whom he'd shown the tape had seen him.

Steve Levin hadn't watched the videotape before. He looked at it in the darkened courtroom with intense concentration, his body leaning forward, his head shaking from side to side. When it was over, he went out into the corridor, where a mob of reporters was waiting to hear his reaction. "It was a pack of lies," he said. "I knew my daughter, and Jennifer would never have done any of the things that Robert said. She was not an irrational, crazy kid. I don't even believe she would have gone into the park at four thirty in the morning. I believe she was taken there. And I don't see how anybody on the jury can believe that videotape."

The tape rings true, juror Forman thought. Parts of it anyway.

It's so outrageous it comes across strong, juror Wallace thought.

A female juror believed it utterly. Robert, she felt, had spoken with pained sincerity.

•   •   •

Robert had listened to the day's proceedings with a composed, untroubled demeanor. Dressed in his neat blue blazer, he had sat tall in his chair, paid close attention to the judge, occasionally penned a note on a pad of yellow paper, and for the most part comported himself like a well-behaved honor student attending a complex lecture course in a required but not particularly relevant subject.

He generally appeared that way in court, even though at night, when testimony and tangled arguments were over, he went carousing with his friends, drinking and partying as he had done for years. On the night the videotape was played, he was particularly merry. In the red-eye hours he visited the West Side building of a well-known female drug dealer whom he used to frequent in his palmier days and whose phone number had been in his address book the night he was arrested.

Detective Sheehan testified early in February. His barrel chest hulking forward, his powerful arms long and dangling, he strolled to the witness chair, leaned back, and let Fairstein lead him through his experiences on the day Jennifer's body was found. Bob Chambers was sitting in the third row on his left. But he didn't look at Bob. He just directed his gaze at Fairstein or the jury, and kept a good-natured expression on his face.

He was different when Litman began to cross-examine him. Warier. Tougher. And when Litman began trying to shake his testimony, he wouldn't budge an inch. Especially when Litman tried to get him to say that he hadn't seen dirt on Jennifer's face when he saw her body in Central Park, or that if he had, it was because the detectives who'd arrived before him had mishandled the corpse and lain it face down on the ground. "I saw dirt," he kept insisting.

Litman got frustrated and grabbed a handful of photographs. "You saw dirt on her face you say?" he asked again, waving the photographs in the air.

"Yeah." Sheehan nodded.

"But there isn't any dirt on her face in these pictures," Litman said, triumphantly flinging the pictures down onto the arm of the witness chair. "And these pictures were taken *before* you arrived at the scene."

Sheehan studied them with his lips compressed. Then, *"I see dirt,"* he said.

"You do?"

"Yeah."

Litman grimaced, twisted his mouth as if he'd just bitten into raw garlic. Then he looked at the jury with an aggrieved expression that seemed to say, This guy is lying, see for yourself, and distributed the pictures to the panel.

Sheehan didn't care that Litman was trying to make him out a liar to the jury. He was happy he'd rattled him. Dismissed from the stand, he paraded the courthouse corridor proudly. "Didja see Litman's expression when I told him I saw dirt?" he said to a reporter. "Jeez! It was something! I got to him!"

He may have recommended Litman to the Chamberses. But he wasn't, he seemed to be saying, going to take any defense attorney's shenanigans lying down.

She had to be allowed to show the jury the photographs she had of Jennifer at Dorrian's just hours before she was killed, Linda Fairstein argued during a bench conference that week.

It wasn't fair, Litman said. Jennifer was wearing earrings in the photographs. He had long ago persuaded Judge Bell not to permit the prosecution to suggest during the trial that Robert had robbed Jennifer, on the grounds that there wasn't any evidence of theft. Now Fairstein was going to circulate pictures of Jennifer wearing earrings! It wasn't fair. Some juror might start wondering why she had on earrings before she was killed and none when her body was found.

Fairstein desperately wanted the jury to see the pictures. It wasn't just because of the earrings—though that was a big part of her wanting to show them. It was also because the pictures made a point about Jennifer's appearance before she was killed. They showed a vibrant, beautiful Jennifer, her eyes shining, her lips parted expectantly, and above all her neck swanlike and unscarred. The pictures were absolutely necessary to her case, she shouted at Litman.

Judge Bell settled the fight. The jurors could see the pictures, he decided. But bits of tape would be pasted over Jennifer's ears. And he would admonish the jury not to speculate about what might be under the tape.

"Step up." "Approach." "Let me hear your reasoning." The lawyers were always bringing up matters that Judge Bell decided required private conferences. Sometimes he conducted the conferences on the record, court reporters taking down the arguments. Sometimes he held them off the record. Sometimes he conducted them at his bench. Sometimes—many times—he sent the jury to its little deliberation room, rose from the bench, and withdrew with the lawyers to his robing room, where not just the jury but the press, too, could not overhear what was being discussed.

Bell felt that privacy was essential, that the conferences addressed extremely sensitive issues which both sides appropriately wanted kept secret from jury and press. But in fact some of the conferences concerned routine matters, the kinds of issues that other judges handled in open court. And some of them, precisely because of the freedom that secrecy affords, became marathon sessions, long-winded, repetitive, tautological debates that filled almost entire days.

Not all the jurors minded. Behind the courtroom in their tiny deliberation room they napped and played cards and computer games. But some jurors were resentful of the delays. Every time these lawyers waste an hour arguing, juror Forman thought, they're wasting an hour of my life. I've got to get out of here, forewoman Debra Cavanaugh thought, and they're making it impossible for me to do so. She was a buyer in the fashion industry, and shortly before the trial had started she had accepted a new job with a company in England, promising to start in March.

If the mushrooming private conferences irritated some members of the jury, they utterly infuriated the press. "I've never seen a trial conducted with so much secrecy," one experienced courtroom reporter complained to a colleague on a day the judge's bench remained empty for hours. "You see that American flag behind the judge's chair?" a newscaster erupted bitterly on another such day. "Well, it doesn't belong there. This sham isn't being conducted like an American trial at all."

Judge Bell didn't know the degree to which the private conferences were angering the press. Nor did he know that some reporters had started a game called "Judge Bell's Quote of the Day." The purpose of the game was to list Bell's occasional malapropisms and inadvertent self put-downs, such remarks as "I think as I go along," and "I frankly could not understand most of what Mr. Litman was saying."

Bell had made the remarks lightly and unguardedly. But they were hung up on a bulletin board in the courthouse pressroom along with a ballot on which reporters voted for their favorite among the forewoman's ever-varying and ultrachic outfits.

Dr. Maria Alandy testified on the twentieth day of the trial, describing the myriad bruises she had seen on Jennifer's body, including the one inside her mouth—the laceration that had made her think that the girl might have been gagged and then beaten. When she was done, she speculated about how long Robert might have exerted pressure on Jennifer's neck. "Compression of the neck in this case," she said, "would have been applied at least twenty to thirty seconds. Or possibly even longer."

"Are you able to say with a degree of medical certainty how much longer?" Fairstein asked.

"Judging from the presence of deep abrasions on the neck, and the irregularity and prominence of the abrasions," Alandy said, "the pressure could have been maintained even more than a minute."

Showtime, juror Robert Nickey, mortician, said to himself when Litman
stepped up to cross-examine Alandy. Like a majority of the jurors, he
found most of the trial exceedingly dull. Except when Litman rose.

Alandy's changed her tune since she testified before the grand jury, Jack
Litman thought as he started to question her. She told the grand jury
the pressure on Jennifer's neck might only have been applied for fifteen
seconds. I'm going to bring that out right away. He gave her a dismissive
glance, the look one delivers to a liar, and said accusingly, as if he'd caught
her out in some dire malpractice, "In the grand jury, you said this strangulation would have taken a minimum of fifteen to twenty seconds, didn't
you? And that was the day after you had examined the body."

"Yes. But—" Alandy said.

He gave her no chance to explain. "Is that right, Doctor?" he snapped.

"Yes," she admitted.

He was satisfied after that, and moved on to other matters. Among
them was the suggestion that contact with cloth, such as the long sleeves
of a shirt, might have made the abrasions on Jennifer's neck look as prominent as they did. "Do you agree, Doctor," he asked, that many of the
marks you saw on Jennifer's neck *might* have come about because of fric-
tion between cloth and the neck?"

"Yes." Alandy nodded.

Litman didn't say Robert had been wearing a long-sleeved shirt. What
Robert had been wearing when he killed Jennifer was never established.

"In the Chambers trial Defense Attorney Jack Litman today revealed that
a long-sleeved shirt could have caused some of the marks on Jennifer
Levin's neck," Marilei Lew Lee heard on the radio that night. She thought
back to the clothes she and Phyllis had carried to Mrs. Hammerstein's
house the day after the killing. There'd been no long-sleeved shirt in the
pile of laundry. Just short-sleeved ones. Including the bloodied baseball

shirt she'd held to the light and examined before turning on the washing machine.

The thought of doing that batch of laundry made her remember something else that had happened months ago. Just before the pretrial hearings Phyllis had told her she looked sick and ought to go home to Brazil for a while. She'd said she wasn't sick, and besides, she didn't have the money to go home. And then next thing she knew, Mrs. Hammerstein, who was extremely generous—she'd given Phyllis a big check for Robert's defense—was saying she'd heard from Phyllis that Marilei wasn't feeling well and handing her a round-trip ticket to Brazil.

"Don't hurry back," Phyllis had said when Marilei got the ticket. "Stay the summer."

Why did Phyllis hustle me out of the country? Marilei wondered now. Did I know something I wasn't supposed to know? Was it anything to do with the shirt?

She thought about getting in touch with Linda Fairstein, who had left messages for her all fall. But she was afraid to return the messages. Phyllis had told her that if she went down to the district attorney's office she might get in trouble with Immigration.

One of Fairstein's most important witnesses testified several days later. He was Dr. Alan Garber, the jogger who had told McEntee the day after Robert's arrest that he'd seen a couple he presumed to be Robert and Jennifer rocking or humping in the park. Since that time, he had changed his story, decided that what he had seen had not been sexual activity but the prologue to or aftermath of a killing.

Fairstein intended to use him to prove her contention that Robert and Jennifer had not had sex in the park. If she could prove that, she could cut a huge hole in Robert's entire version of the events on the night he killed Jennifer.

"Dr. Garber," she said as the doctor, a plump-faced specialist in internal medicine, took the stand, "would you describe to us please what you saw in the park as you approached the area behind the Metropolitan Museum?"

"As I was running," Dr. Garber said, "I noticed two figures. One person was shaking the other person. Leaning over the other person and shaking. The person on top seemed like a white man."

"Could you tell us exactly what you were able to see that led you to the impression that the person on top was a white man?"

"I could see a light shirt and broad shoulders and hair that looked like Caucasian hair."

"Was it shoulder length?"

"No, it was not."

"Could you tell us please what you were able to observe about the second person?"

"The second person appeared to be lifeless."

A few moments later Dr. Garber revealed that despite having noticed what appeared to be a lifeless person, he'd ignored what he'd seen, exchanged a few casual words with a fellow jogger, and continued exercising. He'd jogged completely around the reservoir, and only then, some fifteen minutes later, returned to where he'd noticed the startling sight.

"Would you describe what happened as you came back?" Fairstein asked him.

"As I came back, I saw the two people in the same position. The top person was shaking the bottom person."

Fairstein sat down satisfied. She had told the jury during her opening that there had been no sex between Robert and Jennifer in the park. "Only violence. Only death," she had said. Garber had substantiated her remark.

Litman couldn't wait to get his chance at Garber. He was on his feet the second Fairstein moved toward her chair. "Now, sir, is it correct that you told Detective McEntee, when you spoke with him on August 27th,

1986, that the person you saw on top was rocking?" he demanded of Garber.

"Yes, I did," the internist admitted. His plump face looked nervous and his hands were trembling.

"Now, you were running." Litman said. "You stopped at some point behind the Museum. You looked over and you saw silhouettes. Is that right?"

"No. I saw them *as* I was running," Garber said. But it wasn't whether the doctor had been running or standing still that concerned Litman. "Did you see *silhouettes*, sir?" he demanded.

"What do you mean by 'silhouettes'?" Garber hedged.

Litman frowned angrily, his expression trying to inform the jury that a man's life was at stake and the witness was pussyfooting with words. "When you spoke to the prosecutor," he said, "did you use the word 'silhouettes'?"

"I may have," Garber said. Then: "Yes."

"So why don't you tell us what you meant when you used the word," Litman continued, his voice contemptuous. "Silhouettes. Outlines for bodies. Is that right?"

"Yes."

"And would it be fair to say that it was dark at the time?"

"Yes."

"And there were no streetlights on at the time?"

"Yes. That's correct."

Litman had succeeded in casting doubt on Garber's ability to see anything at all, let alone on whether he had seen that the person on top was a male. Now he moved in for the kill. "You kept on running. Is that right, sir?"

"Yes."

"And the next morning, which was August 27th, 1986, you read an article in the *New York Times* that mentioned that a woman had been strangled in the park. And you called Detective McEntee. And you told him that you believed they were doing something sexual. Is that correct?"

"Yes," Garber sighed.

Fairstein tried to rescue the situation. "Dr. Garber," she asked on her re-direct examination, "did you observe the two people you saw in the park doing anything sexual?"

"No. I did not."

"Then would you tell us the reason you told Detective McEntee they were doing something sexual?"

"I wanted to minimize what I had seen."

"Would you explain to the jury what you mean by the word 'minimizing'?"

"I had seen someone shaking another person and, I don't know why I didn't do anything, but I didn't," Garber replied lamely. "When I first spoke to someone, I just wanted to report that I had seen something.

A few minutes later, Fairstein, afraid the jury would look unfavorably on a medical man who had seen an act of violence under way and failed to report it, got him to amplify on his answer. "I minimized what I saw because of fear," Dr. Garber said. "My wife was pregnant and about to have a baby. And I don't know why else."

I have a problem with Garber's suddenly changing his story, juror Korn-hauser thought. I don't buy that "my-wife-was-pregnant" nonsense.

Garber didn't minimize anything, juror Forman thought. How can he say he minimized something when he went out of his way that first day to telephone the police.

He's a sniveling little coward, juror Mosconi thought.

He's honest, compelling, and moving, juror Wallace thought.

Dr. Werner Spitz, the chief medical examiner of Detroit, was the last and most important prosecution witness, a stooped, gnomish white-haired man with bombastic Napoleonic self-assurance. Under Fairstein's questioning, he told the jury that there was only one way that Jennifer's neck and chin could have gotten the maze of scrapes that marred them. Her assailant must have choked her with her own blouse, must have grabbed her by it, twisted it, and shoved it up under her throat with his fist so that it became, in effect, a noose. Still, he said, the girl had at one point gotten free of the noose. There were telltale marks on her neck to show she'd done so. But although her moment of freeing herself should have given her attacker at least a few seconds in which to reconsider his violence, the assailant hadn't done so. Intending to kill, he had resumed his deadly efforts, tightened the noose again, and compressed his victim's vulnerable neck for at least thirty seconds and possibly as long as several minutes.

Under cross-examination, Spitz never wavered. But he was so stubborn and so vituperative toward Litman that several jurors began to dislike him and as a result to put little faith in his opinion.

Ellen Levin had kept her head down during much of Spitz's testimony, and eventually she left the courtroom. But she was not as miserable as she had been during many of the previous weeks of the trial. A true miracle had occurred. A child had been born. The child was Samantha Jennifer, daughter of Jennifer's sister, Danielle. Samantha Jennifer would never replace Jennifer, Ellen knew. But she was a kind of resurrection.

Ellen had seen the baby in the hospital right after she was born and marveled at her beauty. She had a little fringe of dark hair that made her look like a monk, and an expression on her face that seemed almost like a smile.

Seeing the baby in the nursery had been pleasure enough. But then there'd been something even more wonderful. A real tribute. Danielle had asked Ellen to stay with her for a few days when she took Samantha Jennifer home. Ellen had been terribly pleased. But she'd also been worried. Because she didn't know that much about babies. Because in her day everyone had used nurses when they came out of the hospital. But then things had come back to her. Little things. Like that babies like to sleep on their stomachs. And that if they don't suck properly, you can put a little sugar and water on the nipple. Which was a great thing to remember, because the baby didn't suck properly when they got her home. But Ellen told Danielle about the sugar and water, and Danielle said, "Oh, I forgot! They told me that in the hospital. And they gave me a little bottle of glucose to take home with me!" So Danielle went and got the glucose, and the baby sucked and began to take the nipple, and Ellen felt a tremendous, restful, nurturing joy.

She was feeling it still in the courthouse when Spitz testified. Life had hit her hard. But she wasn't down on her knees anymore.

When she rested her case, Linda Fairstein was exhausted. She was also frustrated. She had seen her witnesses humiliated and discredited, lost the battle to suggest Robert had robbed Jennifer, been unable to make use of his early lies to the police, and even been denied permission to develop a theory she had dearly wanted to develop—the theory that Robert, before killing Jennifer, had gagged her with her denim jacket. She'd been denied the permission because Litman had persuaded Bell that the scientific evidence to support this theory was too new and unreliable. Now Fairstein longed to take a breather, to go away for a few days or, better yet, stay home and sleep. Sleep late and deep, without the obsessive thoughts and memories of the day's arguments that kept pervading her dreams.

But in a trial, she knew, there is no rest, and immediately she began trying to line up witnesses who could rebut those Litman was planning to put on. There were all sorts of people he'd hinted he might produce. Nora Bray, the girl at whose apartment Robert and Jennifer had slept together the night before Jennifer left for California. Steve Saracco, who'd been handling the case before it was reassigned to her. Bob Chambers. Maybe even Phyllis Chambers.

·   ·   ·

Saracco was one of the first witnesses that Litman called. He didn't know what Litman wanted from him. Maybe, the ex-Marine thought as he waited, chain-smoking, to take the stand, he wants to make something out of the fact that I didn't order a search warrant for Robert's clothes the night he was arrested. Maybe he's hoping to imply I took a slipshod approach to the case. Well, if he does that, I know what I'm going to say. I'm going to say that we didn't need the clothes. Because we *knew* who killed Jennifer.

But Litman didn't give him the chance to deliver the line he'd rehearsed. He didn't even ask about the search warrant. He just kept asking about Jennifer's panties, and whether he'd known while Robert was confessing that any panties had been found. Saracco said he hadn't known, and Litman used the answer to cast doubt once again on the police story about finding the panties far from the body. If they had found them there, he implied to the jury, and if the location was so significant, how come they hadn't even mentioned the panties to Saracco?

Saracco was on the stand only a few minutes, but he learned something from the experience that astonished him. It was that there was no carryover between being a prosecutor and being a witness. It didn't matter that he'd tried maybe a hundred murder cases. When he sat in the witness box, he got terribly nervous. And it struck him that being a prosecutor was one hell of a lot better than being a witness.

In Brazil, people who went to police stations could disappear. Marilei, who had gotten another message from Linda Fairstein, was filled with apprehension about hearing from her, but at last she forced herself to go down to her office one evening. When she did, she answered all of Fairstein's questions. She told her everything she remembered about the day that Jennifer died—about talking to Phyllis about Robert's scratches and even about washing his bloodied shirt.

Fairstein wasn't particularly interested in the shirt. But she was very interested in the fact that Phyllis had put peroxide on Robert's scratches, for during the summer hearings Phyllis had testified that the scratches had seemed so insignificant she'd hardly even noticed them. "If Phyllis testifies," she said to Marilei, "I may ask you to do so, too."

"Oh, God, I hope not, I hope not," Marilei said.

But that wasn't the worst thing that happened that evening. The worst thing was that Fairstein showed her Jennifer's death pictures. She felt like swooning when she saw the girl's naked splayed-out body. And then when she didn't faint, but instead made herself look at the pictures, compelled herself to stare unblinkingly at the lurid red welts all over the girl's neck, she realized in an instant that despite what Phyllis and Robert had been telling her all year, the girl could not have died in an accident.

It made her dreadfully upset. But she thought she understood why Robert had strangled Jennifer. Maybe the girl started bossing him, she said to herself. Maybe the girl say, No, don't do that. Do this. Start here. Stop there. And Hrobert think of his mother, how she push him, pull him, and how she is all the time with him, with him, and when he is holding the girl by the throat, he doesn't let go, because he isn't really killing a girl, he is killing his mother.

The day after Marilei saw Jennifer's death pictures, the jury visited the scene of the crime. The trees were wintry bare, the air was dense with fog, the ground was covered with mud. Robert waited in a detective's car while the jurors, silent and shivering, examined the tree under which Jennifer's body had been found and the tree under which the prosecution believed she had first been assaulted.

From his desk in the courthouse pressroom, Mike Pearl answered the phone that afternoon. "What were the jurors wearing?" Esther Pessin of UPI wanted to know. She was home with the flu and had been unable to make the trek to the park. "What was the forewoman wearing?"

"You're sick," Pearl told her. The walls were hung with the trophies of his career, sheet after yellowing sheet of his front-page stories about murder and mayhem. "Forget it. You're not going to be able to write about it, so why do you need to know?"

"I just have to," Pessin wailed. "I can't bear missing a detail. I'm obsessed."

Pearl shrugged as if she was nuts, but began flipping through his notebook and spelling out the clothing for her. "Number Five had on a men's fedora," he said. "And tall boots. The forewoman had on a black leather jacket you'd have killed for. Smooth. With a—whaddya call it—a peplum."

"I can't believe this," Tim Clifford of *Newsday* called out. "She just asked me the same questions! Tell her to lie down and watch it on TV tonight."

But Pearl understood Pessin's obsession. He too had been thinking of nothing lately but the Chambers case. The presidential primaries. The NATO summit. People, even some editors, considered that stuff important. But the fact of the matter was that it wasn't. What was important were only five things. Kids. Animals. Famous names. Violence. And sex. At least to a reporter. Any two of those things got a reporter a lead story. Any three got him a front-page lead. The Chambers case had three out of the five, and had kept getting him—and Esther Pessin, he had to admit—prime placement for over a year and a half.

He was expounding his theory of the Five Important Things to acolytes in the pressroom when he got another call, this one from Jack Litman, whom he'd phoned earlier to get a few extra details about the jurors' trip to the park. "How'm I doing?" Litman asked when he started talking.

"You're doing all right," Pearl said. "But you should smile more." Then he said, "No, I'm just kidding. You're doing fine. You're probably going to win."

Tim Clifford couldn't believe his ears. "Why'd you tell him that?" he asked Pearl as soon as he was off the phone.

Pearl shrugged. "I tell 'em all they're gonna win."

"Gee, I don't do that," Clifford said. "I ask them things. I don't offer my opinion."

"They may not want yours," Pearl sniffed. "I've been doing this stuff for thirty, thirty-five years. They know I know." Then he grinned. "Besides, Litman knows he can't get a straight answer out of me."

Clifford wasn't assuaged. "Well, it does look as if the jury might be leaning toward Litman," he said. "But it's because he's dragged the trial out so long with his nonstop cross-examination that the jurors have become his hostages. If they go with him, it'll be because of the damn *Stockholm* syndrome."

.   .   .

Jack Litman may have felt, as some members of the press did, that the jury was in his pocket, for in the next few days he moved swiftly to bring his case to a conclusion. He had already produced a hand surgeon who had supported Robert's version of events by testifying that the bone injury on Robert's right hand suggested not that he had hurt his hand while punching Jennifer but that he'd hurt it because he'd rolled onto it while lying pinned on the ground. Now he produced the medical examiner of Los Angeles, Dr. Ronald Kornblum, author of *Trauma in Hot Tubs*, who further substantiated aspects of Robert's story.

Jennifer's many bruises, the tall and suntanned Kornblum said, could have occurred from her tripping or falling while she was in the park. Her swollen left eye need not have been punched but merely made puffy because of the position in which she landed after Robert flipped her. He also said that the scratches she'd inflicted on Robert could have been just the signs of "playful" sexual activity, and that Robert could have compressed her neck for only five to fifteen seconds. Finally, he opined, "I believe Levin died as the result of an arm choke hold," thus contradicting Dr. Spitz's theory that she had been strangled with her blouse.

When Kornblum was finished, Litman announced to Linda Fairstein that he was ready to rest his case.

Fairstein was taken by surprise. She'd expected Litman to call several more witnesses. She'd lined up rebuttal witnesses. Gotten all prepared. And now it was over. She wondered if Litman had rested so quickly because there was someone he hadn't wanted her to cross-examine. And she wondered if his sudden rest had anything to do with an anonymous phone call she'd received, a phone call informing her that Shawn Kovell lived in the same building as one of the jurors. Could the juror have seen Robert visiting her there? Or seen him do something there that, if Litman had known about it, might have made him hurry to close? She, Litman, and Bell called the juror in and questioned him. But he'd never seen Robert in his building or even exchanged a word with Shawn Kovell.

At last Fairstein came to the unhappy conclusion that Litman had simply decided he'd made his case, said all there was to say. In a way that was worse than any of her speculations. Because his lightning-speed presentation was like a message to the jury—a message that said, Look, my client's clearly so innocent that I don't even have to belabor the matter.

The trial had taken a terrible toll on Steve Levin. He had been sitting in the courtroom almost every day for over two months, unable to attend to his work, unable to concentrate on anything but his daughter's killer and her killer's tricky lawyer. Some days he had grown so tense and angry that he had stood up and briefly glared at Robert, or cursed him under his breath. But on the weekend that Litman ended his case, Levin tried to relax. He drove out to his house in Montauk and on Saturday went surfing.

It was a sparkling sunny day with a trace of spring in the air, and the sea in which he had shared so many happy moments with Jennifer looked calm and manicured. Wearing a wet suit and a helmet, he plunged into the icy water. And he remained in it for half an hour.

He wasn't the only surfer to brave the cold. There were four or five others. But I'm the oldest, he thought, I'm the old man of the sea.

He was only forty-six, but his experiences over the last seventeen months had made him feel like eighty-six.

"Did you see the article in the News?" a reporter said to a newscaster while they waited on a crowded press line the morning that the lawyers were due to give their summations.

"You mean the one about the murder trial that shocked the city."

"Yeah, whaddidya think?"

"I didn't know what trial they were talking about," the newscaster shrugged. "Not this one, that's for sure. I mean, did *you* hear anything shocking at this trial?"

"No," the reporter said, and several of his colleagues nodded their heads, for the trial had in fact contained few surprises and no shocks. Robert hadn't testified, so the unsavory secrets of his past had remained hidden. And despite all the preliminary talk about how Litman was going to blame Jennifer for her own death, the lawyer—perhaps because protests and demonstrations had been mounted on Jennifer's behalf—had been moderate in his attacks on the dead girl. He had simply gone after the prosecution's evidence, done so fairly and legitimately, and fairly and legitimately destroyed it. They'd been cheated, some members of the press murmured. It wasn't as bad as some other times, like the time they'd gotten themselves all psyched up for Sid Vicious's trial and the guy had ruined it all by OD-ing. But still, it was a rotten break.

In the courtroom that morning, a courtoom so packed that the struggle to get seats had erupted into fistfights, Litman told the jury, "You have been here ten weeks, and you still don't know what the prosecution's theory of this case is." It was true. He had blocked and interrupted the prosecution's story so successfully that it had emerged as a jigsaw of lost and ill-fitting bits and pieces. But the jurors needn't be mystified, he went on, for Robert had explained everything there was to explain in his videotaped statement to the police, and that statement could certainly be trusted because, "Was that the kind of story you make up to get out of something?"

When he said this, juror Mosconi nodded.

Litman then proceeded, methodically and slowly, to compare the often flawed evidence and witnesses the prosecution had introduced with Robert's own explanations.

He spoke for four hours; and the whole time he did, Robert's generally vacant eyes were focused and intense, clinging to Litman's face the way a man being rescued at sea clings to a life buoy.

Litman wasn't that strong, Fairstein thought when he had finished. Not as strong as he was when he cross-examined.

She was glad for many reasons, not the least of which was that Litman had angered her by persuading Judge Bell that she shouldn't be permitted—as she had asked to be permitted—to do her summation the next morning. He wants the jury to hear me when they're tired out from listening to him, she thought as she rose and stood before the jury box. And then she snapped the jurors alert with a poignant opening. "Even if you disregard the testimony of every witness who appeared before you," she said, "the photographs of Jennifer Levin celebrating her future at Dorrian's in the hours before her death, lying sprawled on the ground in Central Park later that night, and spread out the next day against the cold backdrop of the autopsy room of the city morgue argue to you the violent nature of her murder better than any testimony."

A few minutes later she was attacking and mocking Robert's story. "He says he was tied down," she said. "And that when he got an arm free, he had no choice but to put it around Jennifer's neck. But where was his other arm? Tied to the Woolworth Building?"

Juror Cole Wallace smiled.

She admitted she didn't know what had motivated Robert to kill Jennifer, but reminded the jury that they didn't need to have a motive in order to convict. Still, she suggested one. Robert's fight with Jennifer might have started, she said, because he was in a rage at being impotent with her, an impotence caused by his consumption of "too many beers and too much tequila." And then she marshaled the medical evidence, asserting that all the experts, including Litman's, had agreed that, in general, it would take fifteen to thirty seconds of pressure on the neck to cause the kinds of hemorrhages that had been found in Jennifer's eyes.

She's gonna pull the watch stunt, now, Litman said to himself worriedly as he heard Fairstein talk about the hemorrhages. She's gonna take out a watch and show the jury how long fifteen seconds can be. Let it crawl by. Ask them to imagine what it's like to be strangled that long. That's always powerful stuff.

But a moment later, Fairstein was ending her four-hour speech. "Don't make the mistake that Jennifer Levin did," she said in a final, once again poignant, coda. "Don't trust Robert Chambers."

She missed a good one, Litman thought. And what she did throughout most of her summation was, she substituted emotion for logic.

Down in the lobby a vast crowd of spectators, gathered to hear the summations, began drifting slowly away. A reporter noticed the psychologist who had helped Litman pick the jury and hurried over to talk to her. "I didn't hear every day of jury selection," she said. "Bell only let a few press people in at a time. But I was there the day Juror Number Twelve was selected, and I could see why you wanted him, but not why Fairstein let you have him. He was terrifically argumentative. The kind of guy that hangs a jury."

"There are several like that!" the psychologist, Andrea Longpre, said proudly.

The following morning—it was March 17, St. Patrick's Day—Judge Bell gave his instructions to the jury, which from now on would be sequestered, confined to their deliberation room all day, put up in cheap hotels at night. He told them that if they could not convict Robert of intentional or depraved indifference murder, they could consider lesser charges. One was manslaughter in the first degree, a crime which the law defines as a defendant's causing death to someone while not intending to kill but merely to cause serious physical harm. The second was manslaughter in the second degree, a crime which the law defines as a defendant's causing death to someone while intending neither to kill nor harm him, but as a result of consciously disregarding the possibility that his actions may cause death. The third was criminally negligent homicide, a crime which the law defines as a defendant's causing someone's death without either intent or conscious awareness that he might, by his actions, do so—what the rest of us call an accident.

Any of these crimes might fit the evidence, Bell explained. It was up to the jury to decide. But before proceeding to the lesser charges, they must first reach a unanimous decision about each of the murder charges.

The jurors, who for nearly three months had been enjoined from discussing the case with anyone, even one another, were like children dismissed from school that morning. They were voluble, excited, exhilarated, and each person believed that what he thought about the case would prove to be what the others thought. Then they took a vote. Three people were in favor of convicting Robert of intentional murder. The others were opposed.

Ellen Levin broke her silence that afternoon, and for the first time since Jennifer had died gave a brief television interview. "Jennifer was a great kid," she said. "She was responsible, loyal, loving, and land. She had a gift for making people smile just by walking into a room. She was filled with life, and her zest and brightness touched everyone she knew—and even some she didn't know. I hope her spirit will touch the jury as well."

Ellen also remarked, sighing, "I'd been told not to put too much confidence in the justice system. And sure enough, I watched in horror as one by one important pieces of evidence were ruled inadmissible because everyone—even Robert Chambers—is entitled to due process of law. Still, I think Linda Fairstein was able to overcome these limitations."

Then, her eyes hidden behind dark glasses, she hurried away from the cameras.

St. Patrick's Day. For Phyllis the date must have been rich with memories of the time when she had worked as a volunteer for the County Leitrim Society and planned festivities that would add to the glory of the great Irish parade up Fifth Avenue. She had always been surrounded by friends and relatives on St. Patrick's Day, had once even sponsored, with the help of a brother in Ireland, a visit to the States of two hundred people from her home county. This St. Patrick's Day, she was isolated. The friends who at the beginning of the trial had accompanied her to court and sat supportively in her row had ceased doing so. . . . Other friends had ceased calling her. But she wasn't entirely friendless. An old acquaintance from the Greys, a woman who had not previously come to court, had done so this morning and after the judge had charged the jury, had asked Phyllis sympathetically if there was anything she could do to help.

Phyllis had thought the question over and then suggested that it would be nice if her friend made her some food for dinner tonight.

The friend had agreed, and toward dinnertime, Phyllis sent Robert over to her house to pick up the meal. When he returned with it in his arms, she unwrapped it and saw that it was corned beef and cabbage. And that all around the platter her friend had sprinkled shamrocks.

"Should I tell the jurors they can have time off on Sunday to go to church?" Judge Bell asked Litman and Fairstein on Friday, the second day of deliberations. Out in the corridor, where spectators and members of the press were sitting cross-legged on the floor, sipping sodas, playing poker, or watching television on minute screens, there was a carnival atmosphere; but even inside the courtroom the usual solemnity and decorum had eased. Bob Chambers was sitting with his shoes off, his black-socked feet resting wearily on a magazine. The Levin family, enlarged by the presence of a host of peripheral relatives, was chattering animatedly.

Litman seemed lighthearted, too. "No, Your Honor," he said. "Don't say anything about church."

"Why not?" Bell asked.

"Because if you do, and they want to go," Litman joked, "I'm going to have to know beforehand what the sermon is. I once had a jury go to church during deliberations, and the sermon was 'Thou Shalt Not Kill.'"

Litman's spirits stayed high all day. The jury had asked for a read-back of Dr. Garber's testimony—testimony that was highly favorable to the defense—and when toward evening a court stenographer finished reciting Garber's words, Litman avuncularly patted Robert on the cheek.

Robert, too, seemed cheerful. He responded with a broad and happy smile.

The Garber read-back didn't help the jurors resolve their disagreement about whether Robert had intended to kill Jennifer. Nor did the fact that they kept playing and replaying his videotaped confession and carefully examining Jennifer's clothes, her soiled, stretched-out-looking panties, her bra with its underwire and intricate stitching, her blouse with its buttons still intact—peculiar if it had served as the murder weapon Spitz had declared it to be. And soon the jurors began to realize that not only couldn't they resolve the matter of what had been in Robert's mind when he killed Jennifer, but they couldn't even agree on how he had killed her. He had choked her with the blouse, Cole Wallace and the two black jurors, Wayne Gaston and Robert Nickey, believed. He had done it with his arm, Gerry Mosconi and two of the women jurors believed. He had done it with neither of those things, Juror Number Twelve, Guy Gravenson, insisted. Robert had used the bra, he said.

To settle the question, they began re-enacting the crime, donning Jennifer's clothes and twisting the blouse and the bra around one another's necks. They also tried lying on the floor with the panties wrapped around their hands, to see how difficult it was to extricate an arm. And after a while, Mike Ognibene, who was slight, sat on the chest of Gerry Mosconi, who was about the same size as Robert, and, playacting at being Jennifer, hovered over Mosconi's genitals and told him to try to flip him over his shoulder.

"I don't want to hurt you," Mosconi said.

"I'm a wrestler," Ognibene reminded him. "I'll be all right."

"I've done some wrestling, too," Mosconi warned.

"Don't worry."

Mosconi lay back, his arms wrapped in the panties, and wriggled a hand free. He flung it forward. Then he reached for Ognibene. But nothing happened. With the bantam wrestler's weight on him, he couldn't raise his body high enough off the floor to make his arm go the distance to Ognibene's neck.

"Try it again," someone called out.

"Fling yourself up," someone else said.

Mosconi did. But it still didn't work. Then on the third try he managed to raise himself higher. He shot his arm forward, it made contact with Ognibene's neck, and the next thing he knew, Ognibene was flying over his shoulder.

When he landed, he hurt his back.

Cole Wallace wasn't impressed. "Big deal," he said. "He's still alive, isn't he?"

By the fourth day of deliberations, the strain of waiting for a verdict was beginning to make Steve Levin feel virtually ill. "I should smile more," he told a reporter, referring to the presumed beneficent health effects of laughter. "I haven't been smiling enough lately."

That afternoon, while neither judge nor jury was in the courtroom, Steve noticed Robert standing at the defense table talking animatedly to his father. Other members of the Levin family noticed this, too, and one of them whispered to Steve in a startled, indignant tone, "Look! He's *smiling*."

"He won't be smiling long!" Steve exploded. Then he stood up, his back ramrod-stiff, and stared ferociously at his daughter's killer. He maintained the posture for a long, chilling minute, until Robert noticed it and turned his back on him.

Inside the jury room the jurors were bickering. "Listen to me!" Guy Gravenson shouted at Gerry Mosconi. He believed Robert was guilty of depraved indifference murder.

"Why should I listen to *you?*" Mosconi snapped back. He believed Robert was guilty of manslaughter.

Cole Wallace didn't agree with either of them. He felt certain Robert was guilty of intentional murder. He began to argue and reargue his reasons.

"Let's move on," one of the uncommitted jurors begged. "At this rate, we'll be here till Easter."

"What if we are!" Wallace shouted. "You people! You people can't see a drop of water for the sea!"

The forewoman, Debra Cavanaugh, couldn't stand the bickering. I've *got* to get out of here, she thought. If I don't, I'm going to have a nervous breakdown.

On the fifth day of deliberations, Arlene Levin felt drained from the stress of waiting for the verdict. "I don't think I can take another hour of this," she told a reporter. "But it's worse for Steve. He feels he's lost Jennifer. That the stress is making the little things about her disappear."

"We're at an impasse," several jurors said that day.

"We're not at an impasse!" Cole Wallace insisted. "Not until we decide how long Robert held onto Jennifer's neck." He was sure Dr. Alandy had said something about the neck's having been squeezed for fifteen or twenty seconds—otherwise there wouldn't have been pinpoint hemorrhages in Jennifer's eyelids. If he could just get his fellow jurors to listen to that portion of her testimony, they'd see that Robert had squeezed Jennifer's neck long enough to have intended to make her die. "Let's get a read-back of Alandy on the pinpoint hemorrhages," he said.

"Why just Alandy?" one of his fellow jurors objected. "Why not Kornblum? How long did *he* say it took to form those hemorrhages?"

"At least fifteen seconds."

"In general. But not always. He said sometimes they could happen in four or five seconds."

"You sure?"

"Yeah. But we can get it read back if you don't believe me."

Few jurors wanted to sit through a read-back of two sections of complicated medical testimony at this point, so Cavanaugh solved the problem. She sent a note out to Judge Bell saying the group wanted the lawyers to stipulate how long Jennifer's neck would have had to be compressed for pinpoint hemorrhages to have formed in her eyelids.

Litman and Fairstein wrangled over the stipulation, but at last agreed on wording, and the next day the jury filed into the courtroom to hear the information they'd requested. They looked weary and wrinkled, and some of them—those who had thought the deliberations would end quickly and consequently hadn't brought sufficient clothing—were wearing other jurors' ill-fitting garments. "The lawyers have gone through the testimony you were asking about," Judge Bell said as soon as they were seated, "and they have come up with a stipulation, which the court reporter will read to you now."

The jury sat forward.

"The pinpoint hemorrhages in the lower eyelids of Jennifer Levin," the court reporter said, "could have been caused in a period of time less than or equal to the amount of time it took to cause her death."

The faces of several of the jurors sagged, and Wallace looked apoplectic. When he got back into the jury room, he began agitating to have Dr. Alandy's testimony read back in full.

His suggestion inflamed some of the group. "Alandy was on the stand three days," one juror pointed out. "If we have to listen to all of that, we'll never get out of here."

"I don't care what Alandy said," another juror insisted. "I'll never believe Robert Chambers capable of intentional murder. He's too nice, too refined."

Arguments swirled through the room, and several frustrated jurors simply stopped talking to several others. But at last a note was sent out to Judge Bell requesting lengthy but specific portions of Alandy's testimony.

"What sign are you?" Gerry Mosconi said to fellow juror Jeanette Nielsen over dinner that night. They were sitting in the run-down dining room of the third-rate Staten Island hotel in which the court had placed them.

"I don't want to talk to you," Nielsen told him. "Tomorrow, when we go back into the jury room, I'll talk to you."

A few minutes later another juror, Elizabeth Bauch, sat down at the table and noticed that Nielsen was having chocolate cake for dessert. "How's the cake?" she asked. "Any good?"

"Get up and try it for yourself," Nielsen snapped. "If I tell you what I think of it, you're not going to believe me anyway."

Ellen Levin was at home. She opened her dishwasher, planning to put away the clean plates, and then suddenly she began flinging her dishes around the room. They smashed, shards skittering and splintering along the floor.

The seventh day of jury deliberations was one of the worst in Judge Bell's long life on the bench. He opened his *New York Post* to find himself excoriated for his handling of the Chambers case. He had conducted the trial in a secretive and un-American fashion, he read in an article by editor Jerry Nachman, had shown an "inexcusable disregard for the principles of open court." But that wasn't the worst of it. He was known "throughout the Criminal Courts Building," he read, "as Ding-Dong Bell."

Was he? Bell was stunned. The attack, he felt, was vicious. But more than that, it was racist.

Still, he didn't want to get in any more trouble with the press, and as the day proceeded he tried to deflect further criticism. When the lawyers said they wanted to speak with him, he made them address him from their tables instead of in private, and he even invited several reporters to sit in the well of the courtroom so that they could hear better.

But late in the day, while court stenographers were reviewing their notes on Dr. Alandy's testimony so that they could give the jury the sections it had demanded, something happened that Bell felt he absolutely couldn't let the press know about. One of the jurors—it was Gravenson—bypassed the forewoman and sent him a private communication, a note indicating he had some sort of personal problem with the way the deliberations were going.

Bell immediately began worrying that the jury could fall apart. He had reason to worry. The forewoman had herself been importuning him to let her leave, and he had several times had to telephone her employers in England in order to get her to stay. Now there might be two recalcitrant jurors. He told Litman and Fairstein about Gravenson's note unhappily—and in secret—knowing he would probably soon again feel the press's wrath.

Gravenson was examined by Bell and the two lawyers the next morning. It was the eighth day of deliberations. "I want to leave the jury," Gravenson said. And then, hoping to ensure his dismissal, he not only insisted that the deliberations were making him physically ill but said the jury was tainted. A juror, he hinted, had lied about his background during the voir dire, and he knew about the lie.

The man struck both judge and lawyers as emotionally overwrought. Fairstein wanted an alternate put in his place. Litman refused to agree.

If he held out against an alternate, he believed, the case might end in a mistrial. He stuck to his ground.

After a while Judge Bell told Gravenson, who was outside waiting to learn if he could be released, to compose himself, go back to his fellow jurors, and try to deliberate with them once again.

Gravenson said he would try.

"If there's a mistrial," Fairstein said to Litman after Gravenson returned to the jury room, "we're going to prosecute Robert on the burglary charges immediately."

"Yes, I could hear the case right away," Judge Bell said. "Next week maybe."

Something was wrong in the jury room, court officer Bill Alwang thought a few minutes later. The jurors weren't just arguing. They were fighting. Physically fighting. Next thing he knew, he heard pounding on the door. He flung it open to see Gravenson standing in front of him, his coat on and a suitcase in his hand. "I'm getting out of here!" Gravenson screamed. "I'm leaving."

Court officer Alwang brought Gravenson out to Judge Bell and the lawyers again.

I can live with a mistrial, Linda Fairstein thought after she'd listened to Bell calm Gravenson down once again, and once again return him to the jury room. I'll just go ahead and try Robert over again. But she was worried about the Levins. She didn't think they could stand the pressure of another trial.

Maybe, she decided, if Litman comes to me and starts talking about a plea again, I'll listen to him this time. It would have been great to have won a murder conviction. But getting Robert to plead guilty to manslaughter wouldn't be a bad ending to her first homicide trial. At least if he pled guilty to manslaughter in the first degree.

Litman didn't like thinking of himself as an imploring attorney. "I don't plead my clients out," he was fond of saying. "Ask anyone who knows me." But by the end of the day, he was beginning to suspect that a plea might be in Robert's best interests. He knew that the DA's office had solid evidence that Robert had been involved in the burglaries they'd charged him with, and he felt pretty sure that if the case came to trial, not only would Robert be convicted but he'd get a stiff sentence. Because he wouldn't be an ordinary first-time burglar. He'd be Robert Chambers, the guy on whom the DA's office had lavished thousands upon thousands of dollars and man-hours, and failed to convict of murder.

Maybe tomorrow he'd start negotiating, he decided. See if he could plead Robert guilty to second-degree manslaughter.

On the ninth day of deliberations—it was the longest time a New York County jury had sat to consider the case of a single defendant—Litman and Fairstein, closeted in Bell's chambers, began hammering out the details of a plea. Outside in the corridors members of the press were feuding over the accuracy of the Post's latest attack on Bell—an article limning him as incompetent and ignorant—and one enterprising photographer was hawking T-shirts on which he'd embossed a picture of Robert. In the jury room a vote was taken. Nine jurors voted to have Robert convicted of intentional murder. Then the nine tried to persuade the holdouts to join the majority. But in the process of defending their views, the holdouts gained converts. When another vote was taken, there were only seven jurors in favor of intentional murder.

Cavanaugh, convinced the jury would never resolve its difficulties, sent a hysterical note to Judge Bell. "I have given to my limit," the note said. "I am planning to leave the country this evening."

Judge Bell and the lawyers knew about the commotion in the hallways and the imminent collapse of the jury. But they put aside worrying about these matters. They were rocketing toward resolution.

Litman asked for the plea he wanted—manslaughter in the second degree. Fairstein asked for the one she wanted—manslaughter in the first degree. Bell pointed out that under the law a person accused of murder could only plead guilty to the next charge down, which in Robert's case meant first-degree manslaughter, so Fairstein won the first round. Litman won the next. He obtained for Robert not the lengthy maximum sentence that was generally handed down for first-degree manslaughter, but a short sentence, one that was customary in cases of second-degree manslaughter: five to fifteen years.

He also got Fairstein to agree that Robert would not be prosecuted for the pending burglary charge, nor for any other criminal acts—she'd informed him that her office had information saying Robert had stolen $7,000 worth of checks from his neighbor Mrs. Murphy and used the money to buy cocaine.

Fairstein accepted most of Litman's demands. But on one matter she wouldn't budge. It had to do with the language Robert would use when he stood up in court to make his plea. She wanted him to say he'd meant to hurt Jennifer; language like that was traditional during a plea, and besides, it was important to the Levins, with whom she'd been consulting throughout the negotiations. They felt that if Robert declared that he'd meant to hurt Jennifer, he'd at last be putting to rest his heartless story of having killed her because she'd brutalized him during sex.

Litman didn't like the idea. He wanted Robert let off the hook, wanted him to be able to use some face-saving language. "Otherwise he may balk," he said.

Fairstein held firm. During the course of the trial she had grown, toughened, become a stronger woman than she'd been when she'd first accepted the case and worried about Litman's experience with homicide and her own lack of it. She insisted on the customary language, and eventually Litman capitulated.

It took hours before all the details were finally worked out, but at last, late in the afternoon, the deal was done, and Robert, who had been little in evidence throughout the deliberations—he had been upstairs with friends, playing cards and bingo in a comfortable little lounge—entered a hushed and solemn courtroom. His face was deathly white. His mysterious blue eyes acknowledged no one.

He didn't want to say he had meant to hurt Jennifer. He didn't want to in the worst way. When Judge Bell asked him, "Is it true, Mr. Chambers, that on August 26, 1986, you intended to cause serious physical injury to Jennifer Levin and thereby caused her death?" he murmured wordily and almost inaudibly, "Looking back on everything, I would have to say yes." Then he began shaking his head violently from side to side and, raising his voice, added, "But in my heart I did not mean for anything to happen."

Judge Bell seemed willing to let the answer suffice. "All right," he said. But Linda Fairstein was on her feet. "No, no, no, no, no," she was calling out. "I want you to ask him about his mind and his hands, not his heart!"

A moment later, Bell was rephrasing the question. "Mr. Chambers, is it true that on August 26, 1986, you intended to cause serious physical injury to Jennifer Levin and thereby caused the death of Jennifer Levin?"

He answered loud and concisely this time. "Yes, Your Honor," he said. But as he spoke, he went on shaking his head, his body saying no as his mouth said yes.

EPILOGUE

I

Rikers. Next the Downstate Correctional Facility in Fishkill. Then Sing Sing. Robert was moved around from prison to prison in the first few weeks of his incarceration, but eventually he was sent to the Great Meadow Correctional Facility in Comstock, New York, and there he settled down to spend the duration of his sentence. He would not be eligible for parole until 1993.

The prison was a maximum security facility, an aging gray pile of rock surrounded by gun-turreted walls thirty feet high and two feet thick. Few sounds of civilization could have penetrated the walls, even had there been much civilization nearby. The town of Comstock, if it could be called a town, contained a post office, a bar, and a handful of sagging wooden houses. Beyond the town, in the quiet distance, New York's Adirondacks and Vermont's Green Mountains made a wall around the prison wall, encircling it with rugged forested peaks.

Robert couldn't see the mountains from his cell, a small room, eight feet wide by twelve feet long, equipped with a bed, a locker, a sink, and a toilet. He didn't like being confined to the tiny space and after a while asked, even though he had earlier claimed to be frightened of what the

303

other inmates might do to him, to be allowed to mingle with the general population. His request was granted, and soon he was working in the prison paint shop, playing baseball and volleyball in the yard, and lifting weights in the gym.

What went on in his mind? Did he think he was unfairly incarcerated? No doubt. One night in the spring of 1988 he told a prisoner in his cellblock, who later conveyed his words to a newspaper, yet another version of what had happened the night he killed Jennifer. "I was snorting cocaine," he said. "I was blitzed out of my mind. I didn't realize I had my hands on her neck so long. I didn't realize I was strangling her, I was so high."

The truth? Or just another story?

Phyllis visited Robert frequently that spring, no matter that the trip was a terrible ordeal. She had to rise in the middle of the night in order to catch the visitors' bus, which departed from midtown Manhattan at about four in the morning and took close to five hours to reach its destination. Then she had to wait for several more hours until she was processed and passed through. But she didn't mind. It was always good to see Robert.

One night she told John Dermont during a dinner at her home that Robert was getting on famously. "He's on the baseball team," she said. "He's got a terrific tan. And in the fall he'll be taking college classes. The professors come in from Skidmore, you know."

Not long afterward, at another dinner—this time at a restaurant in the Armory, the scene of her glory days when she had headed up the Greys— she told Dermont that she had grown disenchanted with the Kennedys. "I've been reading a book about them," she said, "and the book shows that they were power abusers, lawbreakers. I used to want my son to be like one of them. But I don't any more."

The Levins became active in the victims' rights movement. They appeared at rallies and trials, and they brought a $25 million wrongful death suit against Robert. If they won, they announced, they would use whatever money the suit brought them to help victims. It would be a memorial to Jennifer.

Robert, who had received hundreds of communications of support, began answering them with form letters. In October 1988, he wrote to his well-wishers:

To my new family:

As many of you know, I have been involved with a civil lawsuit. Although the amount is tremendously high, I believe that my choice of not fighting the action was the best for all involved. After speaking with my parents and lawyers, I came to the decision to plead "no contest" to end the circus once and for all. . . .

As for my present situation, things here have also been troublesome. In the past couple of months there have been two disturbances in which no one was hurt. However, major changes came about overnight. A few hundred inmates were transferred to other facilities as a security measure. Unfortunately, one of my friends was found guilty, and will be spending the next ten months in the "Box"—a special disciplinary wing. Luckily, I was inside my cell when all of this happened, otherwise I, too, may have received disciplinary hearings.

Unfortunately, my luck ran out last month. I was on my way to the yard to play baseball and I had an extra pair of sneakers with me. I was bringing these to someone else who was also on the ball team. I was locked up for six days and found guilty of directive 106.10—Direct Order. You see, inmates are permitted [only] one pair of sneakers at all times.

The school semester began on September 12th, but I ran into a slight problem with the application. Next term begins in January. I am getting help with determining which courses will be best for me to take. So, things are starting to look up. After all, once one hits rock bottom there's only one way to go—UP!

What was the sneaker incident all about? In January 1989, Esther Pessin, who had read Robert's letter, ran into Bob Chambers on Broadway and asked him this.

"Oh, you heard? Just a mix-up, that's all," Bob said. "Robert told me he actually had permission to have the extra pair of sneakers with him. A guard had given him the permission. But when they asked him who the guard was, he got the name wrong."

Same old Robert, Pessin thought. An excuse for everything. Same old parental cover-up, too.

II

Robert. And Jennifer. Jennifer and Robert. In the spring of 1989 as I was finishing this book, I kept hearing in my head the voices of their friends, teenage voices that were sometimes remarkably insightful, sometimes woefully banal, and most of the time given to recounting observations by reference to films, as if films gave the speakers breadth, made up for what they had not yet experienced in life. The voices made me sad, reminded me of how young Jennifer and Robert had been when the chain of events that prompted my book had occurred; they'd been adolescents, those creatures with adult bodies and passions, but the heads—the narrow perceptiveness and limited world knowledge—of children. Jennifer never got the chance to grow up, I thought often. Robert has. He's nearly twenty-three.

How is he getting on? I found myself wondering one afternoon. To get an answer to the question, I called Linda Fairstein. There was no point in asking Jack Litman. Although many people thought he had done a remarkable job in defending Robert, his client himself didn't seem to think so. He'd pulled away, hadn't even sent Litman his form letters.

"Robert's apparently doing fine," Fairstein, who had become the godmother of little Samantha Jennifer, told me. "He's made friends. And I even heard he had a protector. Pappy Mason."

Mason was a black drug lord who had reputedly ordered the assassination of a New York policeman. "Robert," I said, "always lands on his feet."

"Yes," Fairstein went on. "I heard Mason took him under his wing. Acted as his bodyguard."

I wasn't altogether surprised to be told that Robert had won an influential guardian in prison. Inmates, just like the rest of us, *like* celebrities. Besides, I thought, he had for years associated with members of the underworld, had used them to obtain drugs and to help him fence the goods he stole in order to buy drugs. He would know how to get on with his fellow inmates, sharing as he did with them both history and an essential meanness of spirit.

But I was to learn subsequently that while Robert *was* getting on well with his new associates, the story about his relationship with Pappy Mason was not true. It had arisen from a boast Robert had made to a visitor. Robert had always been boastful. Prison hadn't changed him. He just boasted now about different sorts of things.

What would psychiatrists have made of him? They'd probably have labeled him a "pathological antisocial personality," I decided. That's the dry term that has these days replaced yesteryear's more ominous-sounding "psychopath" or "sociopath." His early use of alcohol and drugs, his vandalism and school failures, his criminal activities and disregard for the truth—all would have pointed to that diagnosis.

He could have been born with a tendency to the disorder. But he wouldn't have turned into a full-blown antisocial personality if he hadn't been raised where, when, and how he was. Predispositions are encouraged or discouraged by environment.

Robert's environment served him poorly. His parents tried from time to time to control his drinking, drug use, and stealing, but just as often they made excuses for him, forgave him, took his word that he had mended his ways. Other adults, people who might have confronted him about his antisocial activities, chose to be lulled by his parents' reassurances. But more important, his friends looked with favor on his behavior. To them, his drug use, drinking, and even stealing were not merely acceptable but glamorous. And why not? Many of them were doing the same things.

Robert, I knew, had always been looking to blame his own transgressions on someone or something outside himself. Thinking about the milieu in which he had come to manhood, I began to feel that in one sense something outside himself *was* to blame—that he was the by-product of the drug epidemic that swept through American youth in the 1980s. If so, then clearly Jennifer Levin was a victim of that drug epidemic. Because whatever happened in Central Park—whether Robert killed her because he wanted to steal from her in order to buy drugs, or because he experienced with her a drug-induced hallucination that she was attacking him, or because he wanted to have sex with her but was impotent as a result of the depressing action of drugs, or because something she did or said set him off into the kind of intense rage that drugs notoriously produce—one way or another, his use of drugs played a role in her death.

I didn't feel that this excused Robert. What I felt was that, although I had listed and limned in my pages all the things that made him and Jennifer special, they were not, ultimately, unique. They resembled hundreds of thousands of American teenagers. And from their story it would be right on target to conclude that there, but for the grace of God and the reach of the epidemic, did go our own children.

But what of Jennifer? What would have become of her? One day as my mind was on summing up, my phone rang and there, out of the blue, was Kitty Schoen, calling to say hello. I was surprised to hear from her, for I hadn't spoken to any of Jennifer's friends in close to a year. "How are you?" I said. "What's been happening?"

"I'm graduating," Kitty said. "And after graduation I'm going to California. To get a job in TV or film production. I've even had one offer already."

Kitty graduating college? The years of her and Jennifer's chaotic adolescence flashed through my brain, and then unexpectedly I remembered my own, recalled them as vividly as if they hadn't happened in the long-ago fifties, but last week, yesterday. They too had been chaotic, laden with rebellion and risk. Yet sometime during or after my college years I'd turned without even knowing it into a hard-working, level-headed adult. Would Jennifer too have undergone such a sea change? Would it have started by now, the way it seemed to have started in the graduating, future-planning Kitty? I thought it might have, but to check out the feeling I telephoned Leilia Van Baker. Jennifer and she had been so similar, Leilia had often told me, that they'd been like two peas in a pod. What was happening with Leilia?

When I reached her—she was twenty-one now and going to Bennington College—I asked what she was up to. "I'm majoring in art," she told me. "I'm doing painting and graphics. I love it. I love it so much that I didn't even want to take a break to go home on holiday this winter. I just wanted to keep working. Painting."

"That's great. That's wonderful news."

"There's more," Leilia said. "I have a boyfriend. I've been seeing him for eight months. If we stay together, who knows? We could get married. Have kids." She giggled. "But meanwhile, I'm thinking that when school's over I'll go into business. Maybe open a gallery."

Yes, I thought. Yes. I can sense now what Jennifer would have been like today, these days. She'd have been like Leilia. Bursting with news. Busy with new interests. New loves. Preparing for a career. For life.

It brought her death back to me. That death had always seemed a sad and terrible waste. Now it seemed an even greater squander.

AFTERWORD

This book does its best to be a full account of events leading up to and succeeding the death of Jennifer Levin at Robert Chambers's hands. The material presented was drawn from a variety of sources. The chief source was the interviews I conducted with over 200 people who were connected to the principal characters or played a role in the investigation and trial. A number of these people were interviewed repeatedly.

In addition to interviews, I made use of a vast collection of other material: police reports; court documents; letters; juvenilia of Jennifer Levin and Robert Chambers; photographs; newspaper and magazine articles; school records and yearbooks; the 2,200-page transcript of a pretrial hearing held in May and June of 1987, and the 7,700-page transcript of the trial itself. I also drew upon my own observations made at various sites mentioned in the text and during my attendance at pretrial hearings, jury selection proceedings, and the three-month trial.

I have changed the names of some of the people mentioned in the book. All of those whose names have been changed are people whose connection to the case was not previously spelled out through the trial or news accounts. Some of them, when I interviewed them, asked me to change their names. Others were not truly named because my information about them was based on sources other than personal interviews.

There are some 110 people named in the text. Fifteen of them bear pseudonyms.

The pseudonyms are from the short stories of F. Scott Fitzgerald. Fitzgerald loved names, was always giving them to characters, even to characters who appeared but momentarily in his scenes. This meant there was a wealth to choose from. But more important, the preppie world he wrote about in many of his stories was an earlier, more innocent version of the one described here.

A few people connected to the case declined to be interviewed for this book; among them were Bob and Phyllis Chambers and Robert himself. I did, however, have a number of informal conversations with Robert during pretrial court sessions. They were enough, I felt, for me to form an impression of his personality.

Concerning the dialogue and interior monologues used in the book: they are drawn from interviews, police reports, and testimony delivered during the trial or hearings. Although neither Robert nor Phyllis and Bob Chambers testified at the trial, Phyllis and Bob did testify at hearings, and there they reported experiences and thoughts.

While I have not interrupted the flow of the action to indicate whether the source for a scene came from an interview, a court session, or both, I have endeavored wherever possible to make clear for the reader the identity—and generally the affiliation and therefore any possible biases—of the individual from whose perspective thoughts or conversations are derived.

In a handful of scenes, I have attributed thoughts to Jennifer or Robert. I did this sparingly and only when I had good reason, based on information provided by my sources, to believe that the attribution was accurate.

Important events were corroborated by two sources wherever possible. When there were discrepancies between one person's account and another's, I chose the account that seemed—based on the insights I had gained through the body of my research—the most reliable.

There are a few other things I'd like to point out here. One has to do with omissions. I felt I couldn't, for reasons of space and pace, include all the twists and turns of the Chambers case. One matter I excluded was this: that I myself was, briefly, involved in the trial. My notes for this book were subpoenaed by Jack Litman. The subpoena was successfully fought.

Another thing I'd like to mention has to do with the sequence of events. Some of the people I spoke with were imprecise about when things happened. For example, according to my notes the woman who sold Jennifer the skirt for her college wardrobe did so "a couple of days before she was killed." But Jennifer was in the Hamptons for several days before she was killed. I therefore hazarded a guess as to just when the scene occurred. There are a few other such guesses as to sequence—but not many.

Also, there were a few occasions when the you-are-there technique I had chosen did not lend itself to explaining a detail in full. One such occasion occurs in the scene when Judge Bell's name is drawn from the wheel. His name was actually in both the regular wheel and the "P" wheel. I did not include this information in the body of the scene because the fact did not emerge until after the time it describes. Another such occasion concerns the scene in which Robert dials the porno hot line. I don't know whether the message he heard in the summer of 1986 is the message I use in the text, as I didn't research the scene until a year and a half later. A third such matter concerns the scene in which David Fillyaw stabs the Columbia student. I had only David's account of events—his videotaped confession—to go on. Perhaps he was lying in his account, and the girl he stabbed never invited him into her room at all.

Finally, I'd like to thank all of those who granted me interviews. From the beginning, I had conceived of this book as a tapestry that would weave together the experiences the Chambers case brought to a wide variety of individuals—to teenagers, parents, lawyers, judges, police, schoolteachers, servants. But the tapestry would have been a weak one indeed without the contributions of my interviewees. I am grateful to all of them for their consideration and attention. And I'm particularly grateful to those who granted me hours and hours of their valuable time.

ABOUT THE AUTHOR

Linda Wolfe is the author of five true-crime books: *The Professor and the Prostitute and Other True Tales of Murder and Madness*, *Love Me to Death*, *Double Life*, *The Murder of Dr. Chapman*, and *Wasted: Inside the Robert Chambers–Jennifer Levin Murder*, an Edgar Award nominee and a *New York Times* Notable Book. She is also the author of *My Daughter, Myself*, a memoir; *The Literary Gourmet*, a classic cookbook; and *Private Practices*, a novel. Wolfe's articles and essays have appeared in a wide variety of magazines, among them *Vanity Fair*, the *New York Times Magazine*, and *New York* magazine, of which she was a contributing editor. She currently writes a column about books for the website www.FabOverFifty.com.

EBOOKS BY LINDA WOLFE

FROM OPEN ROAD MEDIA

Available wherever ebooks are sold

OPEN ROAD
INTEGRATED MEDIA

Open Road Integrated Media is a digital publisher and multimedia content company. Open Road creates connections between authors and their audiences by marketing its ebooks through a new proprietary online platform, which uses premium video content and social media.

Videos, Archival Documents, and New Releases

Sign up for the Open Road Media newsletter and get news delivered straight to your inbox.

Sign up now at
www.openroadmedia.com/newsletters